LLEWELLYN'S

2019

Magical Almanac

Featuring

Elizabeth Barrette, Blake Octavian Blair,
Deborah Blake, Deborah Castellano, Alexandra Chauran,
Chic and S. Tabatha Cicero, Dallas Jennifer Cobb,
Monica Crosson, Melissa Cynova, Autumn Damiana,
Raven Digitalis, Storm Faerywolf, Kate Freuler,
Justine Holubets, James Kambos, Tiffany Lazic,
Najah Lightfoot, Jason Mankey,
Estha K. V. McNevin, Mickie Mueller, Diana Rajchel,
Suzanne Ress, Charlynn Walls, Charlie Rainbow Wolf,
Stephanie Woodfield, Laura Tempest Zakroff,
and Natalie Zaman

Llewellyn's 2019
Magical Almanac

ISBN 978-0-7387-4609-8. Copyright © 2018 by Llewellyn Publications. All rights reserved. Printed in the United States. Llewellyn Publications is a registered trademark of Llewellyn Worldwide Ltd.

Editing/Layout: Lauryn Heineman

Cover Illustration: © Janie Olsen

Calendar Pages Design: Michael Fallon

Calendar Pages Illustrations: © Fiona King

Interior Illustrations: © Elisabeth Alba: pages 18, 21, 66, 69, 179, 182, 237, 240, 243; © Kathleen Edwards: pages 24, 26, 71, 74 194, 199, 245, 248, 280; © Wen Hsu: pages 7, 10, 13, 15, 56, 59, 61, 102, 107, 175, 228, 232, 235, 272, 275; © Mickie Mueller: pages 39, 42, 45, 85, 88, 91, 213, 216, 219, 259, 263; © Eugene Smith: pages 29, 32, 35, 76, 81, 203, 207, 251, 254; © Laura Tempest Zakroff: pages 186, 190, 192; © Amber Zoellner: pages 47, 51, 53, 95, 98, 223, 226, 267, 269

Clip Art Illustrations: Dover Publications

Special thanks to Amber Wolfe for the use of daily color and incense correspondences. For more detailed information, please see *Personal Alchemy* by Amber Wolfe.

You can order Llewellyn annuals and books from *New Worlds*, Llewellyn's catalog. To request a free copy of the catalog, call 1-877-NEW-WRLD toll-free or visit www.llewellyn.com.

Astrological data compiled and programmed by Rique Pottenger. Based on the earlier work of Neil F. Michelsen.

Llewellyn Worldwide Ltd.
2143 Wooddale Drive
Woodbury, MN 55125

Table of Contents

Earth Magic. 7

Written in Stone: Thirteen Essential Crystals and
Their Many Meanings
   by Charlie Rainbow Wolf 8

Magic and Cats
   by Deborah Blake (and Magic the Cat) 17

House Wards and House Guardians
   by Diana Rajchel. 22

Disabilities and Witchcraft
   by Elizabeth Barrette .29

Urban Elemental Gardens: Crafting Magic in Small
Outdoor Spaces
   by Tiffany Lazic 38

Witchy Business: Navigating the Online
Magickal Marketplace
   by Kate Freuler 46

Rethinking the Wheel of the Year
   by Stephanie Woodfield 55

Air Magic 61

The Milagro Magic
   by Natalie Zaman. 62

Psychic Housecleaning
   by James Kambos. 71

Raziel: The Archangel of Magic
   by Chic and S. Tabatha Cicero. 76

The Magic Hat
   by Suzanne Ress 85

After the Ritual: The Remnants
    by Autumn Damiana .93

Magic Apple: The Fruit from the Tree of Life
    by Justine Holubets .101

Almanac Section 109
    Date, Day, Festivals and Holidays, Moon Sign,
    Lunar Phase, Color and Incense of the Day

2019 Sabbats and Full Moons. 114

Fire Magic 175

Finding Light
    by Monica Crosson .176

The Witch's Sigil: Crafting Magick Symbols for
Spellcraft, Ritual, and More
    by Laura Tempest Zakroff 185

Enlighten Up: A New Approach to Cursing
    by Raven Digitalis. .193

The Origins and Alchemy of Éliphas Lévi's
Baphomet
    by Estha K. V. McNevin 202

Scissors as a Magical Tool
    by Mickie Mueller .212

The Inverse Cone of Power
    by Jason Mankey. .221

Hamsa
    by Dallas Jennifer Cobb 228

Water Magic

Water Magic 235

Ethical Considerations for Healing Circles
by Blake Octavian Blair.................236

So You Want to Start a Coven?
by Alexandra Chauran 245

Conjuring the Silver Thread: Cultivating a Spiritual
Bond with the Ancestors of Our Craft
by Storm Faerywolf......................250

Processing Grief
by Charlynn Walls 258

Back to the Basics: Self-Care with the Elements
and Your Tarot Deck
by Melissa Cynova......................265

A Glamour Dinner Party Rite
by Deborah Castellano..................270

Bad Magickal Breakups
by Najah Lightfoot 277

About the Contributors 282

Earth Magic

Written in Stone:
Thirteen Essential Crystals and Their Many Meanings

by Charlie Rainbow Wolf

There are so many pretty crystals and stones easily available these days that it's often a bit of a minefield trying to work out what is the most beneficial and what could wait until another day. I've attempted to take the guesswork out of that for you by listing thirteen foundation stones that I recommend any would-be crystal user include in their collection—no matter how large or small it may be! These stones won't break the bank, and many of them have more than one purpose. As you grow in your experiences using crystals, you will probably want to keep different sets for different things. If you're a beginner or on a tight budget, this is a good place to start.

Thirteen Foundation Stones

Quartz

I can't say enough about quartz crystal. It's my go-to stone for nearly everything. It comes in different terminations (the way the facets come to a point), inclusions (things inside the stone as it was forming), and hues (clear quartz, milky quartz, and more). Quartz is a form of silicon dioxide (SiO_2) and is one of the most abundant minerals on the planet. It's even found in your own brain in the form of silica! Many beaches contain vast amounts of quartz sand too.

What makes quartz so special is the way it's able to be programmed to do things. On a practical level, quartz crystals are used in watches and clocks to keep the time right, because the oscillations of this stone are predictable. On a metaphysical level, it is a crown chakra stone and helps you to connect with ascended masters and your spirit guardians. It can be programmed as a healing stone, a cleansing stone, or a scrying stone, and, unlike some stones, it's easy to clean quartz's energy and reprogram it for another purpose.

Carry or wear quartz to help you deflect negative energy. This doesn't have to be malicious; empaths and sensitives need protecting from any flotsam and jetsam that's out there. Even electromagnetic emissions from your cellphone or computer monitor should probably be dispersed.

Use quartz as a worry stone if you're in a stressful situation. The tangible feel of it in your hands will help you to focus on something other than what—or who—is stressing you. Focusing on the stone has the potential to help you draw confidence as well as soothe your nerves.

In divination, clear quartz usually means clarity. It often points to a window opening up, your thoughts becoming clearer, or you being able to see a new and more appropriate plan of action. It's a good luck stone and can be used to influence any astrology sign (and thus any time of year) or to draw positive energy to any issue.

Carnelian

You could be forgiven for thinking that carnelian looks like glass. It polishes so very shiny, thanks to being a form of chalcedony, which is yet another type of quartz. This stone ranges from a peachy orange to the deepest vermillion and always stands out from the crowd. It is a sacral chakra stone and helps you build confidence and vitality. It's associated with Mars, Aries, and early spring. In divination, it indicates passion and matters of the heart. It's telling you not to settle for second-best but to hold out for what you truly want from all areas of your life.

Rose Quartz

Some quartz colors are worthy of closer inspection, and the beautiful rose quartz is another one of them. This is a wonderful stone when it comes to learning forgiveness, compassion, and self-acceptance. Rose quartz is pink in color and is found in both opaque and translucent forms. It's a heart chakra stone, bringing tenderness and empathy, but it isn't a pushover. It

aligns with Venus, Taurus, and the middle of spring. In divination, it's a sure sign that love is on its way—though that doesn't necessarily mean romance.

Chrysocolla

Chrysocolla is sometimes called the teaching stone because it's got a way of being heard. It doesn't matter how the message is conveyed; this is the stone of musicians and poets and elders. It calms stress so that the soul can be heard through self-expression. Carry or wear it when you're composing, writing, or delivering an important message. It is a throat chakra stone and will enable you to know when to speak and when to listen. It's associated with Mercury, Gemini, and late spring. In divination, it urges you to speak up for what you want and to voice your needs and desires so that the universe will hear you.

Moonstone

Moonstone is so soothing to frayed nerves with its soft texture and its pearly iridescence. It comes in the softest of hues, from the palest milky blue to rainbow and into a deep pewter gray. It's a stone that will aid you in organizing your thoughts and feelings as well as guiding you when it comes to developing insight and psychic awareness. It is a third-eye chakra stone and teaches you the difference between a vision and an illusion. It's aligned with the Moon, Cancer, and early summer. In divination, it points to an older female, the archetypal grandmother and her wisdom, and advocates that you should start paying closer attention to the cycles and rhythms of your life.

Citrine

This is also a form of quartz, and as for amethyst, care must be taken when choosing it. Most citrine on the market today has been heat treated to get the lovely amber color. Citrine comes in as many shapes and hues as amethyst and from the darkest brown to the palest honey gold. This is an excellent stone for clearing out what needs to be dismissed and for soothing your nerves while you do so. Use it as either a sacral or solar plexus chakra stone, depending on its coloring. This stone resonates with the fire signs of the zodiac (especially Leo), the Sun, and midsummer. In divination, it points to energy and new beginnings.

Rhodochrosite

From the palest pink to the deepest rose, often with white or black striations, rhodochrosite demands your attention. It's hard to be down in the presence of this stone. Reach for it when you are trying to balance your karma or get rid of emotional baggage. It's a form of calcite, sometimes referred to as a "spar." It's a truth-seeking stone, which is why it's so beneficial when working through hurt feelings. It aligns with Virgo, Mercury, and late summer. In divination, it's encouraging you to let go of the past, to forgive and open yourself to loving and being loved, and to learn how to play again.

Malachite

It's usually hard to feel stressed when you're gazing up on the exquisite striations of malachite. It's an outstanding protection stone, and like quartz it helps to absorb and diffuse negative energies. It's a good ally in the workplace, for it will shield you from the electromagnetic energies and the harshness of the artificial lighting. It is a heart chakra stone and assists you in finding kindness and understanding. It resonates with Libra, Venus, and early autumn. In divination, it suggests it's time to listen to messages from the heart, whether they're metaphorical or literal. It is also a good sign that emotional stress is ending.

Agate

Agate comes in many colors and many moods, from the beautiful blue lace agate to the snakeskin-like turritella agate, and more. Agate is quartz stone in the form of chalcedony. Agates encourage strength and resilience, enhance creativity, improve self-confidence, and reduce stress and tension. All the different types of agate are aligned with Scorpio, Pluto (and to a lesser extent, Mars), and midautumn. Their exact influence depends largely on their color, so it's useful to have more than one agate in your bundle.

Blue lace agate is powder blue with darker and lighter stripes running through it. This stone soothes and is helpful when you're facing stressful times. It's in tune with the throat chakra, and in divination it usually refers to a younger woman.

Botswana agate looks like a bull's-eye. It's another calming stone, and it works to elevate a low mood when worn or carried. It's usually considered a root chakra stone, and in divination it encourages you to look for answers in existing situations.

Crazy lace agate encourages you to be flexible in your thinking and promotes positive energy. It connects with the spirit world so that you might be able to contact other realms without being afraid of them. It's most often a third-eye chakra stone, and in divination it is advising you to chill out and get some rest and relaxation with your loved ones.

Dendritic agate looks like it has a tree growing in it! These stones range from clear to milky gray, and they soothe frayed emotions. They're generally associated with the root chakra, but green-hued ones will also work with the heart chakra, and the milky ones with the crown chakra. In divination, they encourage you to branch out and advise that this is not the time to try to be too independent.

Fire agate gets its flashes of color from inclusions within the stone. This is a crystal that stimulates protective energy. Put it on the windowsills of your home and carry it with you to ward off negativity. It's mostly a root chakra stone, but is sometimes assigned to the sacral chakra. In divination, it warns against temptations and distractions.

Moss agate often looks like lichen growing on ice. It's a stone of growth and wealth, so put one with your coin purse and use it in the soil if you're a gardener. It's linked to the heart chakra and promotes the purging of negative emotions. In divination, it shows that things are progressing in a good and harmonious way.

The turritella agate with its snakeskin appearance is very much a stone of grounding energy. Its patterns are created from minute fossils trapped within the stone. It connects to the earth and to the ancestors and encourages practicality. It makes sense that it's a root chakra stone, and in divination, it means you need to appreciate what you have and be practical about your goals.

Sodalite

Sodalite is an attractive cleansing stone and a good substitute for the more expensive lapis lazuli. It cleans away what's blocking you from progressing, as well as assists you in purging negative energy from your subtle body. It's a beautiful indigo blue, often with white flecks. This is a throat chakra stone, keeping your words truthful and allowing you to see deception in others. It's associated with Sagittarius, Jupiter, and late autumn. In divination, it cautions you to keep things clean in your dealings with others and advises that perhaps there are things—and people—that need clearing out of your life before you proceed.

Tourmaline

Tourmaline is another stone that comes in a variety of colors. It's the black tourmaline that I include in a crystal set. Its energies are grounded and centered, and it's a very useful stone to have as an anchor. It's a root chakra stone, urging you to ensure that your basic needs are met. Wear or carry this stone if you're dealing with fear or anxiety. It sympathizes with Capricorn, Saturn, and early winter. In divination, it indicates that things may not unfold as quickly as you'd like. This doesn't necessarily mean that there are obstacles in the way; you might just need to take your time and be more thorough.

Fluorite

This is another stone that comes in a variety of colors, from the very palest of mauve and turquoise to the deepest purple and aquamarine. It's a stone of creativity, of new ideas and new ways of looking at things. If you want a stone to get your mind working and your ingenuity flowing, this is it! Rainbow fluorite is my favorite. It's in harmony with all chakras, and has such beautifully soothing bands of translucent color. It's associated with Aquarius, Uranus, and midwinter. In divination, it points to all manner of fertility and creativity and encourages you to find your heart's desire through what you love to do.

Amethyst

Amethyst is one more addition to the quartz family. When shopping for it, take some time to get the real thing, as some inferior stones have been heat treated to get their color. Amethyst comes in many shapes and hues, from druse to points; from the palest violet to the darkest purple; and opaque, clear, or banded. It's a very spiritual stone and works with the crown and third-eye chakras. It's one of the stones that resonates with Pisces, Neptune, and late winter. In divination, it points to some kind of movement. Usually, this is spiritual growth of some sort, but it can also indicate a house move.

Storing Your Stones

There's no right or wrong way to keep your stones. I have mine in an interesting bag that I picked up in a thrift store decades ago simply because I liked the resonance of the pouch! You could make your own if you're crafty, and if you do, you'll add your own energy to things and make it even more personal and magical. I've known people who keep their stones in wooden or ceramic boxes, in interesting old jars, and more. Go with what feels right to you, but consider these points when choosing your receptacle:

- Does it need to be portable? If so, then a pouch or purse might be more suitable than a box.
- Is it going to be where other people are able to see it? If that's the case, it might be best if the storage container is opaque rather than transparent, so that the stones stay protected from random energies.
- Is there one main purpose for your stones? As I mentioned previously, I have a set of stones for healing and another (larger) set for divination. If you're going to use your crystals mainly for divination, you might want to think about including some kind of casting cloth in with them. This doesn't have to be ornate; a silk scarf or something similar will get you started.

Conclusion

There's only one more point to add, and it comes with a warning. Crystals are addictive! Once you start collecting and working with them, a whole new world is at your fingertips, and it beacons strongly for you to come explore! You'll find ways to include the beneficial properties of crystals in all aspects of your life, from adding them to your bath, keeping them as protective guardians in your car, using them in energy grids around your home and garden, making gem elixirs, and more! My medicine elder referred to crystals as "the bones of the earth." They're truly a gift from the planet, one which is often overlooked thanks to the technological world in which we live.

Magic and Cats

by Deborah Blake (and Magic the Cat)

Everybody knows that cats and Witches go together like peanut butter and jelly (or vodka and tonic). But have you ever wondered why that is or how cats can help with magical work? Since I just wrote a book all about cat magic and happen to have a black cat named Magic, I thought I'd share a few thoughts on the matter. Naturally, being a cat, Magic will probably add her two claws' worth as well.

Cats and Cat Deities

There is something mysterious and magical about cats, which probably explains their association with Witches through the ages. Their eyes glow in the dark, they appear and disappear as they please, and they often seem to know things that go beyond the scope of what any simple "pet" should. They have been revered and worshipped in many cultures, and it is thought that their connection to humans dates back as far as a hundred thousand years ago in Mesopotamia. That's a long time to be bossing us around!

Cats often act as though you should bow down before them, but really the most commonly worshipped cat-related deity is the Egyptian goddess Bast. Many Witches who work with cats in their practice have at least one statue of this goddess, who is often pictured as a woman with the head of a cat but can also be represented by a regal statue of a black cat wearing a gold collar and earrings.

The Egyptians also worshipped Sekhmet, who was more likely to represent the wild side of cats in the form of a lioness, but it is Bast, or Bastet, who is most revered as the goddess of love, sexuality, motherhood, and, of course, cats.

The Norse goddess Freya was sometimes referred to as the "Mother of Cats" and was often depicted riding in a chariot pulled by two giant cats. She was associated with love, divination, and the transitions that come with death and dying. For protection, you can either work with Sekhmet or the slightly more exotic pre-Inca god Ai Apaec, who was often depicted as an old man with a wrinkled face, long fangs, and cat-like whiskers or sometimes as a jaguar. Hecate, the Greek (and later Celtic) goddess of Witches, is more likely to be shown accompanied by great black hounds. But there is also a tale that tells of a time when she had to transform herself into a cat to escape a monster, and it is said that this is how black cats came to be associated with Witchcraft.

Any of these gods can be called on to aid you in your magical work if you want to integrate cats into your practice. If you are interested in working with a cat god or goddess, try setting out a bowl of milk, some cat treats or toys, and maybe some catnip and then asking one to come for a visit.

Magical Work with Cats

There are two basic approaches to working magic with cats. The first is to do magic to help your cat, and the second is to ask your feline companion for his or her assistance with your own magical work. Needless to say, either way, the cat should get treats (according to Magic the Cat).

Magical work for the benefit of your cat includes a spell to find the right one (especially if you are looking for a familiar), discover a cat's name, help integrate a cat into your home, aid with cat healing, and more. Plus, of course, you can work spells to protect any cat that goes outside, find one who has gone missing, or help ease the passage of one who is dying.

But beyond doing magical work to make your cat's life better, you can tap into their natural mystical gifts to help you with your own magic. For instance, cats can aid in divination. My cat Magic is drawn to both the healing work and tarot reading I do and will jump up on the table and stretch out across the card spread. Mind you, this is less helpful than she thinks it is, since it is difficult to read the cards through her furry black butt. Still, it demonstrates the way cats connect to the mystical energies.

If you are trying to find answers through divination, you can try spreading out tarot cards or rune stones and ask your cat to choose the one you need. If your cat shows up during your rituals, as Magic does with mine, pay special attention to their behavior—they may be receiving information you can use. It is also possible that they are simply supervising your activities, to make sure you get it right. In which case, be sure to reward them with treats (this suggestion also brought to you by Magic the Cat).

Feline Power Animals

The domestic cat is not the only feline associated with magical work. Some Witches find it helpful to work with power animals, also known as totems or animal allies, some of which come in catlike forms. The most common are probably the mountain lion (also called a cougar or a puma), lynx, tiger, lion, black panther, leopard, cheetah, and the small but fierce bobcat. Each of these animals has its own attributes and strengths, so if you are looking for a power animal to work with, it is worth doing a little research to find out which one best matches your needs and personality.

Of course, sometimes we don't choose our power animals—they choose us (much like cats themselves). If you notice an animal showing up repeatedly, either in person or in some representative form, such as in pictures, as statues, on television, or in books, it is possible that the universe is trying to tell you something. You can also seek out your power animal. This is often done through shamanic journeying but can also be achieved through trance work of differing types or lucid dreaming. You can also ask the gods to send you the power animal that is right for you. If that doesn't work, try asking your cat. Perhaps he or she will give you a hint.

The Cat as Familiar

Cats may boost your own magical abilities, which is probably one of the reasons why Witches have used them as familiars through the centuries. This doesn't require any special actions on your part; it simply comes with the territory. But if a cat doesn't wish to be involved with your Witchcraft practices—Magic is the only one of my many cats who has ever shown any interest—never try to force it on them. It will not go well for you. Also, Bast is probably watching. Just saying.

That being said, cats do seem to have a natural affinity for Witchcraft and Witches. (Which is not to say that there aren't plenty of Witches who like dogs. I like dogs too. Magic the Cat just won't let me have one.) If you are lucky enough to have a cat who acts as your familiar, be sure to say thank you. You will also want to be careful with some of the usual witchy tools we all use, such as fire, sharp athames, and herbs, some of which are dangerous to cats. Never force a cat into a situation that might be dangerous or unhealthy.

You can use some of your cat's bits and pieces in spellwork—things like a cat's whiskers, claws, and fur can be helpful. But please make sure that these ingredients are derived without hurting the cat. Whiskers and claw tips are shed naturally and can probably be found around the house, and fur can be attained by brushing your cat—an activity that most cats find pleasurable and which has the side benefit of cutting down on hair balls!

If you are making a charm bag to protect your home, you can put a couple of cast-off or clipped claws into it. If you are working healing magic for a sick cat, you might want to integrate a tiny bit of his or her own fur to tie the cat to the spell.

If you are looking for a familiar, you can do a spell under the Full Moon and ask Bast to send you one. Then go to a shelter, or some other place with cats that need homes, and see if any particular cat seems to be attracted to you. Keep in mind, however, that you should never get a cat only to have a familiar. Be prepared to love and live with any animal you take in, whether or not the cat turns out to have an interest in magical work. After all, all cats are magical in their own ways, and they bring us gifts that go far beyond their contributions to our Witchcraft.

Cats and Magic and Witches, Oh My!

I was a cat person long before I realized I was a Witch, but once I knew I was one, it certainly went some way toward explaining my stronger-than-average connection with cats. While not every Witch has—or wants—a cat, many of us find that we seem to have a particularly mystical pull toward the feline species.

As Magic the Cat will tell you, cats enrich our lives in many ways, from helping with our magical work to easing the stresses of a difficult day. In my opinion, they are truly gifts from the gods. In Magic's opinion, those gifts should be rewarded with treats. Who am I to argue?

House Wards and House Guardians

by Diana Rajchel

Adding a layer—or several—of protection to your home is more important than it has ever been. We live in volatile times, and most of us in a culture where few learn how to manage their emotions well. Even those who enjoy pockets of geographic peace or who have relatively low psychic sensitivity can feel buffeted by the chaotic winds of contention. Warding our homes against some of these emotional weather patterns is a necessary part of magical people living their lives rather than living from extinguished fire to extinguished fire.

Most homes have a spirit of their own. The land beneath will also have innate spirit. You can encourage a happy house spirit by minimizing clutter, making sure all energy in the house has a job to do, and maintaining as much good will as you can with your neighbors. (The latter may fall the furthest out of your control.) Regular cleansing and clearing removes pockets of stagnant energy that reduces places for "astral nasties" to hide.

Spaces and Challenges

While certain elements of protection magic remain the same—mainly the need for anchors of physical or energetic protection and a continuous fuel source—the shape and size of where you live dictates the types of wards you need. Houses require protective wards that include the land. Apartments have fewer entrances but more people, so filtering the energy that breaches shared walls becomes more important. People living in single rooms can apply the rules of apartment protection to their own smaller spaces.

Even those who live in tents or outdoor situations can still practice warding. While most can't consistently use physical objects to store the energy, they can practice temporary and easily movable wards and may benefit from invisibility workings. This does go beyond protective shields to protection of your space as you move through the world. While few things are ever foolproof—sometimes stuff just gets in—a warding and guarding practice can add that little element of safety to life that helps on the occasions when something busts through.

Most space warding and cleansing require fire techniques and take fuel from smoke in the forms of candles and incense. While flame and air are an effective means of destroying and dispersing negativity, those with asthma or allergies need other options. These alternatives can also help those who prefer not to share their beliefs and practices with their housemates. Use this far from comprehensive chart to determine what alternatives best serve you and your home:

Problem	Substitute
Fire/candles are not allowed.	There are few effective substitutes for living flame, but you can use LED illumination if the intention involves spreading light; you may also want to use copper wire folded into a triangle on top of salt in a glass jar as an energy trap.
Incense and smudges cause health issues.	Use smudge sprays or aromatherapy misters.
Salts and crystals will be removed.	Pick innocuous items like decorative salt shakers to store the minerals.
Unable to hang items with occult symbols.	Find toys and other items that serve your imagination and turn them into wards—a butterfly is a powerful spiritual symbol that most people find nonthreatening.

Wards

A ward is a metaphysical lock and alarm system. Wards can consist solely of energy or be physical objects imbued with protective energy. All wards need to be programmed and from time to time have their energy renewed.

Before building your wards, keep in mind a few best practices:

Magic multitasks poorly. You can create words that serve multiple purposes—keep off fire, flood, and door-to-door evangelists, as well as keep out your mother-in-law's ghost. Too many purposes spread the protective energy thin, weakening its effect. This forces you to recharge it far more frequently than a single-purpose ward. A good practice is to choose three symbols to represent three wardings: one for harm on the physical plane, one to block out anything uninvited from the spiritual, and one to block out energy sent in anger.

When planning your home wards, look beyond inside-outside barriers. Ward all the doors and windows that form a barrier between the indoors and the outdoors. You also need to look at other ways energy enters the house: fireplaces, vents, and sink drains are examples of more physical entrances. Electrical outlets, televisions, and mirrors sometimes give access to energies entering the home.

When you begin to build your wards, especially those made entirely of energy, remember that metaphysical energy can fit in between the slower-moving energy of atomic solids. You can take that warding symbol and mentally push it through your ceiling to the top of your roof.

Metaphysical energy has a dominant emotional component. This is how your wards—and you—"feel" the intent of what attempts to enter your home. We create wards to help cultivate safe, happy spaces.

Energy-Only Wards

If you want to build a ward using only your energy or energy that you channel from natural elements, then this is just one of many methods you can use. First, decide what you want your ward's intention to be and choose or create a symbol that aligns with that purpose. Runes and pentacles are popular symbols for protecting property, but they are also commonly used. It may act like setting a too-easy password on your email account. If you prefer to use something less common (and thus harder to hack), you may want to research symbols such as old family crests or tarot cards or repurpose scientific notation glyphs.

Find a place to stand or sit, relax your body as much as possible, and rub your palms together to create heat. Place your hands in front of you an inch apart so that you can feel the energy your body has raised. Breathe into the space between your hands to increase that energy. Conjure in yourself the emotion you want to make your ward express (self-confident calm for physical protection, perhaps a "roll off the back" peace for psychic), and with that emotion shape the energy between your hands into the desired symbol. Taking a giant breath, exhale and lift the symbol like someone releasing a wild bird. Imagine it landing in the area you want protected, throwing out anchors in all directions to cling to your home.

Physical Object Wards

Any object typically treated as decoration or a toy can serve as a physical ward. Some prefer common symbols, such as the pentacle and evil eye, to charge and then hang decoratively in their homes. You may find that you prefer to use pictures that you hang on the wall, spiritual statues, gaming figurines, or items you craft yourself with protective energy in mind.

When charging a physical ward, you can use the same process as you do for the energy-only wards, but instead of sending the energy toward the area you want warded, you place your hands on the object and imagine the energy permeating the object. Once charged, place the objects in areas where you feel you need the most protection. You may tweak the intentions on each object so that items near your door guard from intruders, items in your office protect you from unnecessary interruptions, and items in your bedroom put a stop to nighttime astral visitors. Physical wards can go three to six months before needing a recharge, and if you perform a house cleansing and blessing monthly, you can sneak in a passive refresh of their energy.

House Guardians

House guardians differ from wards in that you (usually) don't create them. Guardians are sentient beings that protect your home and family in exchange for offerings. The nature of the offerings changes based on the origin of the given spirit. These spirits can include human ghosts of an exceptionally positive headspace, ancestors, fairies, house wights (spirits attached to the collective spirit of the household), daemons (neutral spirits that can be paid to do a job), deities, animal totems, and angels. You can also create your own house guardian—called a servitor or a tulpa—although this takes some practice and more maintenance than making offerings and maintaining positive relationships with already existent beings. The advantage of creating your own guardians is that, since you made them, they will have only your agenda to fulfill.

What guardians you encourage in your home can change based on your religious or magical tradition, your geographic region, and personal experiences you've had. For instance, many people who grew up in Christian traditions may perform a four corners prayer, which calls angels to guard the four corners of a home (or room) and to keep out negative influences. This practice may continue even as this person moves into a Wiccan household—or may stop in favor of cultivating house wights or other beings that seem more appropriate to that person's phase of life.

If you want active house guardians, you must create a contract with them. This contract looks like an informal employment agreement. You ask for a service, such as keeping intruders and door-to-door evangelists away from your home, and in return you offer the spirits a payment, such as incense, chocolate, or small bowls of wine or juice at regular intervals. Some spirits may require something daily, others weekly. Always put out an offering for any house protectors at the Full Moon. If you use food, leave it for seven days and then dispose of it. Every month, evaluate the service you receive. If the protections prove unsatisfactory, release the spirit.

Robert Frost once wrote that "good fences make good neighbours." He was just talking about practical boundaries, but the truth extends to the metaphysical ones as well. House warding extends beyond a routine house cleansing and blessing. The ever-important monthly cleanse and bless can metaphorically oil the locks on your doors and windows. House wards and spirits add the equivalent of armed guards and a security system. These protections serve double duty: they keep the outside world from intruding into the energy regulation of your home, and they also prevent what you do inside your home from disrupting the lives of your neighbors.

Disabilities and Witchcraft

by Elizabeth Barrette

People have varying levels of functionality, both mental and physical. Some have small issues that limit a few tasks. Some have large issues that make everything harder. These may be soft limits that can be gotten around or hard limits that cannot. It is much easier to cope with challenges given support from friends, family, and covenmates. So if you have a disability, look for ways you can still pursue Witchcraft; if you know someone who is disabled, treat them with compassion and encourage them to pursue their own goals.

While most people are fully abled at any given time, many people have also experienced temporary disabilities. When planning how to manage disability in a magical and spiritual context, remember that even healthy people are one bad illness or car crash away from needing accommodations for a while. There are even happy causes for temporary limitations. It is a lot simpler to adapt your coven practices for a pregnant friend who can't stand for more than fifteen minutes if you have already thought about handling mobility issues. So let's look at some of the options.

Tolerance versus Inclusivity

There are two levels of acceptance when it comes to disability. Tolerance means putting up with people and providing minimum accommodations. They may be able to get in but won't necessarily feel welcome, and this is why many disabled people wind up isolated. A park that has curb cuts but little or nothing for disabled people to do once they get in there is merely tolerant. Inclusivity means actively encouraging people of all abilities to join in and designing the space and events so they can mingle comfortably. One-piece picnic tables aren't very accessible from a wheelchair, but if there's one with separate benches or chairs, then it's easy to move the unneeded seats to make room for a wheelchair. If possible, aim for inclusivity, not just tolerance.

Another aspect of inclusivity is representation. "Nothing about us without us" is an excellent rule of thumb. It means asking people with disabilities what they want or need and then acting on that. Ideally, encourage them to take active roles in coven leadership. It is much easier to attract a diverse membership if potential contacts can tell that you already have a mixed group working together, not just tokens. If your crone uses a walker decorated with runes, then the young man with cerebral palsy is more likely to ask about joining because he can see what accommodations you're already providing for your crone.

There is an important difference between temporary guests and permanent coven members. Many accommodations that work once in a while are difficult or impossible to keep using on a frequent basis. Conversely, accommodations that are cost-effective in the long term may be utterly unaffordable in the short term. For instance, we happen to have two steps at the door of our house. For a while we had a friend in a wheelchair visiting for some of our events, and it was no trouble to spare a couple of folks to boost the wheels over the steps. If that had been a housemate or coven member, however, we probably would've wanted to build a ramp. So when you're thinking about tolerance versus inclusivity, consider the level and frequency of need before deciding which accommodations to offer.

In some cases, facilities or organizations are required to make certain accommodations. Tolerance is generally considered a moral imperative, but there are practical benefits too. Any disability teaches a person to think outside the box; creative problem-solving is useful in all organizations. Each disability has its own quirks and occasionally perks, such as a deaf person running the smoothie bar because a shrieking blender doesn't bother them. "Intentional neighboring" is a community concept in which people trade off to compensate for each other's strengths and weaknesses. A person with PTSD might happily do the pet grooming that an elder can no longer do comfortably, while the elder makes phone calls the other guy's nerves can't take. This works on a coven scale too. The more different people you have, the easier it becomes to find someone for each task so everything gets done.

Types of Disabilities

A disability is any condition that prevents someone from doing things or requires them to do things in a different way from the usual. For instance, a fully blind person cannot see at all but can learn to read Braille instead of inked text. There are many different types of disability, which can range from minor to major and may be temporary or permanent. Someone with a broken leg may need crutches or a wheelchair for a couple of months while the bone heals and then be fine. Someone who has lost a leg may walk with a prosthetic leg or may prefer a wheelchair—or even use both at different times. Disabilities can be visible, such as bad burn scars that limit mobility, or invisible, such as a traumatic brain injury that wrecks many mental skills.

Disabilities are more common than most folks realize. About 56.7 million people in America have a recognized disability, which is roughly 19 percent of the population. Among the more common examples are mobility impairment (30.6 million); lifting/grasping limitations (19.9 million); trouble with instrumental activities of daily living, such as preparing meals or using the phone (15.5 million); trouble with other activities of daily living, such as dressing or eating (9.4 million); vision impairment (8.1 million); hearing impairment (7.6 million); and anxiety or depression (7 million). There are many other physical and mental conditions

that limit what people can do or require creative solutions to do things. Some folks have limitations that are not generally considered disabilities but may cause similar challenges.

Laws regarding disclosure and accommodations vary widely in what they require and who is or is not obligated to follow them. Ideally, you should check your local laws regarding individuals and organizations to see what applies to you. In general, it is not acceptable to demand intimate health information from people; they don't have to disclose a disability. On the bright side, you don't need to know their health issues; you only need to know what accommodations they require. Frame your questions gently and in terms of what people need.

Another good rule of thumb is "reasonable accommodations." Many things can be done free or cheaply, just by changing the order or location of activities or by finding a volunteer to give someone a hand in the potluck line so they don't drop their cane while juggling their plate. However, anything sold to people with disabilities tends to be ruinously expensive, which means that some accommodations are possible in theory but unaffordable in practice, while others are just too complicated for untrained people to manage. A frank discussion about what's reasonable or not will save you a lot of stress, especially if you do it in private rather than having an impromptu argument during a ritual. Check your local resources, because even if you can't offer a certain accommodation, sometimes there are organizations that will provide free equipment or services to people with a disability—for instance, getting a sign language interpreter at a large event.

If you want to make your coven more inclusive, there are two logical ways to start. Should you already have some members with a disability, first check with them to see if more accommodations would make it easier for them to participate. Otherwise, consider working on one broad type of disability at a time, starting with the most common (mobility impairment). Examine your practices and places to see what improvements could be made. Do what you can, and then move on to another disability. That will make it easier to accept new members, whatever they happen to need.

In any case, disability-friendly covens and other Pagans should specify that in their publicly visible materials. Not all groups are tolerant, let alone welcoming, so people learn to watch for clues. Just saying "We welcome all ability levels" is helpful. "This venue is fully wheelchair-accessible" or "This will be a silent ritual" are even more informative. "If you need assistance or accommodations for special needs, please ask (contact information)" encourages people to seek help instead of hanging back because they don't want to bother you. If you display pictures of your members or events, ask visibly disabled members whether or not they are comfortable appearing there. Many aren't, but that just contributes to folks not feeling welcome when they look at group snapshots. Visibility helps if people are willing.

Types of Accommodations

Accommodations are tools or techniques that compensate for a disability and allow people to do more stuff. There are countless variations on this theme but a few big clusters that are useful for solving common problems. Understand that while some solutions work for many different disabilities, there is no such thing as universal design. That's because some disabilities have opposite needs. For example, deaf people benefit from having large open spaces with clear lines of sight so they can see what people are saying or signing; they don't do as well when enclosed by lots of walls or in dim lighting. Blind people benefit from having plenty of walls to follow with a hand, cane, or guide dog. They aren't bothered by dim light, but they may find large open spaces disorienting and difficult to navigate. People with mobility issues may need flat surfaces and places to sit down, whereas people with high energy may need lots of vigorous activity before they can sit still during ritual. Sensory issues go both ways: some folks are sensation avoiders and some are sensory seekers, and they really aren't comfortable in the same environment.

So in planning accommodations, you need to do several things. First, look for things that are accessible to more people, such as renting a venue with both stairs and ramps. Options are good. Second, check the people who will be at that event for their particular needs and prioritize those over abstract check-lists. If you have deaf people but no wheelchair users, prefer the big bright hall with six steps over the place with ramps but cramped rooms and crummy lights. Third, if you have members with conflicting needs, consider catering to each at a different time or location. A person with an assistance animal and some-one with asthma or fur allergies may not be compatible in close proximity, but could each be accommodated in a different room or session. Fourth, consider your own needs and limitations, as they may change over time. Think creatively when approaching challenges, since many can be overcome. Finally, if you're bor-rowing space, understand that you cannot trust claims unless you verify them yourself. People forget about that one step up to the toilet. Check it personally.

Here are some ideas for accommodations that can help with many types of disability:

Walking, climbing, and rolling: Hold events on firm, flat space that doesn't require steps or steep slopes to access. If indoors, ask for clearance width of wheelchairs, walkers, and so on, and carry a measure through the space to make sure everything will fit. Make sure the distance from parking to ritual space is com-fortable for people to travel. If you schedule events in wilder space such as parks, it helps to give a distance and difficulty level: "The handfasting will be one-quarter mile down Bluebird Trail (rated Easy)."

Standing and sitting: Standing on a soft surface like grass or carpet is much better than hardwood or concrete. Comfortable, padded chairs are better than bare wood or metal. Discreetly ask how long people can stand comfortably. Fully seated rituals are better if you have members with mobility or standing issues.

Another option is dividing ritual tasks—for instance, seated drummers and moving dancers. Of course, some people dance in wheelchairs, so let your participants decide.

Lifting, holding, and doing: For people who struggle with a lot of little tasks, it's often helpful to have a volunteer assistant. They may need a hand with holding the chalice, fastening their coven robes, and so forth. Be as matter-of-fact as possible; everyone needs help sometimes. This is a place where affordable aids can be super useful, such as ergonomic grips or Velcro straps.

Reading and writing: Print ritual text in large type or do without a script. Use whiteboards or notepads with high-contrast ink instead of blackboards or electronic screens for large group presentations. Drawing in dirt or sand can work great too. Braille typewriters are expensive, but a stylus and punchboard are cheap. For colorblindness, use symbols in addition to colors for elements or deities.

Hearing and speaking: Offer communication via text message or email instead of phone. Provide ritual outlines in text, and visual cues for actions. Book a sign language translator at large events. If you have deaf covenmates who sign, seriously consider learning at least the basics of their sign language. A smartphone or notebook is great for quick conversations with someone who cannot hear or speak well, whether that's a permanent limit or fresh dental work. Nonverbal folks may do fine with a visual interface such as icons.

Feeling and being: Set up a quiet corner or room in case of emotional overload or energy upheavals. Good shields are soothing to most folks. Avoid sudden noises, flashes, or other surprises in ritual. Let people take breaks if necessary, especially during daylong sabbats or other major events. Reassure anxious people that it's okay to feel stressed and they can participate as much or as little as they feel comfortable. Help depressed folks find satisfying activities within their available energy level. Festivals can provide a booth for emotional first aid as well as physical first aid.

Food and drink: Allergies and other dietary limitations are skyrocketing, so every group should take care with this. Also, some medications are incompatible with certain substances. At potlucks, put a card on each dish with its ingredients. When serving a group, favor things that avoid the most common allergens. Our coven rules are (1) nobody has to be able to eat everything on the table, (2) there has to be something that everybody can reasonably fill up on, and (3) for any allergy that could require an ambulance if triggered, that item doesn't go on the table when that person is present.

Better living through chemistry: If your coven has a no-drugs policy, please emphasize that it applies to things that impair clear thought, not to things required for clear thought! If you work outdoors, allergy supplies may be widely needed in the warm season. In a group with several folks on maintenance medication, you might remind everyone to make sure they've taken everything they should have before important activities begin.

Magical and Spiritual Concerns

Some disability issues interact with magic and spirituality in ways that create different dynamics than the mainstream. One example is that including people with disabilities can broaden other people's perspectives. For example, a coven with deaf members might do some silent rituals, or one with blind members might work in darkness sometimes. A coven whose members have

36

PTSD, anxiety, depression, or other mental issues might choose chthonic work or guided meditation to explore deep areas of the psyche. This all leads to very different experiences in circle compared to the usual techniques. On that note, it is common for a group to have people with several different limitations, in which case rotating the focus among them would make for fresh experiences on a regular basis.

Don't forget what we might think of as mystical disabilities. Some things are described so consistently in Pagan references that anyone who can't do it that way will have serious trouble making progress. For example, almost all magic is described in visual terms; people who think more in audio terms struggle to master basic skills such as grounding, centering, and shielding because the instructions don't make sense to them. Change the description to audio metaphors and they may do just fine. Some people can't sense energy. If everyone else in the group can, the one who can't will probably feel left out and may have a hard time following what everyone else is doing, unless you account for that in your ritual planning.

These aren't things you'll find in standard materials on disability, but they can absolutely make your coven life more complicated. The same basic process applies, though: ask the person what would help them and do that if at all possible. Think about what they want to accomplish and different ways to try doing it. Don't fall into the habit of thinking that there is "one true way" to do things.

Selected Resources

Cohen, Judy. "Disability Etiquette: Tips on Interacting with People with Disabilities." Eastern Paralyzed Veterans Association. Accessed November 3, 2017. https://ada.osu.edu/designguidance/disability%20ettiquite.pdf.

Kirshman, Norman H., and Roger L. Grandgenett II. "ADA: The 10 Most Common Disabilities and How to Accommodate." *LegalBrief Law Journal* 2 (1997). http://legalbrief.com/kirshman.html.

United States Census Bureau. "Nearly 1 in 5 People Have a Disability in the U.S., Census Bureau Reports." July 25, 2012. https://www.census.gov/newsroom/releases/archives/miscellaneous/cb12-134.html.

Urban Elemental Gardens: Crafting Magic in Small Outdoor Spaces

by Tiffany Lazic

In a moment when one is entrenched in an endless trek across a desert of gray concrete, there is nothing that brings the soul to life more than the oasis of color afforded by an urban garden. (Although sometimes an enlightened coffee shop that knows the benefit of a lavender shot in a mocha latte can be a welcomed balm to the soul as well.) Most cities have had the inspired foresight to plan for intercity respites. Some of these "greens" have become the stuff of legend, appearing in stories, films, and other popular culture media to such a degree that finding yourself actually standing in one of these infamous landscapes, such as Central Park (New York) or Hyde Park (London), can feel a bit surreal. But it is not necessary to have access to huge tracts of land in order to bring the legendary, the mythical, and the magical into your life. All you need is a little slice of outside, a hardy plant or two, a couple of special objects, and a spark of imagination.

There are several ways to approach the creation of an urban elemental garden, depending, of course, on the size and layout of the space with which you have to work. Whether working with an elemental system of three (Celtic realms of land, sea, and sky), four (Pagan and First Nations quarters of earth, air, fire, and water), or five (alchemical and Ayurvedic elements of earth, air, fire, water, and aether or the Chinese elements of earth, water, fire, wood, and metal), your garden can become a place to deepen elemental understanding and focus magical intent. Wonderful though it is to be able to have differentiated areas

for each separate element, even a small amount of space will allow for a potently effective multielemental garden.

Earth

It seems almost redundant to talk about creating an earth-focused garden. However you approach any of your garden features, they are going to twig your soul to resonate with the element of earth. That said, there are certain items and objects that can encourage the earth elementals to take pause and maybe even take up residence.

As stewards of the earth's treasures, dwarves love gardens with crystals, which not only bring beauty but offer the added benefit of healing vibrational energy. There are some fairly inexpensive stones and crystals that can allow for a stunning focal point while emanating certain qualities throughout your garden. Use rose quartz to imbue your garden with gentleness and love. Use amethyst to strengthen spiritual connection. Clear quartz is like the glacier water of the crystal world, clearing and cleansing all around it. Special stones that have found me on my travels often make their way into my earth garden. To a casual glance these look like unspectacular stones, but I know that they hold within them the resonance of distant lands and landscapes that are dear to my heart.

In the past, when our children were young and we went through the snail/fish/hamster/guinea pig years, this garden also served as the final resting place for many a beloved animal companion. With a fair amount of space and a selection of tall, thin stones, one can create a small, circular henge, a lovely evocative spot to hold ceremonies for those who have passed. Sitting on a wooden bench, surrounded by special stones and beautiful crystals nestled in a carpet of ground cover, this garden is a wonderful spot to pause in contemplation, feeling the solid and grounded comfort of the earth.

Water

The obvious feature for a water-aligned elemental garden is a pond, naturally. However, if it is not feasible to dig a hole deep enough for a full water feature in the area available to you, a shallow container filled with water will serve the elemental purpose and often double as a favored bathing spot for birds. With increased incidences of West Nile virus, it is important to ensure that any water in your Water garden is not still or stagnant, lest it become a mosquito breeding ground. Stagnancy is also never conducive to effective magical work! Fountains with either electric or solar-powered pumps are an easy solution to constant water flow, and there is nothing like the sound of a fountain's steady, gentle sprinkle to bring a sense of ease and peace to the soul. A pond that is deeper than three feet will

be able to withstand the deep freeze of northern climes without becoming solid ice. This is especially important to keep in mind if you want to introduce live fish (or water nymphs) into your pond.

Holy wells and holy water are a global spiritual theme and have been pilgrimage destinations as places to petition or thank deity for thousands of years. In the same way that stones gathered in travels can be a powerful addition to an earth garden, putting a few drops of sacred water from a holy well into the water of your pond not only creates a connection between your elemental garden and the ancient sacred site, but it also ramps up potency for any magical work done.

Water plants are a given for a pond and are particularly helpful in preventing stagnancy if a fountain is not possible. I find there is something just wondrous about a floating plant, but have learned over the years to be conservative in my water plant acquisition. After several summers of having my small pond completely covered in water lettuce or water hyacinth, I now know that one plant purchased in spring will more than do the job over the course of the summer. Moonflowers, forget-me-nots, and 'Blue Moon' phlox are also gorgeous flowers for this garden.

Water helps us tap into our emotional life, offering the opportunity to release that which may be stuck in us and encouraging the inner waters to flow once again. By burying the grief in the earth garden and merging your tears with the holy waters in the water garden, powerful, healing magical work can happen.

Air

Much as I love the solid comfort of the earth garden and the poignant embrace of the water garden, I have spent so much time cultivating a relationship with the plant devas and neighborhood birds that my air garden has taken on a

hilarious life of its own. With a large array of feeders, it has become quite the bird hot spot, and the seeds that drop to the ground have made for an interesting display of unexpected plants. It seems that anything planted in the air garden just takes off and expands in spades. This was also a major learning experience when it came to planting the mint! In direct contrast to the earth garden, this is a great garden for plants and herbs that like to reach for the sky. Angelica, 'Ruby Giant' echinacea, and Russian sage are a few lovely ones that are easy to establish.

If possible, it is wonderful to craft this garden around or in the vicinity of a tree. Of course, the birds love it, especially if there is a birdhouse or two tucked within the branches. Trees provide so many opportunities to evoke air. If you work with intention ribbons or clouties, the tree in your air garden is a perfect place to hang them post-ritual. It does something quite profound in the soul to see the ribbons accumulate over time, the beauty of your intentions waving gaily in the breeze. You can also hang a strand of prayer flags between the branches. Crafting one with your personal deities is a powerful act of magic in itself, and the flag becomes a constant reflection of dedication. Trees also often present interesting nooks in which to leave offerings to the fairies and nature devas.

Bringing a childlike wonder to the creation of your air garden activates joy and hope. It can be helpful in alleviating heaviness and depression, opening the soul to possibility and light.

Fire

Everyone loves a fiery garden element! Fire pits, outdoor fireplaces, and chimineas are very popular features that create a stunning outdoor space. Space requirements may dictate choice, but even in a tiny space a little ceramic chiminea is a perfect touch to bring a bit of transformational magic to a fire garden. Sadly, one phenomenon that has been hitting some cities is that of garden theft. This tends to be more of an issue with front gardens, of course. I am not at all suggesting the need for an anxious mind in the creation of a lovely magical garden, but awareness is always beneficial. After a few heartbreaking losses from my fire garden, including a huge beautiful chiminea, I chose instead to place inexpensive candleholders and candles in the garden. (I have not had a theft problem since, though a strategically placed dragon might have been helpful as well!)

The flower that just calls out for the fire garden is the sunflower. Whether one stunning, towering beauty or a garden full of bright yellow to fiery-red faces, sunflowers are great for inspiring passion and energy. Marigolds and snapdragons also bring a fiery sense of fun.

Aether

Alchemically speaking, once we have the four other elements in complete balance, we activate aether. Said to be the purer, finer air breathed by the gods, aether is transcendent, taking us out of the earthbound, human realm and illuminating the spirit. Infusing your aether garden with light of all forms is a beautiful way to invoke this element. As solar-powered lights are becoming more readily available at a reasonable price, it does not take much to have a gorgeous light-filled garden that fills the soul with magic! Mirrors and reflective balls help to make a little light go a long way.

Aether teaches us that all things are possible and that spirit can overcome all challenge through what may seem like miraculous feats. Insects are nature's little miracles, often able to accomplish the impossible. There are many, many plants and herbs that attract bees and butterflies. Two favorites are the aptly named bee balm and butterfly weed.

Designing Magic

One of my favorite overheard conversations from many years ago was between my young son and one of his friends as they were coming up the path toward the house. My son was saying, "This is the water garden and this is the fire garden and . . ."

His friend casually replied, "I don't know what you're talking about."

It was such a light, breezy, comfortable exchange, it made me laugh. But it also made me think about what I had unintentionally done when I made the decision to allow magical structure to direct my approach to design, plants, and decorative elements for my gardens.

I realized that, in setting an elemental connection to these gardens, I had opened up another way to experience magic on a daily basis. Our house is just blocks from the downtown core so there is not a huge amount of space with which to work. However, I have found that a few meaningful items nestled—and sometimes hidden—amongst flowers and herbs not only look beautiful but also expand the locale for magical practice into the space beyond the walls of the house.

Our house is our sanctuary. There are many sacred spots, honoring shrines, and working altars set up in various places inside. These elementally aligned gardens have created a sacred circle around our home that not only serves as a magical buffer to the street but also brings the Divine to mind every time we leave or enter the house, if you have the eye and the heart to see.

Whether you are in house, townhouse, condo, or apartment, urban elemental gardens reflect alchemy in action, bringing the above of spirit to the below of color, scent, and natural beauty, and the within of soul to the without of evocative expression. They bring joy to passersby and wonder to those who can see them for what they truly are. And that is magic.

Witchy Business: Navigating the Online Magickal Marketplace

by Kate Freuler

Have you ever dreamed of having your own metaphysical business? Perhaps you've imagined yourself behind the counter in a crystal-filled shop that smells of incense or seen yourself with your own booth at a summer Pagan festival. Maybe you've thought how great it would be to connect with like-minded people while turning a lifelong passion into an online business. If so, you are a lot like me. Running a metaphysical shop has been one of my dreams since I was a child, and making it come true has been transformative and fun.

Nowadays, with online selling venues being so accessible and easy to use, pursuing the dream of having a "witchy business," as I like to call it, is within reach for many of us from the comfort of our own homes without the legal and financial backing required for a brick-and-mortar store.

Lessons in Magikcal Shopkeeping

I've been selling amulets, magickal jewelry, spell bottles, and Witchcraft supplies online for over nine years now and have learned many interesting lessons during the journey—some of them the hard way! We magickal shop owners encounter some unique challenges and responsibilities that are very different from if we were selling, say, clothing or pottery. Dealing in magickal items can become highly personalized, and sometimes my customers trust me with their hidden secrets and desires. It's definitely not a boring job! If you think you are ready to start selling your own witchy wares, here are some pointers to get you started.

1. Play by the Rules

Wait, that's no fun! However, unfortunately for us magickal folks, our services tend to be misunderstood in general and are sometimes under scrutiny by others. As a result, we may find ourselves being questioned or even banned from online marketplaces, usually for making "false claims," when we didn't even realize we were doing anything wrong. This happened to me early on when I listed an amulet described as "money attracting." This was deemed a false claim, even though I honestly believed that was the purpose of the amulet. A false claim is any time we guarantee or imply an outcome, physical or otherwise, with the purchase of an item. We are also not allowed to sell "cures" (no matter how much we may believe they will work), and when describing the attributes for herbs, crystals, or spells, we must choose our words very carefully. These rules sometimes seem unfair and clearly demonstrate that mainstream society still, in this day and age, does not fully understand our beliefs. Regardless, once you've chosen an e-commerce platform on which to sell, you absolutely must follow their terms of use and comply

47

with FDA regulations. If you try to bend the rules, even a little, by saying a certain crystal heals diseases or guarantees lottery winnings, think twice: you can lose your business in a flash and not have a legal leg to stand on.

In some states and provinces, it is even illegal to perform spell-casting services. The intention of these laws is to protect vulnerable people from fraud. For example, I once saw an online ad offering to perform a long-distance disease-curing spell for a hundred dollars; the buyer would not be receiving any tangible object but was simply paying for the promise of a magickal cure. Providing an intangible service like this is not allowed on many e-commerce sites, for the seller can easily appear to be taking advantage of someone who is desperate. However, we *can* sell our amulets, spellkits, and objects as tools to be used by a customer in their own spells, for healing, for money, for love, or for whatever they choose. See the difference? It's a blurry line, but it is there.

2. We Are Representing Our Community

When we put our business out there on the internet, we are representing a worldwide group of Pagans, Wiccans, Witches, and other magickal people. Our group is sometimes judged by society in a harsh and negative way already. If we go out there and conduct shady business, we are perpetrating the stereotype that we are all charlatans, money-hungry frauds, and scammers. Unfortunately, as with everything, there are some bad apples; these are usually not real practitioners of the Craft but people who see a business opportunity and a chance to exploit the needs and weaknesses of others. These sellers give us all a bad reputation. So be realistic and honest in your business, your products, and customer service. If someone contacts you requesting you cast a spell or make an amulet for a goal that you feel is unrealistic or unethical, don't do it. I have had to turn customers away many times because their needs were far-fetched or did not mesh with my own morals.

3. Get Ready for Some Off-the-Wall Questions

I've received emails from potential customers asking for everything from baldness cures to forcing a daughter-in-law to get pregnant against her wishes to killing someone who stands in the way of a love interest. As you see from these requests, there is clearly a major misunderstanding of what Witches actually do. My advice is to answer these questions as politely as possible and decline the sale. You are not obligated to correct others' misconceptions of the Craft. Usually, those looking to display their power over others in a hateful manner don't want to hear the truth anyway. If a customer becomes too demanding or threatening, report them to the website and block them. Do not engage with people who push your boundaries or raise red flags in your intuition.

4. Look Out for Haters

"So what do you do?" is a casual question that often pops up in small talk. Answering "I do Witchcraft!" doesn't always get a positive response. I do find most people in my particular community pretty open-minded, but unfortunately not everyone has that privilege. If you feel you are facing harsh judgment on the topic and would rather not engage in it, you may want to just say you sell gifts or trinkets and leave the Witchcraft out of it; on the other hand, you can use the opportunity to educate people about your beliefs. It's up to you. Also, just as with any business, the Witchcraft market is competitive! Some sellers are not above stealing your ideas, undercutting your prices, or falsely befriending you in order to get your clients. I wish there were some way to avoid this, but that's just the way it is in any market—there are those bad apples again. Follow your instincts regarding who you can trust and team up with.

5. Communicate with Empathy

One of the most common types of client to pop up is beginners. They're new to the path and full of questions. Be kind and patient with these customers, answer their queries, and don't disparage them or talk down to them. Sometimes in the online community people can be rude or discouraging to those just starting out who may have an innocent question or comment. Let's encourage them instead, keeping in mind that we were all newbies once! That being said, you are selling amulets or supplies, not providing tutoring or an online course. If you find someone starts taking up too much of your free time and you do not feel pulled to be their mentor, I suggest diplomatically recommending some books and sending them on their way. If they're really serious about pursuing the Craft, they will do the legwork. Another type of client who appears now and again is nonmagickal people who have turned to spells and Witchcraft out of desperation at difficult times in their lives, such as when they are suffering a loss or struggling in some way. When someone approaches you with what seems like desperation and need—even with a gross misunderstanding of the Craft—handle it with heart. Many times all they need is to feel they've been heard. Send them love, even if you can't do magickal work for them.

The Metaphysical Market

Now that we have the basic advice out of the way, you're ready to get making and selling! When you see all the amazing items up for grabs in the online metaphysical market, you will inevitably become a buyer as well. Either way, thanks to the internet, we can buy and sell almost any charm, spell, or amulet imaginable in a simple click. Witchy buyers and makers alike can reap the benefits of an easily accessible online magickal marketplace. It's wonderful, isn't it? Well . . . not everyone thinks so, and they will not hesitate to tell you so.

"If You Didn't Make It Yourself, It Won't Work!"

If you haven't heard that phrase yet, you will once your shop takes off. There you are minding your own witchy business when you stumble across the blog, tweet, or online persona declaring that store-bought Witchcraft wares are useless—or worse, unethical. It is a rather popular opinion among magickal people that in order for a spell or amulet to manifest a desired outcome, it must be created or performed by the individual themselves and that "buying" these products is a waste of money. What makes it especially scathing is that it is often fellow Pagans, Witches, Wiccans, and like-minded people saying it. If you've ever been on the receiving end of a condemning online debate regarding your handcrafted items (and I have!), you will understand how deflating this can be. However, before getting upset and typing out a regrettable retort, let's first think about this issue, both as an online seller and buyer of magickal goods.

While I agree that the most powerful spells and amulets are made by the practitioner themselves, I also believe that it's

perfectly possible to perform magick for another person and manifest results—even better if the two are combined and the client and spellcaster work together. Here are some tips for people on both ends of the transaction to ensure that the intention and power inside those magickal items isn't getting lost in the mail.

Tips for Sellers

Chances are if a person is purchasing an amulet or spell from you instead of making their own, they may not have the knowledge, time, or resources to do it themselves and trust you to provide not only the physical item but the magick as well. Using the correct materials is important, of course, making sure to align proper herbs and other ingredients with intent, but we all know there is so much more to an amulet than that. This is where the question of charging and empowering comes in, and how we, the shop owners, can make sure that our amulets pack as much power as possible for our clients.

1. Make a Connection

During construction of the item, contemplate any correspondence you've had with the client, their tone, and their needs. Some Witchcrafters find it helps to have a picture of the customer handy to help connect the amulet to them. If that's not possible, you can write their name on a piece of paper and lay the amulet on top of it during whatever empowering ritual you use once it is complete. This creates a connection in the spirit realm between the client and the object.

2. Empower in Bulk

If you are lucky enough that you have built a customer base and are getting lots of orders, you may find it becomes taxing on your energy to personally enchant multiple amulets a day. There are a few simple ways to make it easier. I suggest keeping selenite handy, for it cleanses and charges items simultaneously. Place the amulet on a selenite wand to lend it extra power just before shipping it to your customer. Another trick is to lay your craft supplies out under the appropriate Moon phase to retain an extra boost of power for when you assemble them. Keep them wrapped and separated afterward to ensure they hold the power of the proper Moon phase until use. You can also charge your supplies in batches; say you get a shipment of carnelian stones that you plan to make into courage amulets. Charge all of them at one time with intent, and then set them aside "precharged" for when you construct the final products.

3. Send Clear Instructions

As a final courtesy, make sure you send step-by-step instructions to your clients on how they too can charge the magickal item themselves and attune it with their own energy and goals. You can print the instructions on paper and tuck them in with their order or just email them a copy. Including a customer in the empowerment of their own amulet or spell kit intensifies its strength and gives the client a reassuring sense of control over their situation too.

4. Honesty Is the Best Policy

What if after all this effort the amulet still doesn't work? This is a tricky situation to approach for both parties. I find most customers understand and accept that there are simply some things that will not turn out as planned—the universe can be tricky! This is just another reason why it is especially important to make your client understand their own role in charging and empowering their amulet, helping it work for them in exactly the way they need. Sometimes a challenge you may encounter is the customer not being forthcoming with all the details of the situation, which will render your magick less effective. For example, someone may request you make them a spell kit to catch the eye of a love interest but neglect to mention the object of their affection is happily married with children. You can only work with a person who is honest with you, whether you are selling or buying. It goes both ways!

A Note for Customers

Maybe you are not a maker yourself but are interested in buying some witchy stuff online. You're going to have questions. When you purchase an amulet or charm from a store, is it just wear and go (or burn and go, in the case of candles and incense)? Or is there something you must do yourself to personalize an item to your own needs? Even when buying from a reputable and trusted source, magick is all about intent. Therefore, you need to put some of your own energy into any magickal item you buy.

When you receive an enchanted item, do your own small ritual with it. This can be easy even for a beginner. I suggest first performing a simple cleansing to get rid of any psychic muck that may be picked up in transport. This will not erase the power the seller has put into it but only the unwanted residual energy of travel or being handled by people in the postal system. You can pass the item through incense smoke, leave it under the Full Moon overnight, or, if it is waterproof, pass it under water while envisioning any unwanted vibes washing away, leaving only the

clear, powerful intent that you and the seller have agreed upon. Then, place your amulet on your altar or hold it in your hand and envision its purpose as clearly and specifically as you can. See your goal as if you already have achieved it. If your goal is prosperity, see yourself spending the money you have found, working the job you love, or experiencing the relief of paying off your bills. Transfer this feeling into the amulet and let it combine with the special ingredients and energies the seller has already put there. Your direct intent, combined with the experience, knowledge, and materials of the crafter, will stir up some powerful magickal teamwork.

On that note, don't be shy! Go ahead and ask questions. Communicating with the maker helps them understand your needs and reassures you that you're not being scammed. Any seller who refuses to answer questions, promises unrealistic outcomes, and makes farfetched claims is probably not trustworthy. If you get a bad vibe from a certain shop, you may want to look around for a more relatable, personable seller. Someone who communicates with you in an open, honest and direct way is far more likely to be practicing what they preach than someone who pretends to have superhuman powers and hides behind an egotistical mask of mystery and self-proclaimed power.

So, is it possible to buy an amulet or spell online and still have it work? Yes! But both the buyer and the seller have to put some magickal elbow grease into it. Even in this time of immediate gratification, magick, like most things worth having, takes some good old-fashioned effort, communication, and honesty.

Put Your Heart into It

Whether you are selling deeply personalized custom amulets or just hawking supplies to other Witches, remember that you are a soul first and a business second. A metaphysical business is so much more than just selling trinkets. We are sending our intent out into the world with every order we ship, so fill those packages with love, wisdom, gratitude, and joy. You may even change someone's life, including your own!

Rethinking the Wheel of the Year

by Stephanie Woodfield

I very distinctly remember when I realized my seasonal practices no longer made any sense. It was at a Beltane ritual a few years ago when the priestess began talking about how we were welcoming the warm weather once again, and the joining of the lord and lady would bring the fruitfulness of the coming months ahead. Makes total sense, right? That's textbook Beltane to most Pagans.

Yet all I could think was how ridiculous it was. Because we were in Central Florida. We were outside and it was in the seventies, the land already green and lush around us. Winter in Florida is when a good chunk of the year's produce is grown, so the land had been anything but dormant for "winter." The fruitfulness the priestess was talking about had already reached its height. I wasn't looking forward to the brutal heat to come at all—I was mourning a bit for the cooler days we would soon move past. We were in the dry season, and with the heat that was beginning to grow stronger and the grass and plants that were beginning to turn brown, there has been several wildfires in the area. What we should have been asking the gods for, I thought, was rain. We should be welcoming in the rain of the wet season and asking for an end to the wildfires. We should be respecting that the destruction of the wildfires is needed and not deadly, a part of the life cycle in this part of the world.

I realized in that moment that even though by most Pagan standards we were celebrating Beltane as we should, all we were really doing was repeating what we had been told or read was "correct" for this holiday instead of actually connecting to the changes in the land around us. I thought

about other Beltanes in New England, ones when there was still a chill in the air and we were all elated that we were no longer stuck indoors from the winter weather. I thought of how I was wearing shorts and sweating more on Beltane in Florida than I even had during the peak of summer in Connecticut. The traditional dance of the seasons made sense there, but what about the land I now lived on? How could I honor this place and its cycles? Could the traditional Wheel of the Year even make sense here? If part of being a Pagan was moving with the cycle of the land, then I would have to create new ways to honor my new home, to learn to truly listen to what the land was telling me about itself.

Honoring the Cycles of the Land

Having lived most of my life in New England, I had never really needed to question how I celebrated the seasons. What we think of as the traditional Wheel of the Year comes to us from practices across Ireland, the United Kingdom, and parts of central Europe with climates and seasonal shifts that fall fairly in sync with the seasons in New England and parts of the central United States. Honoring the cycles of the seasons was always a meaningful part of my spiritual practices living in Connecticut. Winter was harsh and there was a joyfulness to welcoming the warmer weather back. But when I moved to the South, I quickly understood that how I had been celebrating just didn't fit any more. I was at quite a loss for what to do. Since the gods that are my primary dedication are Irish and several important mythological events happen on particular holidays, such as Lughnasadh, Beltane, and Samhain, I started off by simply celebrating the event related to the myths I held dear. They were meaningful to me, but still remained divorced from the land.

And so, it became a challenge to understand the landscape I now called home, because if I didn't learn how to connect with it, I wouldn't know how to honor it. It doesn't have four seasons, but it does have its own unique cycles. There is the wet season that begins around Beltane and the dry season, when the weather is more moderate, even chilly at times, and crops are grown. February marks the local strawberry festivals, when the fruit is harvested and there is outdoor entertainment. Summer is brutal, almost in the way winter in New England is harsh. It is when people stay indoors, and the afternoons are marked with lightning and magnificent thunderstorms.

Although most people connect Florida with hot weather, what truly defines the landscape is water, from the freshwater springs and the aquifers that keep the lush landscape vibrant and alive and help form the Everglades to the afternoon downpours in the wet season. What shapes the land the most is water. Most of Florida used to be an ancient coral reef, and part of the land still remembers. And so, I learned to listen to the land and celebrate the cycles I saw in the land around me. I took time to explore the wild places, to understand what the land and the spirits ensouled in it wanted and cared about, and how I might honor them.

Analyzing Traditional Dates

So how do we begin rethinking the seasons? The first thing we must consider is why we are using the traditional Neopagan dates we know today in the first place. Are these the dates our ancestors would have celebrated? Do they work for the environment we live in? In today's world, we like things to run on schedule, to be set in stone. But how our ancestors would have celebrated the land around them would have been more fluid. They would have looked at nature to tell them when it was Beltane or Lughnasadh. When this particular plant started to bloom or when that particular thing began to happen upon the natural landscape. What we think of as Samhain is not quite the date the ancient Irish celebrated on; it would have been closer to November 10. Some Celtic Reconstructionist Pagans still celebrate this date as Old Samhain. Because the Irish did not use the Gregorian calendar we use today, slowly over time the dates for their celebrations stopped lining up with the natural cycle. For a society that relied on planting and harvesting at the correct times to survive, this would have been devastating, and so the dates were moved. Similarly, in Ireland Lughnasadh was celebrated throughout the month of August. Trade, commerce, horse races, and religious festivities marked the gatherings for this holiday. In today's terms, it would have seemed akin to a country fair, minus the deep-fried Twinkies. So that begs the question, is Lughnasadh really on August 1? Is it the entire month? A certain portion of it?

But what about holidays that are marked by astrological events? Those are set days, right? Well, yes and no. When I visited Ireland this past Samhain, one of the places we went was Newgrange. The tour guide brought us into the mound and using a light bulb simulated how it would have looked lit up on the Winter Solstice. It was an absolutely amazing experience, but perhaps the biggest takeaway from the visit was what she told us afterward. She spoke about how people interested could enter the lottery to be one of the special few who got to witness the light enter the mound on the day of the solstice, but she also told us that the light didn't just enter the inner chamber only on December 21 (or whatever date the astronomical solstice fell on) but for about ten days total, a few days before and a few days after the actual astronomical event. So, she asked, when was the actual solstice? December 21, or all the days the chamber was lit up? Which day or days did the Irish celebrate?

Ultimately, this reminds us that there are no set rules for seasonal celebrations. Just because we celebrate on a particular day doesn't mean the Pagans of the past did. And truthfully, it doesn't matter. At the heart of these celebrations is the idea that to become one with the land we must listen to it and see its changing cycles, whether they are subtle or dramatic. And those cycles will not be the same everywhere, so our celebrations should reflect that.

A friend of mine has started celebrating the Wheel of the Year in a very similar way: Beltane has arrived when a

certain bush in her yard begins to bloom, and part of her family's celebration involves harvesting the berries from the bush. Sometimes it is around the first of May, sometimes a week earlier or later, but the point is she listens to the land itself, connecting to the cycles around her, which is in the end the very reason we celebrate seasonal cycles—to connect with the land itself. For me, Beltane is wildfire season, a time to call the rains, and begins when the magnolia trees bloom. Imbolc is the strawberry harvest.

Make a New Wheel

I challenge you to rethink what you have been taught about the Wheel of the Year. Grab a pen and notebook, spend some time in the natural world, and really look at the changes that happen around you. Write these questions in your notebook for each holiday and take your time figuring out the answers.

- What change in the landscape where you live marks the holiday?
- What date would you use?
- What are the major shifts in the landscape?
- How can you celebrate those changes? What meaning do you find in them?

You may decide to completely change how you celebrate some holidays, simply tweak others, or even add holidays based on what you discover.

Whether or not the place you live in reflects the traditional cycles of the Wheel of the Year, I encourage you to rethink how to celebrate the land around you. Build a deeper relationship with the earth you walk upon, and honor the unique ebb and flow of the land around you.

Air Magic

The Milagro Magic
by Natalie Zaman

Pirate's treasure, a dragon's hoard, a genie's cave . . . There's something about a pile of tinkling, twinkling gold and silver that gets my greedy little heart a-fluttering, and it's exactly what I felt when the five-pound box of milagros I ordered from Mexico arrived on my doorstep. You read that correctly. Five pounds. These shiny bits of magic are sold by weight (at least when you're buying lots of little ones)—which is a good thing because when it comes to working with milagros, quantity can be key, and there are an awful lot of milagros in five pounds.

The word *milagro* literally means "miracle" or "surprise" (of the good variety) in Spanish. You'll find the charms in Mexico, the Southern United States, and parts of Latin America, where they were brought over to from Europe, specifically the Iberian peninsula. The concept, however, is actually much older than that.

The milagro is an *ex voto* (Latin for "from the vow")—a token of devotion, offering of gratitude, or petition for intercession. The custom is cross-cultural and dates back to ancient Greece. The *pinax*, a small devotional plaque with figures painted on it, was placed in the temple to thank deities for their power or as a plea for help, a prayer in graphic novel form. Later on, votive paintings called *tamata*, were created by practitioners of Eastern Orthodox religions. These were (and are) images of saints and other holy intercessors to which metal is applied, a means of glorification as well as making the portrait an offering.

Milagro Glossary

Milagros come in hundreds of shapes (that alone makes them an intricate and complex system of symbols), and a single milagro can have many associations: a tiny leg can be used as a petition for healing a broken bone or other leg ailment, just as much as a prayer for safe travel or anything else one might associate with a leg and what it does. Some saints have body parts associated with them (in St. Roque's case, a wounded leg), and so milagros can be representative of their spirits. Essentially, it comes down to the user and purpose. Hold a milagro in your hand. What does it mean to you? What memories does it stir?

The most recognizable milagros are the flat charms—large and small—in gold or silver. Some are actually cast in precious metals, but most are tin and tinted gold or silver. Milagros can also be made of other materials; wax, wood, and clay beads that take the shape of birds, flowers and other icons with symbolic value. On the next page are some typical milagros you might encounter and some traditional and suggested uses. When working with them, think of what the images say to you or what you feel when you touch them and go with that. Prayers, petitions, and magic are most powerful when they come from the heart.

Being raised Catholic, I gravitated to milagros just as I had to other familiar tools: candles, altars, images and statues of saints, and sigils. I work with saints because through them I've found a comfortable connection to sacredness, the universe, and God and Goddess—but I don't believe that milagros belong exclusively in their realm. Do your guiding deities and spirits love milagros? Take some time to meditate and ask them. (I've learned not to take this detail for granted!) Even if they're not a part of your personal history, if these lovely charms make your eyes sparkle with delight, try incorporating them into your magical practice.

Milagros are often seen as a form of folk art and crafting, and I've come to see that as an essential aspect of working with them magically. When you use milagros in spell, devotional, or ritual work, you find yourself making something. Working with them engages the whole person—mind, hand, heart, and soul—and therefore makes for incredibly potent magic: miracles made manifest.

Milagro	Traditional Meanings
Car	Travel, transportation, getting a new car, finding and fixing an issue with a car
Dog	Loyalty, getting a dog or a pet
Eyes	Sight, clarity, healing a problem with the eyes, protection from the evil eye
Heart	Love, physical and/or emotional troubles with the heart, courage
House	Finding or purchasing a home, home protection, a happy home, shelter, a safe haven
Leg*	Troubles with the limb, such as a muscle pain or broken bone; travel
Praying Man or Woman	Making a petition, hope that prayers will be heard
Pregnant Woman	Children, family, fertility, a healthy pregnancy
Star of David	The Jewish faith, someone of the Jewish faith, struggle
Virgin Mary	Blessings, intercession from Mary, protection, anything to do with mothers and mothering

* The same concepts can be applied to other appendages, body parts, and organs: healing wounds in that area or enhancing what the part is used for. For example, an arm can be a petition for strength, a hand, and a helping hand.

Miracles Brought to Light

Beeswax sheets are the perfect medium to wrap, fold, and mold around milagros—and so are perfect for candle magic. I use small metal milagros in my magical work. Working with milagros is all about intention, what you wish to accomplish and whose help you're seeking. Think about that before you begin, and then acquire sheets of beeswax pressed into a honeycomb pattern. The sheets come in different sizes and colors, and while size isn't important, color is, as color embodies its own special energy. For example, if your intention is about love, traditional pinks and reds might be the first colors that come to mind to use. Equally powerful are personal color associations. If you always feel your best—and so find love—when you wear blue, perhaps that would be just as good, or maybe better, to employ. Search your heart to determine what works for you.

You will need:
Sheet of beeswax
Candle wicking
Chalk or permanent marker
Milagros (Think of your intention, and who you would ask for
    help or to whom you would want to express gratitude.)
Hair dryer or heat gun

Unroll a sheet of beeswax so that it lies flat on your workspace. Using the chalk or marker, write out your petition, wish, or statement directly on the wax.

Place a candle wick at one end of the sheet so that the end of the wick lines up with the sheet's edge; this will be the bottom of the candle. The other end of the wick should extend past the other end of the sheet; this will be the top of the candle. Press down on the whole length of the wick to secure it to the wax.

Starting at the bottom of the candle, press a milagro into the wax and say,

Dear (name of saint, deity, etc.) . . .

State your intention or thanks.

Visualize your intention and intercessor. Then, keeping the top and bottom of the candle even, roll the candle once, keeping the wax tight to the milagro. Place another milagro a little above where you placed the first one. State your intention aloud again, visualizing your intention coming to pass or your gratitude being received. Roll the candle again. Continue until you've used up the whole wax sheet.

When you're finished, press the end of the sheet into the candle to secure it. Use the hair dryer or heat gun to soften the wax to make it stick better. Because you're folding the wax around the milagros, you may end up with a triangular, square, or angular candle rather than a round one. If you wish, you can roll another sheet, perhaps in another color, around the first to make a larger, rounder candle.

Alternatively, you can stud a store-bought pillar candle with milagros. Write your intention on the top or bottom of the candle. Use the hair dryer or heat gun to soften the wax on the shaft of the candle; you want the wax to be pliable, but not liquid. When the surface of the candle gets a bit shiny, it should be soft enough to press a milagro into the wax and hold it in place.

Burn a milagro candle on a saint's or deity's special day to add power to your spell. Of course, if your need is urgent, you can burn it right away. Repeat your intention each time you light the candle.

String of Hope

Not all milagros are created equally. Some are simply shapes, while others are cast with bales on top so that they can be nailed to an offering or strung on chains or cords and worn as jewelry.

I like the idea of impermanence; after all, change is the only constant we live with. Create a piece of milagro jewelry to wear your wishes on your sleeve (or elsewhere) and help them come to pass. Again, what you will use will be determined by your intention.

You will need:

A wish or intention. What is your heart's desire? Think about it. Write about it. Search your heart and puzzle out what it is that you really want (or need). It can be an actual, physical thing or something intangible like confidence or friendship. You may also wish to express gratitude or honor. What moves you to create this magic?

Embroidery floss in a color appropriate to your wish. Try using what you personally associate with your intention or use your favorite reference to determine what colors to use.

Milagros that express your intention or honor your deity or spirit of choice. You can use several different charms or multiples of the same. Your jewelry can have a single milagro or a string of them.

Optional: Crystal chips, stones, or beads (with holes drilled through) that support your intention. For example, rose quartz promotes love, jade promotes healing, and tiger's eye promotes success. Use your favorite reference and your intuition to determine what to use for your jewelry.

The jewelry itself is easy to make. Cut an overlong length of embroidery floss (24 to 30 inches) to work with, as you will be knotting each milagro into place. Thread your first milagro onto the floss. When it's positioned where you want it, tie a knot to secure it in place.

Infuse the thread with your intention as you knot it and pass it through your fingers. Imbibe each charm with your desires by stating your intentions aloud as you add it and knot it in place. Ask your deity or guiding spirit for his or her assistance. Continue to thread and knot milagros onto the strand (interspersing them with the crystals if you wish), until you feel it is complete. See this jewelry is an incarnation of your intention, a poem made manifest to enhance your spell—but like a spoken word, it becomes a memory. The point of this jewelry is to lose it; when it leaves you, you know that change will soon be afoot!

Tie the string around your wrist, ankle, or neck so that you're comfortable (depending on the length, you may need to wrap it once or twice), and wear it until it drops off. The string will be picked up by birds and the milagros will be found by those who need them (or perhaps by those who will make your wishes come to pass—the universe works in mysterious ways!).

A Portable Prayer

What are the words you live by? What words move you? What are the words you repeat to yourself when you need to be reminded of your own strength and power? Craft them into a portable, tangible talisman with the help of a handful of milagros.

You will need:

Square of thin cardboard, 9 by 9 inches (A recycled cereal box will work nicely.)

2 pieces of cloth, 9 by 9 inches, in colors and patterns that make you happy

Craft glue

Milagros that relate to your quote (see below)

Heavy sewing needle

Embroidery thread in a color that coordinates with your fabric

Velcro button

Short inspirational quote, prayer, or mantra that holds personal meaning to you printed on a piece of paper or embroidered on a piece of fabric

Glitter glue

Cut a 3-inch square from each corner of the cardboard square to form an equilateral cross. Each "arm" and the center square should be 3 inches tall by 3 inches wide.

Using the cardboard as a pattern, cut two equilateral crosses from your fabric.

Score (don't cut!) the inside square on your cardboard cross so that each arm can be folded down over it.

Brush one side of the cardboard cross with glue and cover it with one of the fabric crosses. Smooth out any bubbles or wrinkles and allow it to dry completely.

Sew a milagro or two to each side arm and the bottom arm on the fabric-covered side. You can also glue them, but a stitch

is stronger. Tie off your thread on the milagro side so that the blank cardboard side of the cross remains flat.

Glue one half of the Velcro button in the center of the top arm. Glue or sew your quote to the center of the cross.

Brush the other side of the cardboard with glue and cover it with the other fabric cross. Smooth out any bubbles or wrinkles and allow it to dry completely. Trim any excess fabric.

Fold the side arms in and then the bottom. Glue the other piece of Velcro to the blank side of the bottom arm (there should be a milagro on the opposite side). Before you secure it, make sure that it lines up with the other portion of the button that you attached previously. To close the talisman, fold in the right arm, then the left, and then the bottom. One piece of the Velcro button should be facing up. When you fold the top arm down, the Velcro buttons will connect and hold it shut. Once all of the Velcro is in place, outline the buttons with glitter glue.

When all the glue is completely dry, outline the cross in glitter glue to cover any seams and blank spaces and seal the fabric to the cardboard. Allow the talisman to dry completely before folding it up.

Carry your portable prayer with you and look at it any time you need a word of encouragement.

More Little Miracles

Milagros can also be incorporated into traditional magical practices. Here are a few ideas to get you started:

- Making a mojo bag, charm bag, or herbal pouch? Add milagros to your blended ingredients or tie a milagro when you knot the pouch to seal it, to add that energy to your working.
- Incorporate milagros into crystal grids to channel and raise energy.
- Do a bit of divination with milagros: place all the milagros you have into a pile or pouch and draw some out. What is their message to you?

Bright blessings!

Resources

Egan, Martha. *Milagros: Votive Offerings from the Americas.* Albuquerque: Museum of New Mexico Press, 1991.

Thompson, Helen. *Milagros: A Book of Miracles.* San Francisco: HarperOne, 1998.

Psychic Housecleaning

by James Kambos

A psychic housecleaning is an excellent way to clear and cleanse the environment of any house or other physical space. It may be used to clear away negative energies after an unpleasant event has occurred or after an unwelcome guest has left. Even if your home doesn't seem to have any bad energies hanging around, a psychic housecleaning will serve to protect you and your family. Whenever possible, it's good to perform a psychic housecleaning before it's actually needed. This will help keep hostile energies away.

Your home isn't the only place that can benefit from a psychic housecleaning. A psychic cleaning could also be done where your coven meets, in an office, or in a business or shop. I've known of a few taking place in dorm rooms.

A psychic housecleaning is a good way to protect and bless any business. I once performed one at a business the day after an employee was fired, and it helped restore positive energy and balance to the shop.

Don't forget—a psychic housecleaning is also an especially good idea to perform when moving into a new house or apartment.

What You'll Need

To perform a psychic housecleaning, you'll need a new plain white candle that can be held and carried easily. A small pillar or taper candle that fits securely into a candleholder that has a handle would be perfect. You'll also need a drop of olive oil to dress or anoint the candle with.

You may also wish to use a small wand or a ritual knife to trace a holy shape, such as a cross or pentagram, in front of doors and windows, but I've found that simply using your pointing finger works just as well.

After I've finished a housecleaning ritual, I like to end it by sprinkling a bit of any purifying herb at all entrances. I use white sage for its all-purpose cleansing qualities. Other herbs and spices you may want to have on hand for this purpose are cinnamon, clove, or lavender. Cinnamon and clove drive out evil forces while cleansing a space. Lavender brings peace and calm. It's good to use after an argument.

Getting Ready

First, I suggest that you should usually perform any psychic housecleaning when you'll be alone and won't be disturbed. If you feel for some reason a particular psychic cleaning may be difficult, please ask a magically inclined friend for help. Also, if the physical space to be cleaned is larger than you think you can handle, then it is a good idea to ask for assistance.

As I mentioned earlier, you'll need to dress or anoint your candle with olive oil. You'll do that now before you actually begin your psychic housecleaning. To dress your candle, take a drop of olive oil and, beginning in the middle of the candle, rub the olive oil toward the wick. Then, using these same steps, repeat but rub toward the bottom of the candle. Dressing the candle in this manner charges it with positive energy. As you rub the oil along the candle, "see" positive energy filling your space and negative forces being repelled. Now your candle is charged with your intent.

Before starting the psychic housecleaning, have any other supplies ready. Have a candleholder on hand. If you intend to use an athame or wand, have it ready. I also have the herb I'll use at the end of the ritual crumbled in a dish.

A Psychic Housecleaning Ritual

Let's begin. If your psychic housecleaning involves a multistory house or structure, start on the top floor while facing the front of the house. If you have a safe, easily accessible attic, you may start there, if you wish. If not, start on the uppermost floor. You'll spiral in a downward clockwise manner. Try to end at your front door.

If your house or apartment is one level, begin and end the ritual at your front door. Always move around your house in a clockwise direction.

First, light the candle. Gaze at the flame. Visualize the candlelight growing until it surrounds you and your home with a glowing protective aura.

To keep you and your home safe during the ritual, say the following words of power. This will help banish any negative forces. If you have a favorite prayer or affirmation that you prefer, then use it instead. Whatever you choose, say it in a strong, clear voice. Now, raise your candle and say your affirmation or these words of power:

With these words and candlelight,
I call upon all negative forces to take flight.
Leave peacefully from every corner and every space.
Depart; let only positive energy fill this place.
Spirits of joy, health, and happiness,
Protect all who live here from grief and sadness.

Begin moving clockwise around your house. Pause at each window, exterior door, or other opening, such as a fireplace. As you pause, use your athame, wand, or finger to make the shape of a holy symbol, such as a cross or a pentagram, at each opening.

Repeat these steps for each floor. If you feel the need, repeat the words of power.

Finally, you should end at your front door, or close to it if possible. Open the door and respectfully extinguish the candle. As an extra measure of cleansing and purification, sprinkle the herb of your choice at each exterior door.

Your home is now psychically cleaned and blessed.

Some Special Considerations

When it comes to psychic housecleaning, you may encounter certain circumstances that will require you to customize your methods. Here are some situations you may have to deal with and tips on how to handle them.

Don't be discouraged if you feel you didn't get rid of all the bad vibrations. A psychic housecleaning may need to be performed more than once.

If you have a room where a violent crime occurred and feel afraid to enter that room—don't enter. Instead, stand at the threshold and bless the room with a holy symbol. Follow the same procedure as you did when blessing a window or fireplace.

Places such as cellars or attics are sometimes filled with creepy-crawly things. Instead of going into spaces such as these, try this: visualize the space in your mind, and then say your words of power. This also works if you're dealing with a space you believe to be haunted.

A psychic housecleaning is a good way to create a safe haven for you and your family. Do it as often as you wish. Once a year is ideal, especially during the spring. Keep in mind that once negative energy has been removed from your home, it's usually gone for good.

Raziel: The Archangel of Magic

by Chic and S. Tabatha Cicero

When you hear the word "angel," what comes to your mind? Is it an image of a chubby-cheeked cherub on a Christmas card? Or is it a symbolic reminder of a religious upbringing that you have grown out of?

While it is true that angels are primarily found within the monotheistic traditions of Judaism, Islam, and Christianity, they are neither unique nor exclusive to those faiths. Angels and archangels have freely crossed cultural and religious boundaries over the centuries.

In the Hellenistic world of late antiquity, pagans also invoked angels. One account tells of a Christian shrine dedicated to the archangel Michael in the Asia Minor city of Colossae, reputed to be the source of a healing spring. Pagans and Christians alike were drawn to the shrine to petition the mighty archangel for his miraculous curative power. Some ancient texts, such as the Græco-Egyptian Magical Papyri, show that polytheists were quite willing to acknowledge and incorporate the angels of Judeo-Christian as "gods."

Nevertheless, the Judeo-Christian tradition, especially including the noncanonical literature, the so-called forgotten books of the Bible, is a primary source for much of our knowledge of angels and archangels. Angels are spiritual beings that are considered to be specific aspects of God, each with a particular purpose and jurisdiction. The word "angel" comes from the Greek *angelos*, which is itself a translation of the Hebrew word *melakh*, meaning "messenger." They have been described as "messengers of the soul." More precisely, an angel is "an intermediary intelligence between the human and the One in the Great Chain of Being," according to Adam Forrest, distinguished Golden Dawn magician and scholar.

The chief significance of angels is not what they are, but rather what they do. Their essential nature is inseparable from their relationship with the Divine: the Transcendent God or the Absolute Source of All. Yet they are also inseparable from their chief human witnesses—mystics and magicians—who encounter and communicate with them.

These divine intermediaries work with the magician in two ways: as emissaries between us and the Divine, and as governors in the spiritual hierarchies who command lesser angels, spirits, and elementals to carry out the goal of the ritual.

Angels invoked in ritual are chosen because of their attributions and correspondences. Prayers and invocations recited to angels for the accomplishment of a specific magical purpose are affirmations that the magician's will is in alignment with the will of the Divine. An image of the angel may be created through the faculty of the imagination. This image will act as a focal point for the magician's willpower and can result in the ritual's ultimate success.

Angel names often end in the suffixes "-el" and "-yah" which are Hebrew god-names, indicating that these entities are aspects "of God." They act as spiritual messengers, helpful intercessors, and intermediaries between divinity and humanity—they are our companions in the Great Work.

Raziel, Herald of the Divine

Magic is the art of the possible. It is the science and art of causing change in both consciousness and circumstance to occur in conformity with will, using means not currently understood by traditional Western science. This definition takes into account the power of the human mind to effect an inner spiritual change that can effectively influence the outer, physical world.

One particular archangel who could be considered the primary angel of magic is Raziel, whose name means "the Secret of God," as well as "the Herald of God" and "the One Sent Forth from God."

Raziel is the archangel of Chokmah, the Second Sephirah or emanation of divine power on the Qabalistic Tree of Life. *Chokmah* means "wisdom"—the essence of illumination resulting from perfect knowledge and perfect understanding. Chokmah is that aspect of the Divine that is complete action and movement as well as the vital, energizing element of existence. The wheel of the zodiac, and all the star lore that accompanies it, is attributed to Chokmah.

Raziel is the ruler of the angelic host known as the *Ophanim* (sometimes spelled *Auphanim*), which means "the wheels," derived from the word *auph,* meaning "to surround or encircle." As head of this group of angels, Raziel is sometimes called *Ophaniel.* The Ophanim are known as the "many-eyed ones" and are sometimes called the *Galgalim,* or "spheres." They are the wheels of the *Mercabah,* or Throne of God, and are sometimes pictured as wheels with spokes and wings. Their duty is to direct the flow of the divine force into form, thus keeping the cycles of manifestation in constant motion. They provide constant energy and motivation in the ritual work of the magician.

The Herald of God also bears the title "Angel of the Mysteries." According to angelic lore, Raziel is "the angel of the secret regions and chief of the Supreme Mysteries" and author of the mysterious Book of Raziel, "wherein all celestial and earthly knowledge is set down," writes Gustav Davidson. This book, reputed to be written on sapphire, was said to have been given to Adam and passed on to the great Hebrew teachers, including Noah and King Solomon. It contained secrets of the stars, the zodiacal signs, the courses of the planets, and the effects they have on every aspect of Creation. The prophet Enoch was said to come into possession of this book and consequently renamed it the book of Enoch.

As God's herald, Raziel is a divine envoy with a specific mission: he is the personification of wisdom whose primary duty is to bestow wisdom on those able to receive it. He is the archangel of creative force and energy. This teacher of wisdom stands atop the White Pillar on the Tree of Life, sometimes envisioned as the Holy Mountain, where each day he proclaims the secrets of the universe in a great, loud reverberating voice. This makes him the perfect archangel of magic. Meditations and rituals that focus on Raziel can be used to increase spiritual awareness, improve psychic faculties, and gain wisdom in all aspects of the magical arts.

Readers can facilitate a connection with Raziel by obtaining a suitable image of him, by creating a dedicated altar to the archangel, by daily meditation, and by a brief invocation ritual that requests his knowledge and aid.

The Image of Raziel

The Golden Dawn teachings tell us "by names and images are all powers awakened and reawakened." We are visual beings, and it is far easier to connect with a spiritual entity if you have a visual image associated with it.

Since Raziel is not one of the more common angels depicted in art, any generic image of an angel photocopied from a historical source or downloaded from the internet will suffice. However, it would be more effective to draw or paint your own image. If you are not artistically inclined, try making a collage from a photocopied image of an angel combined with colors and symbols associated with the angel and his corresponding Sephirah, Chokmah.

Overall Colors

Raziel's main color is gray, ornamented with black and white. Gray is the basic color of Chokmah, while black and white are the "flashing colors" associated with gray, used to highlight sigils, symbols, and other details against the gray background.

Symbols

Key symbols are the zodiacal wheel, all twelve zodiacal signs in their appropriate colors, all seven symbols of the planets in their appropriate colors, an eye, a book, a scroll, a key, a lamp or lantern, a straight line, an equal-armed cross constructed of two straight lines, and any symbol represented in duplicate to indicate the number two (two books, two lanterns, etc.).

Telesmatic Image

The Hebrew alphabet is a hieroglyphic language of images, colors, numeric values, mystical concepts, and more. Therefore, you can elect to build up a magical image of Raziel based on the Hebrew letters of his name: *Resh Zayin Yod Aleph Lamed* (רזיאל). These five letters have the following associations:

Letter	Name	Meaning	Number	Energy	Color
ר (r)	Resh	Head	200	The Sun	Orange
ז (z)	Zayin	Sword	7	Gemini	Orange
י (y)	Yod	Hand	10	Virgo	Yellow-green
א (a)	Aleph	Ox	1	Air	Yellow
ל (l)	Lamed	Ox-goad	30	Libra	Green

Beginning with the letter Resh at the angel's head and ending with the letter Lamed at his feet, the various images, symbols, and colors assigned to the letters of Raziel's name can be combined to form a potent magical image used to represent him. It might look like the following: A bright, youthful angel whose colors range from golden-orange to yellow to green. His bronzed head is framed by golden hair and crowned with the rays of the Sun. He bears a sword in one hand and a book in the other, showing that he is the protector of sacred wisdom. The letters that compose his name are overwhelmingly airy and mercurial, and this could be represented by wispy clouds and gossamer wings surrounding the figure. He may wear a yellow robe or kilt, and his feet may stand upon the rich green grass of a lush pasture. Based on these guidelines, there are few limits on your creativity for building up an appropriate image.

The total gematria (numeric value) of the name Raziel is 248, a number he shares with Auriel, the archangel of earth and the "Light of God." It is also the number of the Hebrew word *gemarah,* which means "teaching" or "study." Raziel is well-equipped to teach the secrets of magic and shed light upon the mysteries of the universe.

Raziel's sigil, or magical signature, can be easily created from the Golden Dawn's diagram of the Rose of Twenty-Two Letters from the Rose Cross Lamen. This sigil can be placed within a circle, cut out, laminated, attached to a ribbon or chain, and worn around your neck as a lamen (a magical pendant) during your work with the archangel. On the reverse side of the lamen you may include the protective figure of the upright pentagram or the image of a winged, spoked wheel to represent Raziel as the leader of the Ophanim.

Building an Altar to Raziel

Whether you have a temple room that is dedicated to your spiritual practice or simply a convenient area of your bedroom available, set aside some tabletop, desktop, or mantel space that can be devoted to the archangel.

If possible, try to orient the altar toward the east, the direction of sunrise. If this is not possible, don't let it deter you. An altar situated in the east will lend itself to ritual worked at any hour of the day, but it is especially advantageous for morning rites. Southern, western, and northern altars are advantageous for midday, evening, and midnight rituals, respectively.

Drape your altar with a neutral gray or soft blue cloth. Upon this, place your image of Raziel—this will be the centerpiece of your sacred space. Place a small white votive candle before the image, and surround the candle with a number of symbols attributed to Raziel. These might include old-fashioned skeleton keys, a small scroll, amaranth flowers or seeds, turquoise or star ruby gemstones, and a journal and pen for writing down any messages you might receive during the working. You can also use all four tarot pips associated with Chokmah: the twos of each elemental suit. For an appropriate incense or essential oil, use musk.

Invoking Raziel

Prepare for the ritual by sitting quietly for a few moments with your eyes closed, breathing rhythmically and relaxing your mind. When you are ready, light the altar candle and anoint your forehead with the essential oil. Gently open your journal to a new page. Gaze upon your image of Raziel and give the following invocation:

> *Eternal and Universal Fountain of Love,*
> *Wisdom, and Happiness;*
> *Nature is the book in which your character is written,*
> *and no one can read it*
> *unless he (she) has been taught in your school.*
> *Grant unto me the attention of your mighty archangel,*
> *Raziel, the Secret of God!*
> *Raziel of the Sapphire Book of Wisdom!*
> *Holy Raziel of the many-winged,*

many-eyed Wheels, the Ophanim!
Key-Master of the Hidden Mysteries,
I invoke you! Raziel!
Oh Circle of Stars compared to which my Soul
is but the younger sibling!
Marvel beyond imagination!
Therefore, by pen and paper, by door and key,
and by lamp and light of my entire being,
do I invoke you, whose name and Power are Secret.
Oh Raziel!
Oh Secret of Secrets that is hidden
in the being of all that lives,
Secret and most Holy!
Angelic guardian of that Source of Light,
Source of Love, and Source of Liberty!
Be here now and at my side from this day forward
to aid me in my quest for Knowledge,
That I might remain forever in your abundant Wisdom!
So mote it be!

When you feel a connection with the archangel, you may ask for spiritual wisdom. Possible questions include the following:

- What portion of your spiritual essence can you share with me at this time?
- Can you teach me about the Sephirah Chokmah?
- Can you teach me about the Ophanim? In what magical operations may the aid of these angels be most appropriately and beneficially invoked?
- What type of magical operation would work best for my specific purpose?
- What teaching which could be of particular benefit to me at this point in my life and Work (or in relation to a specific situation)?
- Is there a particular skill that you can teach me?
- Show me a temple of your realm. What is the name or title of this temple? What is its particular function?
- Can you teach me a new meditation?
- Can you teach me a new mode of healing or enhance my understanding or practice of an existing mode of healing?

- Can you teach me a new mode of divination, or enhance my understanding or practice of an existing mode of divination?
- Can you teach me a new technique of magic or enhance my understanding or practice of an existing mode of magic?
- Can you teach me how I can help others (or another) at this time? (Name specific circumstances.)
- How can you help me advance in the Great Work?
- Can you teach me a new prayer or invocation?
- Can you help me understand arcane knowledge about (name topic—be specific)?
- Can you give me a word, name, sign, or symbol that will help me connect with you when I am away from this sacred altar?
- What can I do to enhance my psychic abilities?
- Teach me how I may balance my magical life with my mundane life so that both are enhanced for the better.

Be sure to write down any communication you receive in your journal. Thank Raziel before ending the rite.

Don't worry if your early sessions don't immediately result in communication. The practice of magic is just that—a practice. Your connection with the archangel will improve with time and effort. Avoid the trap of high expectations and you will find yourself pleasantly surprised in the long run. Above all, do the Work. You will find that Raziel has much to teach.

Sources

Cicero, Chic, and Sandra Tabatha Cicero. *Tarot Talismans: Invoke the Angels of the Tarot.* Woodbury, MN: Llewellyn Publications, 2006.

Coleman, Wade. *Sepher Sapphires: A Treatise on Gematria.* Austin, TX: Golden Dawn Trust, 2004.

Davidson, Gustav. *A Dictionary of Angels.* New York: The Free Press, 1971.

Forrest, Adam. "This Holy Invisible Companionship." In *The Golden Dawn Journal.* Bk. 2, *Qabalah: Theory and Magic.* Edited by Chic Cicero and Sandra Tabatha Cicero. St. Paul, MN: Llewellyn Publications, 1994.

Godwin, David. *Godwin's Cabalistic Encyclopedia.* St. Paul, MN: Llewellyn Publications, 1994.

The Magic Hat

by Suzanne Ress

When my eldest daughter was six years old, she discovered, at the back of a closet, an old hat box. Inside was a beautiful millinery creation that I had inherited from my late great aunt, a very stylish lady in her day. It was a curvy pillbox-shaped hat from the 1950s made of cream-colored velvet suede and decorated with bands of sparkling rhinestones. My daughter tried it on, and it was as if a magical crown had suddenly transformed her from a 1990s child to an ageless fairy wise woman. She wore it all weekend—helping my husband in the vegetable garden, playing dolls with her friend, riding her bicycle, eating meals.

It reminded me of my own special hat. When I was eleven and visiting my grandparents, I found a shaped

black artist's beret with an attached peacock feather amongst the clothes and accessories in my grandmother's "dress-up" closet. I tried it on and looked in the mirror, and that settled it—I wore it everywhere for the rest of my two-week visit. It made me feel more like myself. When it was time to go home and return the hat to the closet, it was as if a part of me were missing.

Perhaps more than any other item of clothing, a hat has the power to transform who you feel you are. But just as a special hat can reinforce or change your identity, sometimes head coverings are used to do the opposite. A few years after several friends and I formed our coven, we decided we should have cloaks to wear for esbats and sabbats. I sewed each member an ankle-length white hooded cloak with cream-colored lining and silver cord ties at the neckline. It never would have occurred to me to make cloaks without hoods. If anything, I could have made hoods without cloaks! Covering our heads, necks, and hair, all of us dressed identically, proved to be an effective way of pooling our individual powers into a much larger and more potent group power for magic work. With our cloaks on and the hoods drawn up, we all look the same and can work equally toward whatever common good we choose.

Auras and Halos

What is it about our heads that, covering them, has such a marked effect on our identities?

Human head hair has long been considered a reflection of a person's soul. Magic spells involving a specific person often call for a lock of that person's hair to represent her. Once upon a time, lockets, tiny antique frames, and even buttons contained a lock of a loved one's hair. It was believed that in the hair a part of the person remained.

In olden times, and even nowadays in some cultures, women were expected to keep their hair bound and covered in public. Long, flowing, uncovered hair represented psychic and sexual power, inappropriate in a world dominated by males and with a single male God. Women who refused to conform, going bareheaded and with their long hair loose, were considered dangerous and branded as witches. Condemned witches often had their heads shaved to render them powerless. On men, long flowing loose hair has long been associated with wizards and pagans in general.

The hair lies within a human's aura, not quite a part of the outside world but not invisible and interior, either. Unlike the skin, hair can be cut away painlessly. Because it grows on the head, in the light of the aura, it seems natural that it would absorb a lot of the energy of the aura itself.

The word "aura" comes from Greek and means "breeze" or "puff of air," which I take to mean the general feeling or energy that surrounds a person or place. When I was a child, my mother, a fan of Edgar Cayce's work, told us she could see auras. She said each person has a different color and intensity of aura, according to their nature. We begged her to tell us what color our auras were. She said she couldn't be rushed; she would need to meditate for a while and be in the right frame of mind. I wanted very badly to believe that people had visible auras, but deep down I was skeptical.

Finally, my mother read my aura. She stared at me with half-closed eyes for a very long time, just us two in a quiet room, and by and by she revealed to me that the aura she'd seen around my head and shoulders was pink. When I asked her what a pink aura meant, she said she didn't know; that was just what she saw. My sister's was blue, she said. Apparently, though, it was exhausting to read auras, for she never got around to doing my three younger siblings'.

Perhaps not coincidentally, many people over the years have told me I look best in and that they associate me with a pinkish coral color.

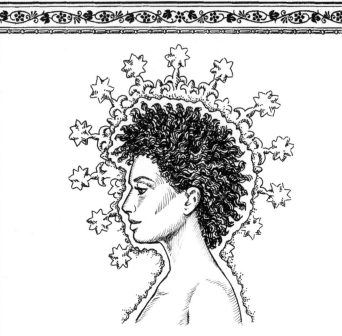

"Halo" also comes from Greek and means "disk of the Sun or Moon." To my mind, auras and halos are the same thing. Individuals with very strong, deep spiritual lives are likely to present strong white or golden auras. There was a time in the past when it was perhaps not so uncommon to see auras, or halos, when they were strong. Artists from every culture regularly painted spiritually holy people with white or golden halos around their heads.

Leadership

To honor a great leader, a crown was placed on their head as a symbol of an exceptional aura and as a solar or lunar symbol. It set them apart from ordinary folk. Crowns have been used since prehistoric times to designate the leader of a tribe, group, or population. When the crown is first placed upon the individual's head in the coronation ceremony, it is this act that symbolizes the giving of collective power to an individual, or the transfer of power from the old leader to the new one. This, too, is a prehistoric ritual. Crowns have always been made with precious or rare materials, whether gold and jewels or unusual and beautiful feathers, foliage, and fruits.

One of the Western world's most beloved monarchs, Queen Elizabeth II of the United Kingdom, wears a tiara for formal occasions; for official royal functions she wears a crown. One needn't be a monarch to wear a tiara, but the crown's full circle around the head represents monarchical power and leadership and can only be worn by the leader. Queen Elizabeth II, now over ninety years old, is never seen in public without a hat, and her carefully selected collection of brightly colored bucket-shaped, brimmed hats, which to me all look like magic hats, have become her personal fashion signature; these set her apart from any other woman in the crowd. In June 2017 the queen presented a Brexit-focused agenda to Parliament wearing a large bright blue hat with a circle of yellow flower centers on the front. The hat bore a striking resemblance to the European Union flag, from which Britain was taking its leave. Officially, the monarch's political views are supposed to remain unknown, but many people believed her flag-hat to be a clear, silent statement against Britain's exit from the European Union.

Religious leaders too wear special headgear. Popes, cardinals, and bishops wear a sort of beanie called a *zucchetto* (Italian for "little pumpkin") for ordinary use, its color establishing the man's rank in the Catholic hierarchy. For important occasions, these religious men wear a miter, which is a tall, peaked hat, something between a cone hat and a turban. It is open in the middle, so the crown of the head remains uncovered. These miters are made of white or gold cloth decorated with jewels and heraldic symbols, much like crowns.

Mongolian queens of the Middle Ages wore very tall conical hats decorated with peacock feathers called *boqta*.

In 1420, Marco Polo brought several boqta back to Venice, and shortly thereafter, European royal women began wearing the *henin*, a pointed cone hat with streaming veils. These hats may have seemed original to medieval Europeans, but Mongolian queens were not the first to wear tall cone-shaped hats.

Conical hats were worn in the Bronze Age between 1400 and 800 BCE by Celtic shamans for ceremonies. These were made of thin gold sheet metal decorated with symbols denoting lunar and solar calendars. They were very tall—almost three feet from the rim to the point. Scholars studying these golden cone hats have determined that they served a dual purpose: to set the shaman apart from the ordinary people, marking him as the leader, and to determine, using the charted mathematical symbols chased into the gold, the dates of practically any astronomical event during the lunar or solar year, such as the solstices, equinoxes, and eclipses, as well as exact temporal divisions such as days, weeks, months, and years (remember, there were no clocks then).

Four of these golden cone hats have been found so far, in France, Germany, and Switzerland. The gold sheet was originally placed over a frame of organic material, willow branch perhaps, which has since rotted away. The designs, which are expertly worked in the repousse and chasing methods, include circles, disks, and eye shapes. These symbols illustrate the Metonic cycle, a complex nineteen-year cycle relating the Sun's and Moon's orbits to quantify time. The Metonic cycle was named for the Greek astronomer Meton of Athens (500 BCE), who supposedly discovered the accuracy of the nineteen-year cycle, but the Iron Age Celts were already using this same mathematical system to predict seasons and astronomical phenomena at least one thousand years earlier!

Because only the shaman knew how to use these symbols for calculating the best times for planting and harvesting, it was believed that he had magical powers. It was the magnificent golden hat that gave him these magical powers of prediction and seeing into the future. Major arcana card number one of the Marseilles Tarot deck, which is believed to be the first, shows the Magician wearing a round-crowned hat. The hat's brim forms a lemniscate. In later decks, the hat disappeared, but the lemniscate, a mathematical symbol for infinity, and hence infinite knowledge, remained, floating above the magician's head. Surely legends of the golden conical hats worn by ancient Celtic shamans were carried down into medieval times when the tarot decks were first produced, making the first card of the "great secrets," the Magician, the master of all that followed.

Wise men and wizards were the first to wear conical hats, but Witches soon followed. For only with a magical hat could magic be performed, and the conic hat was known to be magical. The Sorting Hat from the Harry Potter series is a fictional magic conical hat that once belonged to the wizard Godric Gryffindor and is now used at Hogwarts School to sort the incoming students into appropriate houses, according to their individual

abilities, talents, and character. The Norse god Odin, comparable to the Greek god Hermes, was a prototypical wizard figure who sometimes wore a conical hat and flowing cloak and performed magical spells and charms. And who hasn't seen, or at least heard of, a modern sleight-of-hand magician's black top hat? These fictional, legendary, and invented magic hats owe their origins to the golden cone hats of the Iron Age.

Make a Magic Hat

Following in the ancient Celtic tradition, why not make a magic cone hat for ceremonial usage? Construction of the hat can be as easy as making a card-weight paper cone and brim, glued and stapled together and covered with appropriately colored, black, or white fabric or felt. Decorations can be made with sequins, rhinestones, and small beads sewn or glued into place. If you want something more elaborate, emblems, runic writings, and pictures could be embroidered in colored and metallic threads onto the fabric layer before attaching it to the cone frame.

The frame could be more authentic, depending on how much time and skill you have. Soft willow blanches soaked in water can be bent and woven into a cone-shaped frame and left to dry that way. There are also several beautiful knitted and crocheted witch hat patterns available on the internet, if you are a knitter.

Once the hat is made to your satisfaction, add a small pocket or secret compartment inside, unknown to all but the wearer. Write magic words, incantations, or spells on a piece of grainy paper during a Full Moon ceremony and consecrate the paper. Fold it and keep it hidden in its secret pocket inside the magic hat. These are the words that will imbue the hat with power and make it magical, but only for the Witch or wizard who knows how to use them.

After the Ritual: The Remnants

by Autumn Damiana

The ritual or casting of the spell has concluded. You have returned the remaining energy to the earth, passed around the cakes and ale, taken down the circle, put away your altar tools, and done whatever else you need to do to wrap things up. So now what? Regular practitioners know the value and necessity of "keeping house" on the altar or in the sacred space area, which usually involves a periodic cleaning and inventory of the items there. What is being used? What is no longer needed? What do I do with all this leftover stuff?

This last question has been particularly frustrating for me, because there is no definitive answer. Whatever the working, there are almost always materials remaining afterward. Most existing rituals and spells explain what is needed and how to use each component, but there is not enough information that explains what to do with these same components when the ritual or spell has concluded. These include candles, incense, salt, herbs, crystals, containers, pictures and drawings, offerings, and so on. Some get completely used up, and some are dedicated to a purpose—for example, coins or bills kept in a wallet to attract wealth, which are then spent or donated after the spell has manifested. But then there are some materials that are simply residual and have no place or function—and they hang around on the altar and need to be dealt with.

If you are a member of a tradition that has a method for handling these leftovers, then by all means, go with that. I personally don't think that there is a right or a wrong way of doing this. If you are a solitary or your coven, circle, or group is also uncertain about what to do with these odds and ends, then you have many options. However . . .

- Salt, herbs, and spices should always be disposed of. They have spent their magic on your working and must be discarded.
- Wine, beer, mead, juice, and so on, that has been poured for the ritual and is used in a ritual setting but is not

consumed should also be disposed of, as should any water (unless it is being charged or blessed for later use).

- Libations and food offerings (for the Gods, the elements, the spirits of the land, Mother Earth, etc.) need to be given to them as is their due.
- Seasonal and holiday items should be taken away in a timely manner. Clear or cleanse what you are keeping (vases, statues, tableware, etc.) and dispose of everything else (flowers, food, decorations, etc.) according to the directions below.

Now, when trying to determine what to do with other remnants, you need to ask yourself three questions:

1. Is part of the working dependent upon what I do with the materials?
2. What is the ethical or environmental way to disperse or dispose of materials?
3. Am I comfortable with reusing or repurposing materials?

Leftovers Directly Tied to the Working

Most rituals and spells that have such stipulations will explain how the components used need to be handled. For example, a "witch bottle" made for protection is most commonly buried on the spellcaster's property to serve as an instrument of protection or security. The same can be true for luck, love, and health charms, though sometimes these need to be put under your pillow or kept on your person. If there are no such instructions, then how you handle the leftovers really depends on what your goal is or what you are trying to accomplish. It also depends on your mindset, magically speaking. In some traditions, there are those who believe that everything used in a ritual or spell has residual energy that should be used only for that working. Reuse and disposal of these materials is seen as both taboo and counterproductive. Hoodoo and older (sometimes hereditary) Witchcraft are two such practices in which this is the case. In these traditions, you "seal a spell" or "fix a spell in place" using your spell materials according to these general rules:

- Bury them in your yard, place them in your house, or keep them on your person if you want to keep something close to you.

- Put them near to or buried under your front door if you want to attract something.
- Burn them if you want to destroy something.
- Throw them into a body of moving water if you want something to flow away from you.
- Throw or place them to the east to make something begin or gain in strength.
- Throw or place them to the west to make something end or wane in strength.
- Bury, leave, or scatter them in a cemetery, at a crossroads, or somewhere far out in nature if you want to rid yourself of something really negative or end something permanently.

Dispersal and Disposal

Dispersal of ritual materials refers to spreading them out in some way (strewing herbs, for example). Sometimes the dispersal is part of the ritual itself, as previously discussed. Disposal, on the other hand, is exactly what it sounds like: getting rid of something or throwing it away.

Traditional dispersal or disposal of ritual or spell ingredients works with the power of the elements. You can bury them in the earth, toss them into a body of moving water, burn them in a fire, or scatter them to the winds. These are the tried-and-true methods that work fine if you live in a rural area or are lucky enough to have a large piece of property. In this case, it's probably okay to bury candle stumps in the ground, throw something into a lake or pond (depending on what it is, of course), or find a country crossroads where you can leave your materials. Other practitioners are not as fortunate and need to be both more mindful and more creative when dispersing and disposing of their ritual remnants.

I don't always adhere to the traditional dispersal and disposal methods. As I see it, there are too many impractical and sometimes unethical methods being used, depending on what you are disposing of. For example, it is an intuitive idea to bury salt or scatter it on the ground, given that salt is both a representation of the earth element and a natural substance. However, too much salt concentrated in one place will kill plants living there and prevent new ones from growing. In reality, it is much safer to wash the salt away in a river, in a stream, or even down the drain. It will be diluted and won't harm the soil or natural flora. The same is true for libations. Most liquids like liquor or juice will be readily absorbed into the ground, but it might be better to also wash them away with water, since they can attract insects like ants, wasps, and cockroaches.

Food offerings require special consideration. I think it's okay to leave a bit of food now and again in a remote environment for insects and animals to eat, but not in populated areas, where many people already feed the wildlife. Human food, whether processed or not, is not a part of these animals' natural diets, and feeding them can actually disrupt their instinctual habits of foraging for their own food and can make them dependent on handouts. In addition, it can also make wild animals lose their fear of humans, which results in more roadkill and more of these animals apt to become common pests, like opossums and raccoons. You can offer up food to the Divine just as easily by burying the food or putting it into a compost pile. The important idea is to be aware of what you are doing to the environment when you are dispersing or disposing of anything. If it goes outside, structure your spell or ritual ingredients accordingly—use biodegradable materials and evaluate what can potentially happen to them once they are out of your hands.

As modern Witches, whether we live in rural areas, suburban ones, or more high-density environments, there are new alternatives to how we can disperse or dispose of ritual leftovers. I don't think it is wrong, for instance, to place something in the garbage that would traditionally be buried in the ground. What matters here is the intent behind it. Some would say that to "throw something away" like this is disrespectful, but since the garbage ultimately goes to a landfill or is incinerated, is it? I personally like to differentiate between the garbage can (landfill) and the yard waste can (compost). I put ritual herbs, natural cording or strings (like cotton or raffia), incense, matchsticks, and other biodegradable ritual materials in the yard waste can—it seems a more dignified way to "bury" the items. But the garbage can will work just as well.

The same is true of anything you would like to be carried away by water. It depends on what you are disposing of—would it be acceptable to put it in local ponds, rivers, lakes, or the ocean? If the answer is yes, then you can pour the materials down the sink, shower drain, or toilet because these are also streams of water. This can be a great way to get rid of small amounts of herbs, bits of food, incense ash, and various liquids but again, if this feels disrespectful or somehow wrong to you, then don't do it. On the other hand, if you really want to banish or get rid of some nasty energy, then flushing it down the toilet might work! Make sure to practice common sense when disposing of anything through your plumbing. Use your garbage disposal in your sink and cut things into tiny pieces if you plan to flush them down the toilet. And *never* dump anything in the drain (including the garbage disposal) or the toilet that might clog the pipes, such as wax, oil, sticky or doughy pieces of food, or any plant matter that is stringy or fibrous. Very few ritual leftovers are ideal for water disposal, so be selective with this method.

Burning materials can be both easier and more difficult, depending on your circumstances. If you have a wood-burning fireplace or wood stove, a fire pit, or a burn pile (like for leaves), then you are in luck. Burning an item is one of the most complete ways to dispose of it and offers a feeling of finality, although some people like to burn things so that the smoke from the fire carries the energy toward the heavens. Small items, like photos or pieces of paper, can be burned in a cast-iron cauldron, but be cautious. Make sure your cauldron is sitting on a fireproof surface and is not near anything flammable. Do not burn anything in your cauldron while indoors, and when you use it for burning outside, I recommend that you keep a fire extinguisher on hand just in case.

Air disposal is simple, but it only works for very small, very light items that are biodegradable—the kind that can be whisked away by the wind, like ashes. If you opt for this method, you can either wait for a blustery day or a storm approaching, or you can find a safe high point (a mountain peak, the top of a tall building, or even your roof) and toss your materials off to be taken away by the air currents. Alternately, you can let the element of air take your leftovers via a car or boat ride, but keep in mind that you might get pulled over for littering if anyone sees you throwing things out the window!

And let's not forget recycling. When you are done with that spell jar or those tea candles, you may want to simply recycle the glass and the metal candle cup. Recycling is in many ways just like disposal, but in an environmentally responsible way. If there is anything that you are prepared to let go of on your altar, see if you can recycle it. Most glass, metal, and many plastics can be recycled in an ordinary recycling bin. Fabric, such as an old altar cloth, doesn't even need to be in good condition if you can find a textile recycling center because the fibers can be repurposed. Also, in many cases, if you ask around, you can find another Witch, magical practitioner, coven, or group that will be happy to take something off of your hands that you no longer need or want if it's still usable. As a last resort, you can magically clear or cleanse these items and donate them to a local charity or thrift store, where someone else can buy and enjoy them.

How to Reuse and Repurpose Leftovers

This can be a touchy topic, as I mentioned earlier, because not everyone believes that it is a good idea to reuse or repurpose ritual supplies. However, I think that it is environmentally and ethically responsible to try. Again, clearing and cleansing works with the power of the elements. Use smudging or incense, leave items in the rays of the Sun or the Moon, bury them in the ground or in a pot of soil, purify them in rainwater or in a magical bath, hang them out in the air or to catch the winds, or clear them using salt, herbs, cleansing crystals, sound, or any combination of these methods. Here are some other guidelines:

Crystals and Stones: Just like altar tools, I see no reason that a crystal or stone can't be cleared or cleansed of energy when you want to use it again, because the residual energy can be broken down. If it continues to feel "weird" after a cleansing, then you should probably discard it.

Candles: If you use a candle as the focal point of your spell, then it is not advisable to reuse it. Maybe you should relight the candle periodically and meditate on its purpose to help guide the spell on its way. A candle that has simply been used for illumination, to represent a god/goddess, or burned during ritual because of its color can be reused. Candle stubs can also be repurposed: melt them in a double-boiler with other stubs, strain out the wicks and debris, and pour them into a new candle. I believe that the element of fire melting the wax will purify it and leave it free of previous energies.

Incense: I always reuse commercial incense, because I see it as "new" every time it is extinguished and relit. Incense blends that are prepared for a specific working, however, are a different story. Usually these are herbal or spice blends that are burned on charcoal, and they should be disposed of when the working has concluded. The charcoal, on the other hand, can be reused.

Containers: These include bags, bottles, boxes, and jars. You have to use your discretion when dealing with these. If they have anything connecting them to a particular ritual, such as symbols or sigils, they cannot be used again. Even a plain container, while potentially reusable, may acquire energy, and you might rather dispose of it. The key to deciding what to do with these is to ask yourself how attached you are to the container. If it is a simple drawstring bag or cardboard box that you can part with, then do so. But special containers, such as decorative bottles, keepsake boxes, and apothecary jars, can be cleared or cleansed to be reused again.

Ephemera: Materials that are "ephemeral" (short-lived) include drawings, photos, printouts, any kind of paper, and so on. These are items that by definition will degrade or disintegrate over time. I am in favor of disposing of these once they have been used in a ritual or spell. So, if you are using a favorite photo or keepsake, simply take a picture or make a copy of it to use in your ritual. You can dispose of that afterward and keep the original safe.

Finally, keep in mind that some items will retain weird or negative vibes no matter how you clear or cleanse them. Remember to go with your gut. If it tells you that you should part with something, then do so . . . but if not, then see if you can reuse or repurpose it.

Magic Apple: The Fruit from the Tree of Life

by Justine Holubets

An apple's form itself is magic: the cross section reveals the pentagram-like pith. The apple is a hero of myths, sacred books, and fairy tales all over the world. It also refers to power and prestige. One of the monarchial regalia, the orb with a crown or cross was called an "apple" in Russian translations. The apple's symbology is diverse: life and death, love and temptation, immortality and knowledge are just a few spheres represented by the modest fruit. The variety and controversy around it makes exploration exciting and rewarding for magical, spiritual, and soul well-being.

The Golden Apples of Beauty and Love

In the sacred books the Bible and the Qur'an, the apple was a fruit from the Tree of the Knowledge of Good and Evil. Medieval art depicted this mysterious tree as an apple tree possibly because of the similarity of the Latin words *mālum* ("evil") and *malum* ("apple"). The Old Testament conception of the Fall endowed the apple with a contradictive meaning of wisdom and the seductive female force that was hard to oppose. Solomon's Song of Songs

grants it with sensual meaning when the female speaker describes her lover as "an apple tree among the trees of the forest."

The eternal balancing between reason and passion is well presented in the tarot card the Lovers with its Eden scene: we see a nude couple, an angel above them, and the trees. A serpent coiled around the tree takes us back in time and resembles the mythological apple tree in the Garden of the Hesperides, guarded by the dragon Ladon. It grew from the earth goddess Gaia's gift of branches to Hera on the occasion of her wedding. Its fruits were far from simple—golden apples of heavenly gifts of immortality, wisdom, and beauty. Considering its almost magical nutritional qualities, it is not surprising that apples of Slavic legends were known as "apples of youth," granting eternal youth and beauty yet requiring great efforts to find and obtain them.

Following the ambition to be the best, the most beautiful, and obsessed with a desire to stop time and preserve their physical beauty, many forget about the other interpretation of beauty: a mark of divine gifts that come from within. The eternal light of kindness, compassion, and content felt inside, which the person inevitably radiates outward, attracting people with much more power and intensity than just clothes, cosmetics, or any artificial means of beauty. All these qualities are invisible and immortal gifts yet far more reliable and lasting.

The mythical golden apple reminds us of the side effects of love and beauty—in other words, the consequences of our choices. Paris was to give a golden apple with an inscription "to the most beautiful" to one of three goddesses. Ignoring the power and skill promised by Hera and Athena, he chose Aphrodite, the goddess of love. In return she rewarded him with the love of the most praised woman of that time, the beautiful Helen of Sparta. However, the result was far from a happy ending, triggering one of the most terrible and cruel wars in mythology, the ten-year Trojan War. Seeking passion, we sometimes make the wrong choices and naively think we are blessed by love; our blindness in following these momentary wishes, as in Paris's case, quickly turns our relationships into discord and breakup. There are many love spells that employ the use of apples, from simple ones that involve putting them under the pillow to see the promised partner in a dream, to more complicated ones that involve interpreting peeled apple skin.

If you wish for a love spell, though, beware not to turn a golden apple of love into an apple of discord and provoke an epic Trojan War in your personal life. Instead, it is much more beneficial to try to master perhaps the most difficult art of knowing your wishes and making the right choices. I invite you to follow me in a special ritual to receive the rewards offered by the three immortal goddesses: power and career advancement (Hera), wisdom and intellectual self-realization (Athena), and adventure and passion (Aphrodite).

Ritual: Journey to the Garden of the Hesperides

It is possible to turn a short break into meaningful initiation. The best time to perform this ritual is during a holiday or break from your usual schedule. It should take seven to ten days or can be stretched to up to twenty-one days, depending on how quickly you finish each of the ten tasks. Perform the ritual in solitude or independently from family or friends. Ideally, take a physical journey to a new place that inspires you.

The main goals are to feel gratitude by channeling abundance; to develop a cyclic worldview, necessary for growth in

103

magical practices; and to gather "harvest" for your work and efforts. The apple is one of the symbols of the harvest feast. In Slavic tradition, there is a Savior of the Apple Feast Day, celebrated on August 19, which is meant to remind us of gratitude to Mother Nature for her gifts. It is believed that eating an apple on this day with a wish in mind will help make it come true.

Holding the knowledge of light and darkness, the Hesperides Apple Tree is close in meaning with the Qabalistic Tree of Life, an ordered structure of ten spheres linked with each other by paths. Without going deep into Qabala, we will use its form as a guide. Take ten carefully chosen ripe apples and place them at the position of the Sephiroth, so that you have your personal apple tree before your eyes. The last of Hercules's labors, his search for the apples of the Garden of the Hesperides, is the basis for this spiritual journey. The myth offers perfect practical thresholds for the journey stages.

Each morning we start with a short meditation on the Tree of Life, slowly eating one apple at a time and concentrating on the daily aim. And each evening looking at the seeds left, we write down and reflect on the day's experience in detail.

You will need:
10 apples
Diary for notes
Box for seeds

Day 1: Find the Garden
The location of the Hesperides garden was unknown, which was an additional challenge for the hero. After arriving at your destination, try to pause and feel the place—its nature, people, sounds, smells, and colors. Today your task is to release the tense feeling of constant control. Forget about the clock and watch the time from the sunrise-to-sunset dimension. Eat your first apple, feeling its taste, and try not to perceive it as a snack.

My destination was a resort city in the south of Turkey I have visited many times. After an extremely exhausting winter and burning out from work, I noticed how difficult it was to calm the fuss in my head. I spent the whole first day in the swimming pool, absorbing the warmth of the hot air, saturated with floral aroma and sea breeze, watching dancing sunbeams, playing with the hair of elegant palms, and flirting with the restless orange trees. I was immersed in a trance-like mood.

Reflect on the symbols of the myth. Watch the night sky and think about the guardians of the apples. Watch the shining Hesperides, the stars and planets, which brought you here and lead you; maybe you will see a shooting star that will show your heart the way. Think about the dragon, twined around the tree, the dangerous serpent of passions hidden in the magic crown with kundalini power. Are you ready for his sweet speech and the desires he might awaken in you?

Day 2: Meet a Nymph

Nymphs gave the hero a hint for the next step. Be open and ready to receive any information coming. Listen to and socialize with any person who approaches you. It's the nymphs who send the message. For me, it was a woman with a piercing look whom I met at breakfast. With loose gowns, jewelry, and flower-scented perfume, she stood out from others at the resort. A traveler, hippie, and spiritual practitioner, she loaded me with a treasury of esoteric knowledge, which helped me to tune in to my magical goal.

Day 3: Consult Nereus

Hercules managed to catch and tame the enigmatic shape-shifter Nereus, who revealed the Garden's location to the hero. This day is a challenge to learn the area's culture, through the behavior, body language, and speech of people you came across during the day. Feel yourself a traveler and explorer; discover and compare, and understand yourself better.

For me it was conversations with the hotel's owners, local business tycoons of the old city area: four brothers different in character yet one in their goal-oriented mind. I received plenty of curious conclusions on tourism from an old seller with a diploma in psychology. I enjoyed a discussion with a simple old man, the owner of a rock beach I visited every day, who, turning his philosophical look into the horizon, reminded me of Hemingway's old man, looking out for his marlin. An exotic Turkish culture showed me its faces through the fascinating net of human stories, just as multi-identitied Nereus led me to reflect deeper on my own.

After the first three days, you may feel a slight shift through your entire body, as if you are not you and the reality around you is kind of surreal or Fae-like. Don't forget to eat the apples and feel their taste, imagining how they nurture not only your body but your soul and your experience. Now that you know yourself, it is time to help yourself.

Day 4: Defeat Antaeus

Hercules successfully fought the fierce giants. One of them, Antaeus, could be defeated only by being lifted off the ground, from which he received his huge strength. As you eat your fourth apple, think about the energies you are getting from Mother Earth through the fruit, just like the giant received his power from the ground. The key challenge of today is to become the better version of yourself, disconnect from physical laziness, and feel the joy of victory over uncontrolled obsessions and physical dependences. My personal concern was a drive for food. It was hard, yet I restrained myself from grabbing all the delicious and generous plates of Turkish cuisine and focused instead on the long city walks, hourly swims in the sea, and yoga exercising on the morning's empty beach.

Day 5: Fight Kyknos

Kyknos was another giant, bearing the features of his father, Ares, the god of war and passion. Today is the day of adventure, and it is good to eat a big sweet apple to receive more energy. After yesterday's difficult task, you have to reward yourself. Seek out any cultural event, excursion, tour—everything that brings pleasure to your senses. In Turkey, I watched a spectacular dance performance with powerful music and historical and creative elements; it was an excellent source to boost my energy level.

Day 6: Escape the Altar of Sacrifice

No initiation can occur without some challenge or danger. A tired Hercules, after falling asleep in a faraway land, was captured by locals and was doomed to a ritual sacrifice. Savoring today's apple, be ready for temptations that will be generously offered from everywhere: delicious food, original souvenirs, or promising relationships. Today you arrive at the center of the Tree, at the stage of Eden, so wait for the trial of choice: to go or not to go, to buy or not to buy, to taste or not to taste. Following your simple desires will become your challenge. You may consume the fruit

of temptation and act according to the desires of your ego, as vacations are usually a free time to indulge. However, keep in mind that succumbing recklessly to temptation may destroy your health, budget, or heart. Be mindful of your goal of spiritual transformation and refuse to surrender to every impulse, avoiding being one of many victims on the altar of passions.

After this second stage, you should feel composed, stable and confident in your ability to control your body, senses, and passions. You are one step closer to your final destination, four stages left. Four apples are now at your tree, and it is time to look around and see if you might help others.

Day 7: Release Prometheus, Part 1

Hercules freed the bound Titan Prometheus from his tortures. Today is the day of surprises. It is not the day of initiating but passive waiting; keep your eyes wide open for an opportunity to do a good deed while going about your vacation schedule.

While walking, I helped a lost couple with directions. They appeared to work for a cultural TV channel and were looking for interesting travelers to prepare content on Turkey. They were extremely out of time, and our occasional meeting saved them.

Day 8: Release Prometheus, Part 2

Usually, helping others comprises two aspects: emotional and practical. The first one is sharing a word, a smile, advice, or information; the second is participation in the business of the other party or offering your service. At the beach I received a request for a tarot reading from a local visitor who turned out to be a scientist with plenty of projects and who felt released and inspired after the analysis of his intellectual property perspectives.

Day 9: Gather the Apples

After reaching the garden, Hercules relied on the help of Atlas, the Titan holding the sky on his shoulders. Atlas fetched the apples while Hercules replaced him for a while. Today you are most likely to meet your own guide who would serve as a mediator and will bring you the golden apples. Don't forget to think of your desire when eating your apple. It might be a day full of wonders. Today's apple should have a real magic taste.

Atlas is associated with strength, wit, cunning, and geography. At the end of my journey I met a new person who interestingly resembled a classical hero in terms of his athletic appearance, easygoing spirit, and rich traveling experience. Together we dived, swam, explored the hidden caves along the shore, and jumped from the rocks. I felt myself a sister of my beloved joyful sea nereids, rewarded for my spiritual efforts during the journey.

Day 10: Offer the Apples to the Goddess

In one version of the myth, after Hercules's successful deed, his patroness Athena returns the apples to the Hesperides. The journey is over, and it is time for review. Eat the last apple, feeling gratitude for your experience. Look through your notes and observe the material things you might have obtained throughout the journey, as they can serve as hints too. Including a wonderfully refreshed attitude and friendship, I received a small silver serpent for a present, which seemed relevant to the guardian dragon of the Garden. I perceived it as a sign of my successful connection to the spiritual realm.

To complete the ritual, take the seeds left from the ten magic apples and sacrifice them to the elements: bury them in the ground or throw them in the sea or from the cliff. You return the apples to where they belong, to nature, where other heroes will travel to in search of their own golden magic fruits.

Almanac Section

Calendar

Time Zones

Lunar Phases

Moon Signs

Full Moons

Sabbats

World Holidays

Incense of the Day

Color of the Day

Almanac Listings

In these listings you will find the date, day, lunar phase, Moon sign, color, and incense for the day, as well as festivals from around the world.

The Date

The date is used in numerological calculations that govern magical rites.

The Day

Each day is ruled by a planet that possesses specific magical influences:

MONDAY (MOON): Peace, sleep, healing, compassion, friends, psychic awareness, purification, and fertility.

TUESDAY (MARS): Passion, sex, courage, aggression, and protection.

WEDNESDAY (MERCURY): The conscious mind, study, travel, divination, and wisdom.

THURSDAY (JUPITER): Expansion, money, prosperity, and generosity.

FRIDAY (VENUS): Love, friendship, reconciliation, and beauty.

SATURDAY (SATURN): Longevity, exorcism, endings, homes, and houses.

SUNDAY (SUN): Healing, spirituality, success, strength, and protection.

The Lunar Phase

The lunar phase is important in determining the best times for magic.

THE WAXING MOON (from the New Moon to the Full) is the ideal time for magic to draw things toward you.

THE FULL MOON is the time of greatest power.

THE WANING MOON (from the Full Moon to the New) is a time for study, meditation, and little magical work (except magic designed to banish harmful energies).

The Moon's Sign

The Moon continuously "moves" through the zodiac, from Aries to Pisces. Each sign possesses its own significance.

ARIES: Good for starting things, but lacks staying power. Things occur rapidly, but quickly pass. People tend to be argumentative and assertive.

TAURUS: Things begun now last the longest, tend to increase in value, and become hard to alter. Brings out appreciation for beauty and sensory experience.

GEMINI: Things begun now are easily changed by outside influence. Time for shortcuts, communication, games, and fun.

CANCER: Stimulates emotional rapport between people. Pinpoints need, supports growth and nurturance. Tends to domestic concerns.

LEO: Draws emphasis to the self, central ideas, or institutions, away from connections with others and other emotional needs. People tend to be melodramatic.

VIRGO: Favors accomplishment of details and commands from higher up. Focuses on health, hygiene, and daily schedules.

LIBRA: Favors cooperation, social activities, beautification of surroundings, balance, and partnership.

SCORPIO: Increases awareness of psychic power. Precipitates psychic crises and ends connections thoroughly. People tend to brood and become secretive.

SAGITTARIUS: Encourages flights of imagination and

confidence. This is an adventurous, philosophical, and athletic Moon sign. Favors expansion and growth.

CAPRICORN: Develops strong structure. Focus on traditions, responsibilities, and obligations. A good time to set boundaries and rules.

AQUARIUS: Rebellious energy. Time to break habits and make abrupt changes. Personal freedom and individuality is the focus.

PISCES: The focus is on dreaming, nostalgia, intuition, and psychic impressions. A good time for spiritual or philanthropic activities.

Color and Incense

The color and incense for the day are based on information from *Personal Alchemy* by Amber Wolfe, and relate to the planet that rules each day. This information can be taken into consideration along with other factors when planning works of magic or when blending magic into mundane life. Please note that the incense selections listed are not hard and fast. If you cannot find or do not like the incense listed for the day, choose a similar scent that appeals to you.

Festivals and Holidays

Festivals and holidays of many cultures and nations are listed throughout the year. The exact dates of many ancient festivals are difficult to determine; prevailing data has been used.

Time Zones

The times and dates of all astrological phenomena in this almanac are based on **Eastern Standard Time (EST)**. If you live outside of the Eastern time zone, you will need to make the following adjustments:

PACIFIC STANDARD TIME: Subtract three hours.

MOUNTAIN STANDARD TIME: Subtract two hours.

CENTRAL STANDARD TIME: Subtract one hour.

ALASKA: Subtract four hours.

HAWAII: Subtract five hours.

DAYLIGHT SAVING TIME (ALL ZONES): Add one hour.

Daylight Saving Time begins at 2 am on March 10, 2019, and ends at 2 am on November 3, 2019.

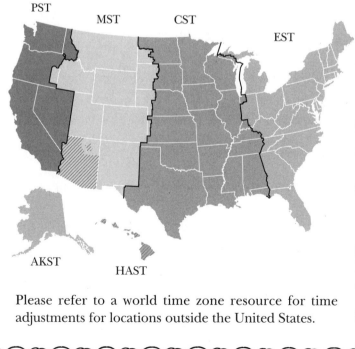

Please refer to a world time zone resource for time adjustments for locations outside the United States.

2019 Sabbats
and Full Moons

January 21	Leo Full Moon 12:16 am
February 2	Imbolc
February 19	Virgo Full Moon 10:54 am
March 20	Ostara (Spring Equinox)
March 20	Libra Full Moon 9:43 pm
April 19	Libra Full Moon 7:12 am
May 1	Beltane
May 18	Scorpio Full Moon 5:11 pm
June 17	Sagittarius Full Moon 4:31 am
June 21	Midsummer (Summer Solstice)
July 16	Capricorn Full Moon 5:38 pm
August 1	Lammas
August 15	Aquarius Full Moon 8:29 am
September 14	Pisces Full Moon 12:33 am
September 23	Mabon (Fall Equinox)
October 13	Aries Full Moon 5:08 pm
October 31	Samhain
November 12	Taurus Full Moon 8:34 am
December 12	Gemini Full Moon 12:12 am
December 21	Yule (Winter Solstice)

All times are Eastern Standard Time (EST)
or Eastern Daylight Time (EDT)

2019 Sabbats in
the Southern Hemisphere

Because Earth's Northern and Southern Hemispheres experience opposite seasons at any given time, the season-based sabbats listed on the previous page and in this almanac section are not correct for those residing south of the equator. Listed here are the Southern Hemisphere sabbat dates for 2019:

February 1	Lammas
March 20	Mabon (Fall Equinox)
May 1	Samhain
June 21	Yule (Winter Solstice)
August 1	Imbolc
September 23	Ostara (Spring Equinox)
November 1	Beltane
December 21	Midsummer (Summer Solstice)

Birthstone poetry reprinted from
The Occult and Curative Powers of Precious Stones
by William T. Fernie, M.D.
Harper & Row (1981)

Originally printed in 1907 as
Precious Stones:
For Curative Wear; and Other Remedial Uses;
Likewise the Nobler Metals

1   Tuesday
New Year's Day • Kwanzaa ends   Moon Sign: Scorpio
Waning Moon   Incense: Geranium
Moon phase: Fourth Quarter
Color: Scarlet

2   Wednesday
First Writing Day (Japanese)   Moon Sign: Scorpio
Waning Moon   Moon enters Sagittarius 3:58 am
Moon phase: Fourth Quarter   Incense: Lilac
Color: Brown

3   Thursday
St. Genevieve's Day   Moon Sign: Sagittarius
Waning Moon   Incense: Nutmeg
Moon phase: Fourth Quarter
Color: White

4   Friday
Kamakura Workers' Festival (Japanese)   Moon Sign: Sagittarius
Waning Moon   Moon enters Capricorn 1:55 pm
Moon phase: Fourth Quarter   Incense: Vanilla
Color: Coral

    Saturday
Bird Day   Moon Sign: Capricorn
Waning Moon   Incense: Sandalwood
New Moon 8:28 pm
Color: Black

6   Sunday
Epiphany   Moon Sign: Capricorn
Waxing Moon   Incense: Frankincense
Moon phase: First Quarter
Color: Gold

7   Monday
Tricolor Day (Italian)   Moon Sign: Virgo
Waxing Moon   Moon enters Aquarius 1:46 am
Moon phase: First Quarter   Incense: Neroli
Color: Lavender

January

8 Tuesday
Midwives' Day (Bulgarian)
Waxing Moon
Moon phase: First Quarter
Color: Red

Moon Sign: Aquarius
Incense: Cedar

---

9 Wednesday
Feast of the Black Nazarene (Filipino)
Waxing Moon
Moon phase: First Quarter
Color: White

Moon Sign: Aquarius
Moon enters Pisces 2:44 pm
Incense: Bay laurel

---

10 Thursday
Feast of St. Leonie Aviat
Waxing Moon
Moon phase: First Quarter
Color: Purple

Moon Sign: Pisces
Incense: Carnation

---

11 Friday
Carmentalia (Roman)
Waxing Moon
Moon phase: First Quarter
Color: Pink

Moon Sign: Pisces
Incense: Cypress

---

12 Saturday
Revolution Day (Tanzanian)
Waxing Moon
Moon phase: First Quarter
Color: Blue

Moon Sign: Pisces
Moon enters Aries 3:18 am
Incense: Patchouli

---

13 Sunday
Twentieth Day (Norwegian)
Waxing Moon
Moon phase: First Quarter
Color: Yellow

Moon Sign: Aries
Incense: Almond

☽ Monday
Feast of the Ass (French)
Waxing Moon
Second Quarter 1:46 am
Color: Gray

Moon Sign: Aries
Moon enters Taurus 1:31 pm
Incense: Narcissus

January

15 Tuesday
Martin Luther King Jr. Day
Waxing Moon
Moon phase: Second Quarter
Color: Black

Moon Sign: Taurus
Incense: Basil

16 Wednesday
Teachers' Day (Thai)
Waxing Moon
Moon phase: Second Quarter
Color: Topaz

Moon Sign: Taurus
Moon enters Gemini 8:00 pm
Incense: Marjoram

17 Thursday
St. Anthony's Day (Mexican)
Waxing Moon
Moon phase: Second Quarter
Color: Crimson

Moon Sign: Gemini
Incense: Apricot

18 Friday
Feast of St. Athanasius
Waxing Moon
Moon phase: Second Quarter
Color: Coral

Moon Sign: Gemini
Moon enters Cancer 10:44 pm
Incense: Alder

19 Saturday
Edgar Allen Poe's birthday
Waxing Moon
Moon phase: Second Quarter
Color: Indigo

Moon Sign: Cancer
Incense: Magnolia

20 Sunday
Feast of St. Euthymius the Great
Waxing Moon
Moon phase: Second Quarter
Color: Orange

Moon Sign: Cancer
Moon enters Leo 10:54 pm
Sun enters Aquarius 4:00 am
Incense: Heliotrope

☺ Monday
Martin Luther King Jr. Day
Waxing Moon
Full Moon 12:16 am
Color: White

Moon Sign: Leo
Incense: Clary sage

January

22 Tuesday

St. Vincent's Day (French)
Waning Moon
Moon phase: Third Quarter
Color: Maroon

Moon Sign: Leo
Moon enters Virgo 10:22 pm
Incense: Ylang-ylang

23 Wednesday

Feast of St. Ildefonsus
Waning Moon
Moon phase: Third Quarter
Color: Yellow

Moon Sign: Virgo
Incense: Honeysuckle

24 Thursday

Alasitas Fair (Bolivian)
Waning Moon
Moon phase: Third Quarter
Color: Green

Moon Sign: Virgo
Moon enters Libra 11:02 pm
Incense: Balsam

25 Friday

Burns Night (Scottish)
Waning Moon
Moon phase: Third Quarter
Color: Purple

Moon Sign: Libra
Incense: Orchid

26 Saturday

Australia Day
Waning Moon
Moon phase: Third Quarter
Color: Gray

Moon Sign: Libra
Incense: Ivy

◑ Sunday

Holocaust Remembrance Day
Waning Moon
Fourth Quarter 4:10 pm
Color: Yellow

Moon Sign: Libra
Moon enters Scorpio 2:31 am
Incense: Marigold

28 Monday

St. Charlemagne's Day
Waning Moon
Moon phase: Fourth Quarter
Color: Ivory

Moon Sign: Scorpio
Moon enters Cancer 1:57 pm
Incense: Hyssop

January

29 Tuesday
Up Helly Aa (Scottish)
Waning Moon
Moon phase: Fourth Quarter
Color: Gray

Moon Sign: Scorpio
Moon enters Sagittarius 9:33 am
Incense: Ginger

30 Wednesday
Martyrs' Day (Indian)
Waning Moon
Moon phase: Fourth Quarter
Color: Brown

Moon Sign: Sagittarius
Incense: Lavender

31 Thursday
Independence Day (Nauru)
Waning Moon
Moon phase: Fourth Quarter
Color: Turquoise

Moon Sign: Sagittarius
Moon enters Capricorn 7:47 pm
Incense: Mulberry

January Birthstones

By her in January born
No gem save Garnets should be worn;
They will ensure her constancy,
True friendship, and fidelity.

Modern: Garnet   Zodiac (Capricorn): Ruby

February Birthstones

The February-born shall find
Sincerity, and peace of mind,
Freedom from passion and from care,
If they the Amethyst will wear.

Modern: Amethyst   Zodiac (Aquarius): Garnet

February

1   Friday

St. Brigid's Day (Irish)
Waning Moon
Moon phase: Fourth Quarter
Color: Pink

Moon Sign: Capricorn
Moon enters Virgo 2:13 pm
Incense: Yarrow

---

2   Saturday

Imbolc • Groundhog Day
Waning Moon
Moon phase: Fourth Quarter
Color: Blue

Moon Sign: Capricorn
Incense: Rue

---

3   Sunday

St. Blaise's Day
Waning Moon
Moon phase: Fourth Quarter
Color: Amber

Moon Sign: Capricorn
Moon enters Aquarius 8:03 am
Incense: Eucalyptus

☽ Monday

Independence Day (Sri Lankan)
Waning Moon
New Moon 4:04 pm
Color: Silver

Moon Sign: Aquarius
Incense: Lily

---

5   Tuesday

Lunar New Year (Pig)
Waxing Moon
Moon phase: First Quarter
Color: Scarlet

Moon Sign: Aquarius
Moon enters Pisces 9:02 pm
Incense: Cedar

---

6   Wednesday

Bob Marley's birthday (Jamaican)
Waxing Moon
Moon phase: First Quarter
Color: Topaz

Moon Sign: Pisces
Incense: Bay laurel

---

7   Thursday

Feast of St. Richard the Pilgrim
Waxing Moon
Moon phase: First Quarter
Color: Purple

Moon Sign: Pisces
Incense: Jasmine

February

8 Friday
Preševen Day (Slovenian)
Waxing Moon
Moon phase: First Quarter
Color: White

Moon Sign: Pisces
Moon enters Aries 9:34 am
Incense: Mint

---

9 Saturday
St. Maron's Day (Lebanese)
Waxing Moon
Moon phase: First Quarter
Color: Brown

Moon Sign: Aries
Incense: Pine

---

10 Sunday
Feast of St. Scholastica
Waxing Moon
Moon phase: First Quarter
Color: Orange

Moon Sign: Aries
Moon enters Taurus 8:28 pm
Incense: Hyacinth

---

11 Monday
National Foundation Day (Japanese)
Waxing Moon
Moon phase: First Quarter
Color: Gray

Moon Sign: Taurus
Incense: Narcissus

◑ Tuesday
Abraham Lincoln's birthday
Waxing Moon
Second Quarter 5:26 pm
Color: Red

Moon Sign: Taurus
Incense: Bayberry

---

13 Wednesday
Parentalia
Waxing Moon
Moon phase: Second Quarter
Color: Brown

Moon Sign: Taurus
Moon enters Gemini 4:32 am
Incense: Lilac

---

14 Thursday
Valentine's Day
Waxing Moon
Moon phase: Second Quarter
Color: Green

Moon Sign: Gemini
Incense: Myrrh

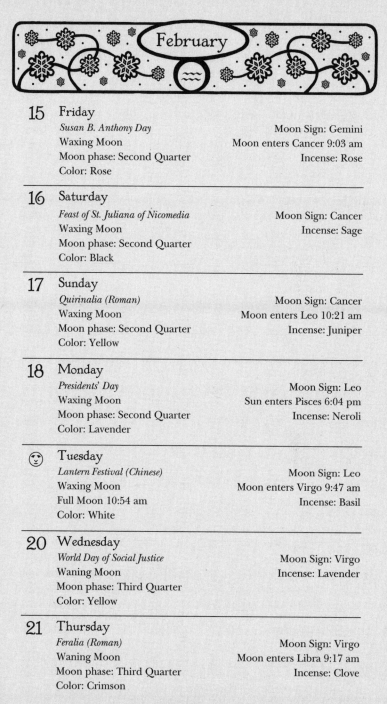

February

15 Friday
Susan B. Anthony Day
Waxing Moon
Moon phase: Second Quarter
Color: Rose

Moon Sign: Gemini
Moon enters Cancer 9:03 am
Incense: Rose

16 Saturday
Feast of St. Juliana of Nicomedia
Waxing Moon
Moon phase: Second Quarter
Color: Black

Moon Sign: Cancer
Incense: Sage

17 Sunday
Quirinalia (Roman)
Waxing Moon
Moon phase: Second Quarter
Color: Yellow

Moon Sign: Cancer
Moon enters Leo 10:21 am
Incense: Juniper

18 Monday
Presidents' Day
Waxing Moon
Moon phase: Second Quarter
Color: Lavender

Moon Sign: Leo
Sun enters Pisces 6:04 pm
Incense: Neroli

☺ Tuesday
Lantern Festival (Chinese)
Waxing Moon
Full Moon 10:54 am
Color: White

Moon Sign: Leo
Moon enters Virgo 9:47 am
Incense: Basil

20 Wednesday
World Day of Social Justice
Waning Moon
Moon phase: Third Quarter
Color: Yellow

Moon Sign: Virgo
Incense: Lavender

21 Thursday
Feralia (Roman)
Waning Moon
Moon phase: Third Quarter
Color: Crimson

Moon Sign: Virgo
Moon enters Libra 9:17 am
Incense: Clove

February

22 Friday
Caristia (Roman)
Waning Moon
Moon phase: Third Quarter
Color: Pink

Moon Sign: Libra
Incense: Thyme

23 Saturday
Mashramani Festival (Guyana)
Waning Moon
Moon phase: Third Quarter
Color: Gray

Moon Sign: Libra
Moon enters Scorpio 10:56 am
Incense: Patchouli

24 Sunday
Regifugium (Roman)
Waning Moon
Moon phase: Third Quarter
Color: Gold

Moon Sign: Scorpio
Incense: Almond

25 Monday
St. Walburga's Day (German)
Waning Moon
Moon phase: Third Quarter
Color: White

Moon Sign: Scorpio
Moon enters Sagittarius 4:19 pm
Incense: Rosemary

◖ Tuesday
Zamboanga Day (Filipino)
Waning Moon
Fourth Quarter 6:28 am
Color: Maroon

Moon Sign: Sagittarius
Incense: Cinnamon

27 Wednesday
Independence Day (Dominican)
Waning Moon
Moon phase: Fourth Quarter
Color: Brown

Moon Sign: Sagittarius
Incense: Honeysuckle

28 Thursday
Kalevala Day (Finnish)
Waning Moon
Moon phase: Fourth Quarter
Color: White

Moon Sign: Sagittarius
Moon enters Capricorn 1:48 am
Incense: Carnation

1 **Friday**
Matronalia (Roman)
Waning Moon
Moon phase: Fourth Quarter
Color: Coral

Moon Sign: Capricorn
Incense: Violet

---

2 **Saturday**
Lantern Festival (Chinese)
Waning Moon
Moon phase: Fourth Quarter
Color: Indigo

Moon Sign: Capricorn
Moon enters Aquarius 2:06 am
Incense: Ivy

---

3 **Sunday**
Doll Festival (Japanese)
Waning Moon
Moon phase: Fourth Quarter
Color: Yellow

Moon Sign: Aquarius
Incense: Marigold

---

4 **Monday**
St. Casimir's Fair (Polish and Lithuanian)
Waning Moon
Moon phase: Fourth Quarter
Color: Gray

Moon Sign: Aquarius
Incense: Lily

---

5 **Tuesday**
Mardi Gras (Fat Tuesday)
Waning Moon
Moon phase: Fourth Quarter
Color: Black

Moon Sign: Aquarius
Moon enters Pisces 3:11 am
Incense: Cedar

---

6 **Wednesday**
Ash Wednesday
Waning Moon
New Moon 11:04 am
Color: White

Moon Sign: Pisces
Incense: Marjoram

---

7 **Thursday**
Vejovis Festival (Roman)
Waxing Moon
Moon phase: First Quarter
Color: Turquoise

Moon Sign: Pisces
Moon enters Aries 3:27 pm
Incense: Balsam

125

March

8 Friday
International Women's Day
Waxing Moon
Moon phase: First Quarter
Color: Purple

Moon Sign: Aries
Incense: Cypress

9 Saturday
Teachers' Day (Lebanese)
Waxing Moon
Moon phase: First Quarter
Color: Blue

Moon Sign: Aries
Incense: Pine

10 Sunday
Tibet Uprising Day
Waxing Moon
Moon phase: First Quarter
Color: Orange

Moon Sign: Aries
Moon enters Taurus 3:10 am
Incense: Hyacinth
Daylight Saving Time begins at 2 am

11 Monday
Johnny Appleseed Day
Waxing Moon
Moon phase: First Quarter
Color: Silver

Moon Sign: Taurus
Incense: Hyssop

12 Tuesday
Girl Scouts' birthday
Waxing Moon
Moon phase: First Quarter
Color: Red

Moon Sign: Taurus
Moon enters Gemini 11:48 am
Incense: Ginger

13 Wednesday
Feast of St. Leander of Seville
Waxing Moon
Moon phase: First Quarter
Color: Brown

Moon Sign: Gemini
Incense: Lavender

◐ Thursday
Pi Day
Waxing Moon
Second Quarter 6:27 am
Color: Green

Moon Sign: Gemini
Moon enters Cancer 5:49 am
Incense: Jasmine

15 Friday
Fertility Festival (Japanese)
Waxing Moon
Moon phase: Second Quarter
Color: Rose

Moon Sign: Cancer
Incense: Orchid

16 Saturday
St. Urho's Day (Finnish-American)
Waxing Moon
Moon phase: Second Quarter
Color: Blue

Moon Sign: Cancer
Moon enters Leo 8:57 pm
Incense: Sandalwood

17 Sunday
St. Patrick's Day
Waxing Moon
Moon phase: Second Quarter
Color: Amber

Moon Sign: Leo
Incense: Frankincense

18 Monday
Sheila's Day (Irish)
Waxing Moon
Moon phase: Second Quarter
Color: Ivory

Moon Sign: Leo
Moon enters Virgo 9:41 pm
Incense: Clary sage

19 Tuesday
Minna Canth's birthday (Finnish)
Waxing Moon
Moon phase: Second Quarter
Color: Gray

Moon Sign: Virgo
Incense: Geranium

☺ Wednesday
Ostara • Spring Equinox
Waxing Moon
Full Moon 9:43 pm
Color: Yellow

Moon Sign: Virgo
Moon enters Libra 9:28 pm
Sun enters Aries 5:58 pm
Incense: Bay laurel

21 Thursday
Purim begins (at sundown on March 20)
Waning Moon
Moon phase: Third Quarter
Color: White

Moon Sign: Libra
Incense: Clove

22 Friday

Denver March Powwow (ends Mar. 24)
Waning Moon
Moon phase: Third Quarter
Color: Coral

Moon Sign: Libra
Moon enters Scorpio 10:16 pm
Incense: Mint

23 Saturday

Pakistan Day
Waning Moon
Moon phase: Third Quarter
Color: Indigo

Moon Sign: Scorpio
Incense: Magnolia

24 Sunday

Day of Blood (Roman)
Waning Moon
Moon phase: Third Quarter
Color: Orange

Moon Sign: Scorpio
Incense: Heliotrope

25 Monday

Tolkien Reading Day
Waning Moon
Moon phase: Third Quarter
Color: White

Moon Sign: Scorpio
Moon enters Sagittarius 2:06 am
Incense: Neroli

26 Tuesday

Prince Kuhio Day (Hawaiian)
Waning Moon
Moon phase: Third Quarter
Color: Scarlet

Moon Sign: Sagittarius
Incense: Ylang-ylang

27 Wednesday

World Theatre Day
Waning Moon
Moon phase: Third Quarter
Color: Topaz

Moon Sign: Sagittarius
Moon enters Capricorn 10:07 am
Incense: Honeysuckle

◐ Thursday

Weed Appreciation Day
Waning Moon
Fourth Quarter 12:10 am
Color: Purple

Moon Sign: Capricorn
Incense: Carnation

March

29 Friday

Feast of St. Eustace of Luxeuil
Waning Moon
Moon phase: Fourth Quarter
Color: Pink

Moon Sign: Capricorn
Moon enters Aquarius 9:46 pm
Incense: Thyme

30 Saturday

Seward's Day (Alaskan)
Waning Moon
Moon phase: Fourth Quarter
Color: Brown

Moon Sign: Aquarius
Incense: Rue

31 Sunday

César Chavez Day
Waning Moon
Moon phase: Fourth Quarter
Color: Gold

Moon Sign: Aquarius
Incense: Eucalyptus

March Birthstones

Who in this world of ours, her eyes
In March first opens, shall be wise.
In days of peril, firm and brave,
And wear a Bloodstone to her grave.

Modern: Aquamarine
Zodiac (Pisces): Amethyst

April
♈

1 Monday
All Fools' Day • April Fools' Day
Waning Moon
Moon phase: Fourth Quarter
Color: White

Moon Sign: Aquarius
Moon enters Pisces 10:48 am
Incense: Lily

2 Tuesday
The Battle of Flowers (French)
Waning Moon
Moon phase: Fourth Quarter
Color: Maroon

Moon Sign: Pisces
Incense: Bayberry

3 Wednesday
Feast of St. Mary of Egypt
Waning Moon
Moon phase: Fourth Quarter
Color: Yellow

Moon Sign: Pisces
Moon enters Aries 10:56 pm
Incense: Lilac

4 Thursday
Megalesia (Roman)
Waning Moon
Moon phase: Fourth Quarter
Color: Green

Moon Sign: Aries
Incense: Balsam

☽ Friday
Tomb-Sweeping Day (Chinese)
Waning Moon
New Moon 4:50 am
Color: Rose

Moon Sign: Aries
Incense: Vanilla

6 Saturday
Tartan Day
Waxing Moon
Moon phase: First Quarter
Color: Black

Moon Sign: Aries
Moon enters Taurus 9:06 am
Incense: Sage

7 Sunday
Motherhood and Beauty Day (Armenian)
Waxing Moon
Moon Phase: First Quarter
Color: Gold

Moon Sign: Taurus
Incense: Marigold

April

8 Monday
Buddha's birthday
Waxing Moon
Moon phase: First Quarter
Color: Gray

Moon Sign: Taurus
Moon enters Gemini 5:15 pm
Incense: Clary sage

9 Tuesday
Valor Day (Filipino)
Waxing Moon
Moon phase: First Quarter
Color: Red

Moon Sign: Gemini
Incense: Ginger

10 Wednesday
Siblings Day
Waxing Moon
Moon phase: First Quarter
Color: Brown

Moon Sign: Gemini
Moon enters Cancer 11:31 pm
Incense: Marjoram

11 Thursday
Juan Santamaría Day (Costa Rican)
Waxing Moon
Moon phase: First Quarter
Color: Crimson

Moon Sign: Cancer
Incense: Mulberry

◐ Friday
Children's Day (Bolivian and Haitian)
Waxing Moon
Second Quarter 3:06 pm
Color: Pink

Moon Sign: Cancer
Incense: Cypress

13 Saturday
Thai New Year (ends April 15)
Waxing Moon
Moon phase: Second Quarter
Color: Blue

Moon Sign: Cancer
Moon enters Leo 3:50 am
Incense: Magnolia

14 Sunday
Palm Sunday
Waxing Moon
Moon phase: Second Quarter
Color: Amber

Moon Sign: Leo
Incense: Heliotrope

April ♈

15 Monday
Fordicidia (Roman)
Waxing Moon
Moon phase: Second Quarter
Color: Ivory

Moon Sign: Leo
Moon enters Virgo 6:14 am
Incense: Narcissus

16 Tuesday
World Voice Day
Waxing Moon
Moon phase: Second Quarter
Color: White

Moon Sign: Virgo
Incense: Cedar

17 Wednesday
Yayoi Matsuri (Japanese)
Waxing Moon
Moon phase: Second Quarter
Color: Topaz

Moon Sign: Virgo
Moon enters Libra 7:22 am
Incense: Lavender

18 Thursday
International Day for Monuments and Sites
Waxing Moon
Moon phase: Second Quarter
Color: Purple

Moon Sign: Libra
Incense: Clove

☺ Friday
Good Friday
Waxing Moon
Full Moon 7:12 am
Color: Coral

Moon Sign: Libra
Moon enters Scorpio 8:41 am
Incense: Orchid

20 Saturday
Passover begins (at sundown on April 19)
Waning Moon
Moon phase: Third Quarter
Color: Brown

Moon Sign: Scorpio
Sun enters Taurus 4:55 am
Incense: Pine

21 Sunday
Easter
Waning Moon
Moon phase: Third Quarter
Color: Orange

Moon Sign: Scorpio
Moon enters Sagittarius 11:59 am
Incense: Almond

22 Monday

Earth Day
Waning Moon
Moon phase: Third Quarter
Color: Silver

Moon Sign: Sagittarius
Incense: Rosemary

23 Tuesday

St. George's Day
Waning Moon
Moon phase: Third Quarter
Color: Gray

Moon Sign: Sagittarius
Moon enters Capricorn 6:50 pm
Incense: Cinnamon

24 Wednesday

St. Mark's Eve
Waning Moon
Moon phase: Third Quarter
Color: Yellow

Moon Sign: Capricorn
Incense: Honeysuckle

25 Thursday

Robigalia (Roman)
Waning Moon
Moon phase: Third Quarter
Color: Purple

Moon Sign: Capricorn
Incense: Apricot

◑ Friday

Orthodox Good Friday
Waning Moon
Fourth Quarter 6:18 pm
Color: White

Moon Sign: Capricorn
Moon enters Aquarius 5:27 am
Incense: Mint

27 Saturday

Passover ends
Waning Moon
Moon phase: Fourth Quarter
Color: Indigo

Moon Sign: Aquarius
Incense: Patchouli

28 Sunday

Orthodox Easter
Waning Moon
Moon phase: Fourth Quarter
Color: Yellow

Moon Sign: Aquarius
Moon enters Pisces 6:11 pm
Incense: Frankincense

April

29 Monday
Showa Day (Japanese)
Waning Moon
Moon phase: Fourth Quarter
Color: Lavender

Moon Sign: Pisces
Incense: Hyssop

30 Tuesday
Walpurgis Night • May Eve
Waning Moon
Moon phase: Fourth Quarter
Color: Black

Moon Sign: Pisces
Incense: Basil

April Birthstones

She who from April dates her years,
Diamonds shall wear, lest bitter tears
For vain repentance flow; this stone
Emblem for innocence is known.

Modern: Diamond
Zodiac (Aries): Bloodstone

May

1 Wednesday

Beltane • May Day
Waning Moon
Moon phase: Fourth Quarter
Color: White

Moon Sign: Pisces
Moon enters Aries 6:24 am
Incense: Bay laurel

---

2 Thursday

National Education Day (Indonesian)
Waning Moon
Moon phase: Fourth Quarter
Color: Crimson

Moon Sign: Aries
Incense: Mulberry

---

3 Friday

Roodmas
Waning Moon
Moon phase: Fourth Quarter
Color: Pink

Moon Sign: Aries
Moon enters Taurus 4:18 pm
Incense: Yarrow

---

4 Saturday

Star Wars Day
Waning Moon
New Moon 6:45 pm
Color: Blue

Moon Sign: Taurus
Incense: Rue

---

5 Sunday

Cinco de Mayo (Mexican)
Waxing Moon
Moon phase: First Quarter
Color: Orange

Moon Sign: Taurus
Moon enters Gemini 11:40 am
Incense: Juniper

---

6 Monday

Ramadan begins
Waxing Moon
Moon phase: First Quarter
Color: Silver

Moon Sign: Gemini
Incense: Narcissus

---

7 Tuesday

Teacher Appreciation Day
Waxing Moon
Moon phase: First Quarter
Color: Gray

Moon Sign: Gemini
Incense: Geranium

May

8   Wednesday
White Lotus Day (Theosophical)
Waxing Moon
Moon phase: First Quarter
Color: Topaz

Moon Sign: Gemini
Moon enters Cancer 5:06 am
Incense: Honeysuckle

---

9   Thursday
Lemuria (Roman)
Waxing Moon
Moon phase: First Quarter
Color: White

Moon Sign: Cancer
Incense: Balsam

---

10   Friday
Independence Day (Romanian)
Waxing Moon
Moon phase: First Quarter
Color: Rose

Moon Sign: Cancer
Moon enters Leo 9:14 am
Incense: Orchid

☾   Saturday
Ukai season opens (Japanese)
Waxing Moon
Second Quarter 9:12 pm
Color: Indigo

Moon Sign: Leo
Incense: Sandalwood

---

12   Sunday
Mother's Day
Waxing Moon
Moon phase: Second Quarter
Color: Gold

Moon Sign: Leo
Moon enters Virgo 12:22 pm
Incense: Hyacinth

---

13   Monday
Pilgrimage to Fátima (Portuguese)
Waxing Moon
Moon phase: Second Quarter
Color: Ivory

Moon Sign: Virgo
Incense: Hyssop

---

14   Tuesday
Carabao Festival (Spanish)
Waxing Moon
Moon phase: Second Quarter
Color: Red

Moon Sign: Virgo
Moon enters Libra 2:51 pm
Incense: Ylang-ylang

May

15 Wednesday

Festival of St. Dymphna
Waxing Moon
Moon phase: Second Quarter
Color: Brown

Moon Sign: Libra
Incense: Marjoram

16 Thursday

St. Honoratus's Day
Waxing Moon
Moon phase: Second Quarter
Color: Green

Moon Sign: Libra
Moon enters Scorpio 5:26 pm
Incense: Apricot

17 Friday

Norwegian Constitution Day
Waxing Moon
Moon phase: Second Quarter
Color: Pink

Moon Sign: Scorpio
Incense: Alder

☺ Saturday

Battle of Las Piedras Day (Uruguayan)
Waxing Moon
Full Moon 5:11 pm
Color: Black

Moon Sign: Scorpio
Moon enters Sagittarius 9:21 pm
Incense: Rue

19 Sunday

Mother's Day (Kyrgyzstani)
Waning Moon
Moon phase: Third Quarter
Color: Amber

Moon Sign: Sagittarius
Incense: Eucalyptus

20 Monday

Victoria Day (Canada)
Waning Moon
Moon phase: Third Quarter
Color: White

Moon Sign: Sagittarius
Incense: Rosemary

21 Tuesday

Navy Day (Chilean)
Waning Moon
Moon phase: Third Quarter
Color: Maroon

Moon Sign: Sagittarius
Moon enters Capricorn 3:56 am
Sun enters Gemini 3:59 am
Incense: Bayberry

May

22 Wednesday

Harvey Milk Day (Californian)
Waning Moon
Moon phase: Third Quarter
Color: Yellow

Moon Sign: Capricorn
Incense: Lilac

23 Thursday

Tubilustrium (Roman)
Waning Moon
Moon phase: Third Quarter
Color: Turquoise

Moon Sign: Capricorn
Moon enters Aquarius 1:49 pm
Incense: Carnation

24 Friday

Education and Culture Day (Bulgarian)
Waning Moon
Moon phase: Third Quarter
Color: Coral

Moon Sign: Aquarius
Incense: Cypress

25 Saturday

Missing Children's Day
Waning Moon
Moon phase: Third Quarter
Color: Brown

Moon Sign: Aquarius
Incense: Ivy

☾ Sunday

Pepys's Commemoration (English)
Waning Moon
Fourth Quarter 12:34 pm
Color: Gold

Moon Sign: Aquarius
Moon enters Pisces 2:08 am
Incense: Almond

27 Monday

Memorial Day
Waning Moon
Moon phase: Fourth Quarter
Color: Gray

Moon Sign: Pisces
Incense: Lily

28 Tuesday

St. Germain's Day
Waning Moon
Moon phase: Fourth Quarter
Color: Scarlet

Moon Sign: Pisces
Moon enters Aries 2:32 pm
Incense: Cedar

May

29 Wednesday

Oak Apple Day (English)   Moon Sign: Aries
Waning Moon   Incense: Lavender
Moon phase: Fourth Quarter
Color: Topaz

30 Thursday

Canary Islands Day   Moon Sign: Aries
Waning Moon   Incense: Nutmeg
Moon phase: Fourth Quarter
Color: Purple

31 Friday

Visitation of Mary   Moon Sign: Aries
Waning Moon   Moon enters Taurus 12:43 am
Moon phase: Fourth Quarter   Incense: Vanilla
Color: White

May Birthstones

Who first beholds the light of day,
In spring's sweet flowery month of May,
And wears an Emerald all her life,
Shall be a loved, and happy wife.

Modern: Emerald
Zodiac (Taurus): Sapphire

June

♊

1 Saturday
Dayak Harvest Festival (Malaysian)
Waning Moon
Moon phase: Fourth Quarter
Color: Gray

Moon Sign: Taurus
Incense: Magnolia

2 Sunday
Republic Day (Italian)
Waning Moon
Moon phase: Fourth Quarter
Color: Amber

Moon Sign: Taurus
Moon enters Gemini 7:48 am
Incense: Heliotrope

☽ Monday
Feast of St. Clotilde
Waning Moon
New Moon 6:02 am
Color: White

Moon Sign: Gemini
Incense: Clary sage

4 Tuesday
Ramadan ends
Waxing Moon
Moon phase: First Quarter
Color: Red

Moon Sign: Gemini
Moon enters Cancer 12:17 pm
Incense: Geranium

5 Wednesday
Constitution Day (Danish)
Waxing Moon
Moon phase: First Quarter
Color: Brown

Moon Sign: Cancer
Incense: Honeysuckle

6 Thursday
National Day of Sweden
Waxing Moon
Moon phase: First Quarter
Color: Green

Moon Sign: Cancer
Moon enters Leo 3:16 pm
Incense: Clove

7 Friday
Vestalia begins (Roman)
Waxing Moon
Moon phase: First Quarter
Color: Pink

Moon Sign: Leo
Incense: Violet

June

8 Saturday
World Oceans Day
Waxing Moon
Moon phase: First Quarter
Color: Blue

Moon Sign: Leo
Moon enters Virgo 5:45 pm
Incense: Patchouli

9 Sunday
Shavuot (begins at sundown on June 8)
Waxing Moon
Moon phase: First Quarter
Color: Yellow

Moon Sign: Virgo
Incense: Marigold

◐ Monday
Portugal Day
Waxing Moon
Second Quarter 1:59 am
Color: Lavender

Moon Sign: Virgo
Moon enters Libra 8:29 pm
Incense: Hyssop

11 Tuesday
Kamehameha Day (Hawaiian)
Waxing Moon
Moon phase: Second Quarter
Color: Maroon

Moon Sign: Libra
Incense: Bayberry

12 Wednesday
Independence Day (Filipino)
Waxing Moon
Moon phase: Second Quarter
Color: Topaz

Moon Sign: Libra
Incense: Bay laurel

13 Thursday
St. Anthony of Padua's Day
Waxing Moon
Moon phase: Second Quarter
Color: Purple

Moon Sign: Libra
Moon enters Scorpio 12:02 am
Incense: Myrrh

14 Friday
Flag Day
Waxing Moon
Moon phase: Second Quarter
Color: Rose

Moon Sign: Scorpio
Incense: Thyme

June

15 Saturday
Vestalia ends (Roman)
Waxing Moon
Moon phase: Second Quarter
Color: Indigo

Moon Sign: Scorpio
Moon enters Sagittarius 5:03 am
Incense: Sandalwood

16 Sunday
Father's Day
Waxing Moon
Moon phase: Second Quarter
Color: Gold

Moon Sign: Sagittarius
Incense: Juniper

Monday
Bunker Hill Day (Massachusetts)
Waxing Moon
Full Moon 4:31 am
Color: Silver

Moon Sign: Sagittarius
Moon enters Capricorn 12:13 pm
Incense: Lily

18 Tuesday
Waterloo Day (British)
Waning Moon
Moon phase: Third Quarter
Color: Scarlet

Moon Sign: Capricorn
Incense: Cinnamon

19 Wednesday
Juneteenth
Waning Moon
Moon phase: Third Quarter
Color: Yellow

Moon Sign: Capricorn
Moon enters Aquarius 10:01 pm
Incense: Lilac

20 Thursday
Flag Day (Argentinian)
Waning Moon
Moon phase: Third Quarter
Color: Crimson

Moon Sign: Aquarius
Incense: Jasmine

21 Friday
Litha • Summer Solstice
Waning Moon
Moon phase: Third Quarter
Color: Purple

Moon Sign: Aquarius
Sun enters Cancer 11:54 am
Incense: Rose

June

22 Saturday

Teachers' Day (El Salvadoran)
Waning Moon
Moon phase: Third Quarter
Color: Blue

Moon Sign: Aquarius
Moon enters Pisces 10:01 am
Incense: Sage

23 Sunday

St. John's Eve
Waning Moon
Moon phase: Third Quarter
Color: Orange

Moon Sign: Pisces
Incense: Hyacinth

24 Monday

St. John's Day
Waning Moon
Moon phase: Third Quarter
Color: Gray

Moon Sign: Pisces
Moon enters Aries 10:38 am
Incense: Rosemary

○ Tuesday

Fiesta de Santa Orosia (Spanish)
Waning Moon
Fourth Quarter 5:46 am
Color: Black

Moon Sign: Aries
Incense: Ginger

26 Wednesday

Pied Piper Day (German)
Waning Moon
Moon phase: Fourth Quarter
Color: White

Moon Sign: Aries
Incense: Marjoram

27 Thursday

Seven Sleepers' Day (German)
Waning Moon
Moon phase: Fourth Quarter
Color: Green

Moon Sign: Aries
Moon enters Taurus 9:32 am
Incense: Balsam

28 Friday

Paul Bunyan Day
Waning Moon
Moon phase: Fourth Quarter
Color: Coral

Moon Sign: Taurus
Incense: Mint

June

29 Saturday
Haro Wine Battle (Spain)
Waning Moon
Moon phase: Fourth Quarter
Color: Black

Moon Sign: Taurus
Moon enters Gemini 5:09 pm
Incense: Pine

30 Sunday
The Burning of the Three Firs (French)
Waning Moon
Moon phase: Fourth Quarter
Color: Yellow

Moon Sign: Gemini
Incense: Eucalyptus

June Birthstones

Who comes with summer to this earth,
And owes to June her hour of birth,
With ring of Agate on her hand,
Can health, wealth, and long life command.

Modern: Moonstone or Pearl
Zodiac (Gemini): Agate

July

1 Monday
Canada Day
Waning Moon
Moon phase: Fourth Quarter
Color: Ivory

Moon Sign: Gemini
Moon enters Cancer 9:24 pm
Incense: Neroli

2 Tuesday
World UFO Day
Waning Moon
New Moon 3:16 pm
Color: Maroon

Moon Sign: Cancer
Incense: Ylang-ylang

3 Wednesday
Dog Days of Summer begin
Waxing Moon
Moon phase: First Quarter
Color: Yellow

Moon Sign: Cancer
Moon enters Leo 11:19 pm
Incense: Lilac

4 Thursday
Independence Day
Waxing Moon
Moon phase: First Quarter
Color: White

Moon Sign: Leo
Incense: Myrrh

5 Friday
Tynwald Day (Manx)
Waxing Moon
Moon phase: First Quarter
Color: Purple

Moon Sign: Leo
Incense: Cypress

6 Saturday
San Fermín begins (Spanish)
Waxing Moon
Moon phase: First Quarter
Color: Gray

Moon Sign: Leo
Moon enters Virgo 12:25 am
Incense: Magnolia

7 Sunday
Star Festival (Japanese)
Waxing Moon
Moon phase: First Quarter
Color: Amber

Moon Sign: Virgo
Incense: Frankincense

July

8 Monday
Feast of St. Sunniva
Waxing Moon
Moon phase: First Quarter
Color: Silver

Moon Sign: Virgo
Moon enters Libra 2:07 am
Incense: Narcissus

◑ Tuesday
Battle of Sempach Day (Swiss)
Waxing Moon
Second Quarter 6:55 am
Color: Red

Moon Sign: Libra
Incense: Ginger

10 Wednesday
Nicola Tesla Day
Waxing Moon
Moon phase: Second Quarter
Color: Brown

Moon Sign: Libra
Moon enters Scorpio 5:29 am
Incense: Marjoram

11 Thursday
Mongolian Naadam Festival (ends July 13)
Waxing Moon
Moon phase: Second Quarter
Color: Turquoise

Moon Sign: Scorpio
Incense: Nutmeg

12 Friday
Malala Day
Waxing Moon
Moon phase: Second Quarter
Color: Pink

Moon Sign: Scorpio
Moon enters Sagittarius 11:05 am
Incense: Alder

13 Saturday
Feast of St. Mildrith
Waxing Moon
Moon phase: Second Quarter
Color: Blue

Moon Sign: Sagittarius
Incense: Ivy

14 Sunday
Bastille Day (French)
Waxing Moon
Moon phase: Second Quarter
Color: Gold

Moon Sign: Sagittarius
Moon enters Capricorn 7:05 pm
Incense: Juniper

July

15 Monday

St. Swithin's Day
Waxing Moon
Moon phase: Second Quarter
Color: White

Moon Sign: Capricorn
Incense: Hyssop

Tuesday

Fiesta de la Tirana (Chilean)
Waxing Moon
Full Moon 5:38 pm
Color: Black

Moon Sign: Capricorn
Incense: Cedar

17 Wednesday

Gion Festival first Yamaboko parade (Japanese)
Waning Moon
Moon phase: Third Quarter
Color: Topaz

Moon Sign: Capricorn
Moon enters Aquarius 5:19 am
Incense: Honeysuckle

18 Thursday

Nelson Mandela International Day
Waning Moon
Moon phase: Third Quarter
Color: Purple

Moon Sign: Aquarius
Incense: Apricot

19 Friday

Flitch Day (English)
Waning Moon
Moon phase: Third Quarter
Color: Rose

Moon Sign: Aquarius
Moon enters Pisces 5:19 pm
Incense: Orchid

20 Saturday

Binding of Wreaths (Lithuanian)
Waning Moon
Moon phase: Third Quarter
Color: Indigo

Moon Sign: Pisces
Incense: Rue

21 Sunday

National Day (Belgian)
Waning Moon
Moon phase: Third Quarter
Color: Amber

Moon Sign: Pisces
Incense: Marigold

July

22 Monday
St. Mary Magdalene's Day
Waning Moon
Moon phase: Third Quarter
Color: Lavender

Moon Sign: Pisces
Moon enters Aries 6:02 am
Sun enters Leo 10:50 pm
Incense: Rosemary

23 Tuesday
Mysteries of St. Cristina (Italian)
Waning Moon
Moon phase: Third Quarter
Color: Scarlet

Moon Sign: Aries
Incense: Cinnamon

Wednesday
Gion Festival second Yamaboko parade (Japanese)
Waning Moon
Fourth Quarter 9:18 pm
Color: Brown

Moon Sign: Aries
Moon enters Taurus 5:42 pm
Incense: Lavender

25 Thursday
Illapa Festival (Incan)
Waning Moon
Moon phase: Fourth Quarter
Color: Crimson

Moon Sign: Taurus
Incense: Mulberry

26 Friday
St. Anne's Day
Waning Moon
Moon phase: Fourth Quarter
Color: Purple

Moon Sign: Taurus
Incense: Yarrow

27 Saturday
Sleepyhead Day (Finnish)
Waning Moon
Moon phase: Fourth Quarter
Color: Black

Moon Sign: Taurus
Moon enters Gemini 2:29 am
Incense: Pine

28 Sunday
Independence Day (Peruvian)
Waning Moon
Moon phase: Fourth Quarter
Color: Yellow

Moon Sign: Gemini
Incense: Almond

July

29 Monday
St. Olaf Festival (Faroese)
Waning Moon
Moon phase: Fourth Quarter
Color: Gray

Moon Sign: Gemini
Moon enters Cancer 7:31 am
Incense: Lily

30 Tuesday
Micman Festival of St. Ann
Waning Moon
Moon phase: Fourth Quarter
Color: White

Moon Sign: Cancer
Incense: Basil

 Wednesday
Feast of St. Ignatius
Waning Moon
New Moon 11:12 pm
Color: Yellow

Moon Sign: Cancer
Moon enters Leo 9:18 am
Incense: Bay laurel

July Birthstones

The glowing Ruby shall adorn
Those who in warm July are born;
Then will they be exempt and free
From love's doubt, and anxiety.

Modern: Ruby
Zodiac (Cancer): Emerald

August

1 Thursday
Lammas
Waxing Moon
Moon phase: First Quarter
Color: Turquoise

Moon Sign: Leo
Incense: Clove

---

2 Friday
Porcingula (Pecos)
Waxing Moon
Moon phase: First Quarter
Color: Rose

Moon Sign: Leo
Moon enters Virgo 9:20 am
Incense: Vanilla

---

3 Saturday
Flag Day (Venezuelan)
Waxing Moon
Moon phase: First Quarter
Color: Blue

Moon Sign: Virgo
Incense: Sandalwood

---

4 Sunday
Constitution Day (Cook Islands)
Waxing Moon
Moon phase: First Quarter
Color: Orange

Moon Sign: Virgo
Moon enters Libra 9:30 am
Incense: Hyacinth

---

5 Monday
Carnival of Bogotá
Waxing Moon
Moon phase: First Quarter
Color: Lavender

Moon Sign: Libra
Incense: Hyssop

---

6 Tuesday
Hiroshima Peace Memorial Ceremony
Waxing Moon
Moon phase: First Quarter
Color: Red

Moon Sign: Libra
Moon enters Scorpio 11:31 am
Incense: Bayberry

☾ Wednesday
Qixi Festival (Chinese)
Waxing Moon
Second Quarter 1:31 pm
Color: White

Moon Sign: Scorpio
Incense: Honeysuckle

August

8 Thursday

Farmers' Day (Tanzanian)
Waxing Moon
Moon phase: Second Quarter
Color: Green

Moon Sign: Scorpio
Moon enters Sagittarius 4:35 pm
Incense: Carnation

9 Friday

Nagasaki Peace Memorial Ceremony
Waxing Moon
Moon phase: Second Quarter
Color: Pink

Moon Sign: Sagittarius
Incense: Violet

10 Saturday

Puck Fair (ends Aug. 12; Irish)
Waxing Moon
Moon phase: Second Quarter
Color: Brown

Moon Sign: Sagittarius
Incense: Sage

11 Sunday

Mountain Day (Japanese)
Waxing Moon
Moon phase: Second Quarter
Color: Yellow

Moon Sign: Sagittarius
Moon enters Capricorn 12:50 am
Incense: Eucalyptus

12 Monday

World Elephant Day
Waxing Moon
Moon phase: Second Quarter
Color: Ivory

Moon Sign: Capricorn
Incense: Clary sage

13 Tuesday

Glorious Twelfth (United Kingdom)
Waxing Moon
Moon phase: Second Quarter
Color: Maroon

Moon Sign: Capricorn
Moon enters Aquarius 11:35 am
Incense: Cedar

14 Wednesday

Independence Day (Pakistani)
Waxing Moon
Moon phase: Second Quarter
Color: Yellow

Moon Sign: Aquarius
Incense: Lilac

August

Thursday
Ghost Festival (Chinese)
Waxing Moon
Full Moon 8:29 am
Color: Crimson

Moon Sign: Aquarius
Moon enters Pisces 11:49 pm
Incense: Balsam

---

16 Friday
Xicolatada (French)
Waning Moon
Moon phase: Third Quarter
Color: White

Moon Sign: Pisces
Incense: Thyme

---

17 Saturday
Black Cat Appreciation Day
Waning Moon
Moon phase: Third Quarter
Color: Gray

Moon Sign: Pisces
Incense: Rue

---

18 Sunday
St. Helen's Day
Waning Moon
Moon phase: Third Quarter
Color: Gold

Moon Sign: Pisces
Moon enters Aries 12:33 pm
Incense: Frankincense

---

19 Monday
Vinalia Rustica (Roman)
Waning Moon
Moon phase: Third Quarter
Color: Silver

Moon Sign: Aries
Incense: Narcissus

---

20 Tuesday
St. Stephen's Day (Hungarian)
Waning Moon
Moon phase: Third Quarter
Color: Scarlet

Moon Sign: Aries
Incense: Geranium

---

21 Wednesday
Consualia (Roman)
Waning Moon
Moon phase: Third Quarter
Color: Brown

Moon Sign: Aries
Moon enters Taurus 12:37 am
Incense: Lavender

August ♍

22 Thursday
Feast of the Queenship of Mary (English)
Waning Moon
Moon phase: Third Quarter
Color: Turquoise

Moon Sign: Taurus
Incense: Myrrh

○ **Friday**
National Day (Romanian)
Waning Moon
Fourth Quarter 10:56 am
Color: Rose

Moon Sign: Taurus
Moon enters Gemini 10:34 am
Sun enters Virgo 6:02 am
Incense: Rose

24 Saturday
St. Bartholomew's Day
Waning Moon
Moon phase: Fourth Quarter
Color: Black

Moon Sign: Gemini
Incense: Patchouli

25 Sunday
Liberation of Paris
Waning Moon
Moon phase: Fourth Quarter
Color: Gold

Moon Sign: Gemini
Moon enters Cancer 5:05 pm
Incense: Heliotrope

26 Monday
Heroes' Day (Namibian)
Waning Moon
Moon phase: Fourth Quarter
Color: Ivory

Moon Sign: Cancer
Incense: Lily

27 Tuesday
Independence Day (Moldovan)
Waning Moon
Moon phase: Fourth Quarter
Color: Gray

Moon Sign: Cancer
Moon enters Leo 7:53 pm
Incense: Ylang-ylang

28 Wednesday
St. Augustine's Day
Waning Moon
Moon phase: Fourth Quarter
Color: Topaz

Moon Sign: Leo
Incense: Marjoram

August

29 Thursday
St. John's Beheading
Waning Moon
Moon phase: Fourth Quarter
Color: Purple

Moon Sign: Leo
Moon enters Virgo 7:57 pm
Incense: Apricot

 Friday
St. Rose of Lima Day (Peruvian)
Waning Moon
New Moon 6:37 am
Color: White

Moon Sign: Virgo
Incense: Mint

---

31 Saturday
Islamic New Year
Waxing Moon
Moon phase: First Quarter
Color: Indigo

Moon Sign: Virgo
Moon enters Libra 7:08 pm
Incense: Magnolia

August Birthstones

Wear Sardonyx, or for thee
No conjugal felicity;
The August-born without this stone,
'Tis said, must live unloved, and lone.

Modern: Peridot
Zodiac (Leo): Onyx

September

1 Sunday
Wattle Day (Australian)
Waxing Moon
Moon phase: First Quarter
Color: Amber

Moon Sign: Libra
Incense: Eucalyptus

2 Monday
Labor Day • Labour Day (Canada)
Waxing Moon
Moon phase: First Quarter
Color: White

Moon Sign: Libra
Moon enters Virgo 7:35 pm
Incense: Neroli

3 Tuesday
National Feast of San Marino
Waxing Moon
Moon phase: First Quarter
Color: Black

Moon Sign: Virgo
Incense: Ginger

4 Wednesday
Feast of St. Rosalia
Waxing Moon
Moon phase: First Quarter
Color: Yellow

Moon Sign: Virgo
Moon enters Sagittarius 11:08 pm
Incense: Lily

5 ☽ Thursday
International Day of Charity
Waxing Moon
Second Quarter 11:10 pm
Color: Crimson

Moon Sign: Sagittarius
Incense: Carnation

6 Friday
Unification Day (Bulgaria)
Waxing Moon
Moon phase: Second Quarter
Color: Coral

Moon Sign: Sagittarius
Incense: Orchid

7 Saturday
Independence Day (Brazilian)
Waxing Moon
Moon phase: Second Quarter
Color: Blue

Moon Sign: Sagittarius
Moon enters Capricorn 6:37 am
Incense: Ivy

8 Sunday

Grandparents' Day
Waxing Moon
Moon phase: Second Quarter
Color: Yellow

Moon Sign: Capricorn
Incense: Hyacinth

9 Monday

Remembrance for Herman the Cheruscan (Asatru)
Waxing Moon
Moon phase: Second Quarter
Color: Gray

Moon Sign: Capricorn
Moon enters Aquarius 5:24 pm
Incense: Hyssop

10 Tuesday

National Day (Belizean)
Waxing Moon
Moon phase: Second Quarter
Color: Scarlet

Moon Sign: Aquarius
Incense: Cinnamon

11 Wednesday

Coptic New Year
Waxing Moon
Moon phase: Second Quarter
Color: Brown

Moon Sign: Aquarius
Incense: Bay laurel

12 Thursday

Mindfulness Day
Waxing Moon
Moon phase: Second Quarter
Color: Green

Moon Sign: Aquarius
Moon enters Pisces 5:52 pm
Incense: Clove

13 Friday

The Gods' Banquet (Roman)
Waxing Moon
Moon phase: Second Quarter
Color: White

Moon Sign: Pisces
Incense: Cypress

☺ Saturday

Holy Cross Day
Waxing Moon
Full Moon 12:33 am
Color: Black

Moon Sign: Pisces
Moon enters Aries 6:32 pm
Incense: Pine

15 Sunday

International Day of Democracy
Waning Moon
Moon phase: Third Quarter
Color: Gold

Moon Sign: Aries
Incense: Juniper

---

16 Monday

Independence Day (Mexican)
Waning Moon
Moon phase: Third Quarter
Color: Silver

Moon Sign: Aries
Incense: Lily

---

17 Tuesday

Constitution Day
Waning Moon
Moon phase: Third Quarter
Color: Red

Moon Sign: Aries
Moon enters Taurus 6:31 am
Incense: Ylang-ylang

---

18 Wednesday

World Water Monitoring Day
Waning Moon
Moon phase: Third Quarter
Color: Topaz

Moon Sign: Taurus
Incense: Marjoram

---

19 Thursday

Feast of San Gennaro
Waning Moon
Moon phase: Third Quarter
Color: Turquoise

Moon Sign: Taurus
Moon enters Gemini 4:58 pm
Incense: Jasmine

---

20 Friday

St. Eustace's Day
Waning Moon
Moon phase: Third Quarter
Color: Pink

Moon Sign: Gemini
Incense: Violet

◯ Saturday

UN International Day of Peace
Waning Moon
Fourth Quarter 10:41 pm
Color: Indigo

Moon Sign: Gemini
Incense: Sandalwood

September

22 Sunday
Hobbit Day
Waning Moon
Moon phase: Fourth Quarter
Color: Orange

Moon Sign: Gemini
Moon enters Cancer 12:50 am
Incense: Frankincense

23 Monday
Mabon • Fall Equinox
Waning Moon
Moon phase: Fourth Quarter
Color: Ivory

Moon Sign: Cancer
Sun enters Libra 3:50 am
Incense: Narcissus

24 Tuesday
Sukkot begins
Waning Moon
Moon phase: Fourth Quarter
Color: Gray

Moon Sign: Cancer
Moon enters Leo 5:19 am
Incense: Bayberry

25 Wednesday
Doll Memorial Service (Japanese)
Waning Moon
Moon phase: Fourth Quarter
Color: White

Moon Sign: Leo
Incense: Lavender

26 Thursday
Feast of Santa Justina (Mexican)
Waning Moon
Moon phase: Fourth Quarter
Color: Purple

Moon Sign: Leo
Moon enters Virgo 6:37 am
Incense: Balsam

27 Friday
Meskel (Ethiopian and Eritrean)
Waning Moon
Moon phase: Fourth Quarter
Color: Rose

Moon Sign: Virgo
Incense: Thyme

☽ Saturday
Confucius's birthday
Waning Moon
New Moon 2:26 pm
Color: Blue

Moon Sign: Virgo
Moon enters Libra 6:03 am
Incense: Magnolia

September

29 Sunday

Michaelmas
Waxing Moon
Moon phase: First Quarter
Color: Yellow

Moon Sign: Libra
Incense: Almond

30 Monday

Rosh Hashanah (begins at sundown on Sept. 29)
Waxing Moon
Moon phase: First Quarter
Color: Lavender

Moon Sign: Libra
Moon enters Scorpio 5:42 am
Incense: Clary sage

September Birthstones

A maiden born when autumn leaves
Are rustling in September's breeze,
A Sapphire on her brow should bind;
'Twill cure diseases of the mind.

Modern: Sapphire
Zodiac (Virgo): Carnelian

October

1 Tuesday
Armed Forces Day (South Korean)
Waxing Moon
Moon phase: First Quarter
Color: Black

Moon Sign: Scorpio
Incense: Geranium

2 Wednesday
Gandhi's birthday
Waxing Moon
Moon phase: First Quarter
Color: Brown

Moon Sign: Scorpio
Moon enters Sagittarius 7:44 am
Incense: Bay laurel

3 Thursday
German Unity Day
Waxing Moon
Moon phase: First Quarter
Color: Green

Moon Sign: Sagittarius

Incense: Carnation

4 Friday
St. Francis's Day
Waxing Moon
Moon phase: First Quarter
Color: Pink

Moon Sign: Sagittarius
Moon enters Capricorn 1:43 pm
Incense: Mint

◖ Saturday
Republic Day (Portuguese)
Waxing Moon
Second Quarter 12:47 pm
Color: Gray

Moon Sign: Capricorn
Incense: Rue

6 Sunday
German-American Day
Waxing Moon
Moon phase: Second Quarter
Color: Gold

Moon Sign: Capricorn
Moon enters Aquarius 11:42 pm
Incense: Heliotrope

7 Monday
Double Ninth Festival (Chinese)
Waxing Moon
Moon phase: Second Quarter
Color: Silver

Moon Sign: Aquarius
Incense: Rosemary

October

8 Tuesday

Arbor Day (Namibian)

Waxing Moon

Moon phase: Second Quarter

Color: Red

Moon Sign: Aquarius

Incense: Cedar

9 Wednesday

Yom Kippur (begins at sundown on Oct. 8)

Waxing Moon

Moon phase: Second Quarter

Color: Yellow

Moon Sign: Aquarius

Moon enters Pisces 12:05 pm

Incense: Lilac

10 Thursday

Finnish Literature Day

Waxing Moon

Moon phase: Second Quarter

Color: White

Moon Sign: Pisces

Incense: Clove

11 Friday

Meditrinalia (Roman)

Waxing Moon

Moon phase: Second Quarter

Color: Purple

Moon Sign: Pisces

Incense: Violet

12 Saturday

National Festival of Spain

Waxing Moon

Moon phase: Second Quarter

Color: Black

Moon Sign: Pisces

Moon enters Aries 12:46 am

Incense: Sandalwood

☉ Sunday

Fontinalia (Roman)

Waxing Moon

Full Moon 5:08 pm

Color: Yellow

Moon Sign: Aries

Incense: Marigold

14 Monday

Sukkot begins (at sundown on Oct. 13)

Waning Moon

Moon phase: Third Quarter

Color: Ivory

Moon Sign: Aries

Moon enters Taurus 12:24 pm

Incense: Narcissus

October

15 Tuesday
The October Horse (Roman)
Waning Moon
Moon phase: Third Quarter
Color: Maroon

Moon Sign: Taurus
Incense: Basil

16 Wednesday
The Lion Sermon (British)
Waning Moon
Moon phase: Third Quarter
Color: Topaz

Moon Sign: Taurus
Moon enters Gemini 10:30 pm
Incense: Lavender

17 Thursday
Dessalines Day (Haitian)
Waning Moon
Moon phase: Third Quarter
Color: Turquoise

Moon Sign: Gemini
Incense: Apricot

18 Friday
Feast of St. Luke
Waning Moon
Moon phase: Third Quarter
Color: Coral

Moon Sign: Gemini
Incense: Cypress

19 Saturday
Mother Teresa Day (Albanian)
Waning Moon
Moon phase: Third Quarter
Color: Blue

Moon Sign: Gemini
Moon enters Cancer 6:43 pm
Incense: Ivy

20 Sunday
Sukkot ends
Waning Moon
Moon phase: Third Quarter
Color: Orange

Moon Sign: Cancer
Incense: Hyacinth

○ Monday
Apple Day (United Kingdom)
Waning Moon
Fourth Quarter 8:39 am
Color: White

Moon Sign: Cancer
Moon enters Leo 12:29 pm
Incense: Lily

October ♏ ♐

22 Tuesday

Jidai Festival (Japanese)
Waning Moon
Moon phase: Fourth Quarter
Color: Scarlet

Moon Sign: Leo
Incense: Bayberry

23 Wednesday

Revolution Day (Hungarian)
Waning Moon
Moon phase: Fourth Quarter
Color: Brown

Moon Sign: Leo
Moon enters Virgo 3:29 pm
Sun enters Scorpio 1:20 pm
Incense: Honeysuckle

24 Thursday

United Nations Day
Waning Moon
Moon phase: Fourth Quarter
Color: Purple

Moon Sign: Virgo
Incense: Mulberry

25 Friday

St. Crispin's Day
Waning Moon
Moon phase: Fourth Quarter
Color: Rose

Moon Sign: Virgo
Moon enters Libra 4:20 pm
Incense: Orchid

26 Saturday

Death of Alfred the Great
Waning Moon
Moon phase: Fourth Quarter
Color: Indigo

Moon Sign: Libra
Incense: Pine

☽ Sunday

Diwali
Waning Moon
New Moon 11:39 pm
Color: Amber

Moon Sign: Libra
Moon enters Scorpio 4:29 pm
Incense: Frankincense

28 Monday

Ohi Day (Greek)
Waxing Moon
Moon phase: First Quarter
Color: Lavender

Moon Sign: Scorpio
Incense: Clary sage

October

29 Tuesday
National Cat Day
Waxing Moon
Moon phase: First Quarter
Color: Red

Moon Sign: Scorpio
Moon enters Sagittarius 5:58 pm
Incense: Cedar

---

30 Wednesday
John Adams's birthday
Waxing Moon
Moon phase: First Quarter
Color: White

Moon Sign: Sagittarius
Incense: Marjoram

---

31 Thursday
Halloween • Samhain
Waxing Moon
Moon phase: First Quarter
Color: Crimson

Moon Sign: Sagittarius
Moon enters Capricorn 10:38 pm
Incense: Myrrh

October Birthstones

October's child is born for woe,
And life's vicissitudes must know;
But lay an Opal on her breast,
And hope will lull those foes to rest.

Modern: Opal or Tourmaline
Zodiac (Libra): Peridot

1 Friday

All Saints' Day • Día de los Muertos
Waxing Moon
Moon phase: First Quarter
Color: White

Moon Sign: Capricorn
Incense: Yarrow

---

2 Saturday

All Souls' Day
Waxing Moon
Moon phase: First Quarter
Color: Brown

Moon Sign: Capricorn
Incense: Sage

---

3 Sunday

Culture Day (Japanese)
Waxing Moon
Moon phase: First Quarter
Color: Yellow

Moon Sign: Capricorn
Moon enters Aquarius 6:19 am
Incense: Heliotrope
Daylight Saving Time ends at 2 am

☽ Monday

Mischief Night (British)
Waxing Moon
Second Quarter 5:23 am
Color: Gray

Moon Sign: Aquarius
Incense: Hyssop

---

5 Tuesday

Election Day (general)
Waxing Moon
Moon phase: Second Quarter
Color: Maroon

Moon Sign: Aquarius
Moon enters Pisces 6:08 pm
Incense: Cinnamon

---

6 Wednesday

St. Leonard's Ride (German)
Waxing Moon
Moon phase: Second Quarter
Color: Topaz

Moon Sign: Pisces
Incense: Lavender

---

7 Thursday

Feast of St. Willibrord
Waxing Moon
Moon phase: Second Quarter
Color: Turquoise

Moon Sign: Pisces
Incense: Balsam

November ♏

8 Friday

World Urbanism Day
Waxing Moon
Moon phase: Second Quarter
Color: Coral

Moon Sign: Pisces
Moon enters Aries 6:49 am
Incense: Vanilla

9 Saturday

Fateful Day (German)
Waxing Moon
Moon phase: Second Quarter
Color: Blue

Moon Sign: Aries
Incense: Sandalwood

10 Sunday

Martin Luther's Birthday
Waxing Moon
Moon phase: Second Quarter
Color: Gold

Moon Sign: Aries
Moon enters Taurus 6:18 pm
Incense: Eucalyptus

11 Monday

Veterans Day • Remembrance Day (Canada)
Waxing Moon
Moon phase: Second Quarter
Color: White

Moon Sign: Taurus
Incense: Neroli

☺ Tuesday

Feast Day of San Diego (Tesuque Puebloan)
Waxing Moon
Full Moon 8:34 am
Color: Scarlet

Moon Sign: Taurus
Incense: Ginger

13 Wednesday

Loy Krathong Lantern Festival (Thai)
Waning Moon
Moon phase: Third Quarter
Color: Yellow

Moon Sign: Taurus
Moon enters Gemini 3:46 am
Incense: Bay laurel

14 Thursday

Feast of St. Lawrence O'Toole
Waning Moon
Moon phase: Third Quarter
Color: Green

Moon Sign: Gemini
Incense: Mulberry

15 Friday

Seven-Five-Three Festival (Japanese)
Waning Moon
Moon phase: Third Quarter
Color: Pink

Moon Sign: Gemini
Moon enters Cancer 11:15 am
Incense: Mint

16 Saturday

St. Margaret of Scotland's Day
Waning Moon
Moon phase: Third Quarter
Color: Black

Moon Sign: Cancer
Incense: Patchouli

17 Sunday

Queen Elizabeth's Ascension Day
Waning Moon
Moon phase: Third Quarter
Color: Orange

Moon Sign: Cancer
Moon enters Leo 4:57 pm
Incense: Juniper

18 Monday

Independence Day (Moroccan)
Waning Moon
Moon phase: Third Quarter
Color: Ivory

Moon Sign: Leo
Incense: Narcissus

◐ Tuesday

Garifuna Settlement Day (Belizean)
Waning Moon
Fourth Quarter 4:11 pm
Color: Red

Moon Sign: Leo
Moon enters Virgo 8:54 pm
Incense: Basil

20 Wednesday

Revolution Day (Mexican)
Waning Moon
Moon phase: Fourth Quarter
Color: Brown

Moon Sign: Virgo
Incense: Honeysuckle

21 Thursday

Feast of the Presentation of Mary
Waning Moon
Moon phase: Fourth Quarter
Color: Purple

Moon Sign: Virgo
Moon enters Libra 11:20 pm
Incense: Jasmine

November

22 Friday
St. Cecilia's Day
Waning Moon
Moon phase: Fourth Quarter
Color: Rose

Moon Sign: Libra
Sun enters Sagittarius 9:59 am
Incense: Alder

23 Saturday
National Adoption Day
Waning Moon
Moon phase: Fourth Quarter
Color: Indigo

Moon Sign: Libra
Incense: Magnolia

24 Sunday
Native American Heritage Day
Waning Moon
Moon phase: Fourth Quarter
Color: Yellow

Moon Sign: Libra
Moon enters Scorpio 12:58 am
Incense: Almond

25 Monday
Feast of St. Catherine of Alexandria
Waning Moon
Moon phase: Fourth Quarter
Color: Silver

Moon Sign: Scorpio
Incense: Rosemary

☽ Tuesday
Constitution Day (Indian)
Waning Moon
New Moon 10:06 am
Color: Black

Moon Sign: Scorpio
Moon enters Sagittarius 3:11 am
Incense: Bayberry

27 Wednesday
Feast of St. Virgilius
Waxing Moon
Moon phase: First Quarter
Color: White

Moon Sign: Sagittarius
Incense: Marjoram

28 Thursday
Thanksgiving Day (US)
Waxing Moon
Moon phase: First Quarter
Color: Crimson

Moon Sign: Sagittarius
Moon enters Capricorn 7:33 am
Incense: Myrrh

November

29 Friday

William Tubman's birthday (Liberian)
Waxing Moon
Moon phase: First Quarter
Color: Purple

Moon Sign: Capricorn
Incense: Thyme

30 Saturday

St. Andrew's Day (Scottish)
Waxing Moon
Moon phase: First Quarter
Color: Blue

Moon Sign: Capricorn
Moon enters Aquarius 3:13 pm
Incense: Ivy

November Birthstones

Who first come to this world below,
With drear November's fog, and snow,
Should prize the Topaz's amber hue,
Emblem of friends, and lovers true.

Modern: Topaz or Citrine
Zodiac (Scorpio): Beryl

December

1 Sunday
Feast for Death of Aleister Crowley (Thelemic)
Waxing Moon
Moon phase: First Quarter
Color: Amber

Moon Sign: Aquarius
Incense: Marigold

---

2 Monday
Republic Day (Laotian)
Waxing Moon
Moon phase: First Quarter
Color: Lavender

Moon Sign: Aquarius
Incense: Clary sage

---

3 Tuesday
St. Francis Xavier's Day
Waxing Moon
Moon phase: First Quarter
Color: Gray

Moon Sign: Aquarius
Moon enters Pisces 2:11 am
Incense: Ginger

☽ Wednesday
Feasts of Shango and St. Barbara
Waxing Moon
Second Quarter 1:58 am
Color: Yellow

Moon Sign: Pisces
Incense: Lilac

---

5 Thursday
Krampus Night (European)
Waxing Moon
Moon phase: Second Quarter
Color: White

Moon Sign: Pisces
Moon enters Aries 2:44 pm
Incense: Clove

---

6 Friday
St. Nicholas's Day
Waxing Moon
Moon phase: Second Quarter
Color: Pink

Moon Sign: Aries
Incense: Rose

---

7 Saturday
Burning the Devil (Guatemalan)
Waxing Moon
Moon phase: Second Quarter
Color: Brown

Moon Sign: Aries
Incense: Rue

December

8 Sunday
Bodhi Day (Japanese)
Waxing Moon
Moon phase: Second Quarter
Color: Gold

Moon Sign: Aries
Moon enters Taurus 2:29 am
Incense: Juniper

9 Monday
Anna's Day (Sweden)
Waxing Moon
Moon phase: Second Quarter
Color: Silver

Moon Sign: Taurus
Incense: Lily

10 Tuesday
Alfred Nobel Day
Waxing Moon
Moon phase: Second Quarter
Color: Red

Moon Sign: Taurus
Moon enters Gemini 11:47 am
Incense: Ylang-ylang

11 Wednesday
Pilgrimage at Tortugas
Waxing Moon
Moon phase: Second Quarter
Color: Topaz

Moon Sign: Gemini
Incense: Bay laurel

☺ Thursday
Fiesta of Our Lady of Guadalupe (Mexican)
Waxing Moon
New Moon 12:12 am
Color: Purple

Moon Sign: Gemini
Moon enters Cancer 6:23 pm
Incense: Nutmeg

13 Friday
St. Lucy's Day (Scandinavian and Italian)
Waning Moon
Moon phase: Third Quarter
Color: Coral

Moon Sign: Cancer
Incense: Cypress

14 Saturday
Forty-Seven Ronin Memorial (Japanese)
Waning Moon
Moon phase: Third Quarter
Color: Blue

Moon Sign: Cancer
Moon enters Leo 10:56 pm
Incense: Magnolia

December

15 Sunday
Consualia (Roman)
Waning Moon
Moon phase: Third Quarter
Color: Yellow

Moon Sign: Leo
Incense: Hyacinth

---

16 Monday
Las Posadas begin (end Dec. 24)
Waning Moon
Moon phase: Third Quarter
Color: White

Moon Sign: Leo
Incense: Rosemary

---

17 Tuesday
Saturnalia (Roman)
Waning Moon
Moon phase: Third Quarter
Color: Scarlet

Moon Sign: Leo
Moon enters Virgo 2:16 am
Incense: Cedar

☽ Wednesday
Feast of the Virgin of Solitude
Waning Moon
Fourth Quarter 11:57 pm
Color: Brown

Moon Sign: Virgo
Incense: Honeysuckle

---

19 Thursday
Opalia (Roman)
Waning Moon
Moon phase: Fourth Quarter
Color: Crimson

Moon Sign: Virgo
Moon enters Libra 5:04 am
Incense: Apricot

---

20 Friday
Feast of St. Dominic of Silos
Waning Moon
Moon phase: Fourth Quarter
Color: Rose

Moon Sign: Libra
Incense: Orchid

---

21 Saturday
Yule • Winter Solstice
Waning Moon
Moon phase: Fourth Quarter
Color: Gray

Moon Sign: Libra
Moon enters Scorpio 7:57 am
Sun enters Capricorn 11:19 pm
Incense: Patchouli

22 Sunday

Feasts of SS. Chaeremon and Ischyrion
Waning Moon
Moon phase: Fourth Quarter
Color: Orange

Moon Sign: Scorpio
Incense: Eucalyptus

---

23 Monday

Hanukkah begins (at sundown on Dec. 22)
Waning Moon
Moon phase: Fourth Quarter
Color: Gray

Moon Sign: Scorpio
Moon enters Sagittarius 11:34 am
Incense: Narcissus

---

24 Tuesday

Christmas Eve
Waning Moon
Moon phase: Fourth Quarter
Color: Maroon

Moon Sign: Sagittarius
Incense: Cinnamon

---

25 Wednesday

Christmas Day
Waning Moon
Moon phase: Fourth Quarter
Color: Topaz

Moon Sign: Sagittarius
Moon enters Capricorn 4:45 pm
Incense: Marjoram

☽ Thursday

Kwanzaa begins (ends Jan. 1) • Boxing Day
Waning Moon
New Moon 12:13 am
Color: Green

Moon Sign: Capricorn
Incense: Jasmine

---

27 Friday

St. Stephen's Day
Waxing Moon
Moon phase: First Quarter
Color: Purple

Moon Sign: Capricorn
Incense: Yarrow

---

28 Saturday

Feast of the Holy Innocents
Waxing Moon
Moon phase: First Quarter
Color: Indigo

Moon Sign: Capricorn
Moon enters Aquarius 12:21 am
Incense: Pine

December ♑

29 Sunday
Feast of St. Thomas à Becket
Waxing Moon
Moon phase: First Quarter
Color: Gold

Moon Sign: Aquarius
Incense: Almond

---

30 Monday
Hanukkah ends
Waxing Moon
Moon phase: First Quarter
Color: Ivory

Moon Sign: Aquarius
Moon enters Pisces 10:41 am
Incense: Hyssop

---

31 Tuesday
New Year's Eve
Waxing Moon
Moon phase: First Quarter
Color: White

Moon Sign: Pisces
Incense: Basil

December Birthstones

If cold December gives you birth,
The month of snow, and ice, and mirth,
Place in your hand a Turquoise blue;
Success will bless whate'er you do.

Modern: Turquoise or Blue Topaz
Zodiac (Sagittarius): Topaz

Fire Magic

Finding Light

by Monica Crosson

It was November, and autumn had only just touched the Pacific Northwest, burnishing the landscape with shades of pumpkin, ochre, and brick red. The air was tinged with apple and wood smoke as we prepared ourselves for the pleasures of darker days: candlelight and cozy fires, holiday baking, and s'mores around a crackling fire. I wasn't worried about the forecast of record-breaking cold and precipitation for our area. I wasn't concerned about the darkness—spring always comes, and we are filled, once again, with light.

My husband, Steve, had been complaining for weeks about shortness of breath and heart palpitations. One night when I woke up and he no longer could sleep lying down, I insisted he go to the doctor. The next day, to my surprise, he called me not with information concerning what he had thought was a bout with asthma, but that he had been transported by ambulance from the doctor's office to the hospital. He was in complete heart failure and most likely wouldn't have survived another twenty-four hours. I had been on him for years about taking better care of himself, so my first reaction was anger.

"This is your fault!" I cried into the phone. "I told you to take better care of yourself, and you didn't. You're not twenty years old, Steve!"

"I know," he spoke softly. "I promise I'll do better."

"What are we going to do?" I sobbed.

"Isn't it you who always says spring will come and we will be filled with light?"

"It feels very far away right now."

The recovery took weeks and the list of medications was long. I took on more work, keeping in mind it would only be for a couple of months. And as I witnessed the weather predictions come true in the form of heavy snow that made commuting treacherous, I reminded myself that spring would come and there would be light. The snow piled, heavy and deep—one, two, three feet. I white-knuckled it to work and back and made sure Steve kept his appointments. I helped our daughter, Chloe, with her schoolwork, and every evening, I made a thirty-mile round trip to pick up my son Elijah at the bus stop. He used our county's public transit system to commute to the college he attends.

But I suppose I had been too busy to notice that my oldest son had lost the light behind his beautiful eyes. Demons from his past had returned and gnawed hungrily at his mind. I have never mentioned his bipolar illness in my writing simply because he doesn't want to be known as "Monica's bipolar son" but rather as Joshua, writer, artist, musician, and Goddess-loving, really cool guy.

On one horrible evening he could no longer take it, and he slipped into January's darkness. Unable to locate him and fearing he may harm himself, we called the sheriff, who found him barefoot and shivering along the riverbank several miles from our home. Joshua hadn't told anyone that he had stopped taking his medication months before. He thought he was okay, failing to realize it was the medication that made him okay. He was checked into a mental health facility near Seattle. When I picked him up several weeks later, we reminded each other that there would be a spring and the light would come back into our lives.

February brought influenza into our home. It was Elijah who worried me the most. The flu triggered his asthma and he struggled to breathe, but he was a trooper. It was finals week, so he sucked on his inhaler and continued his studies. I didn't think about Steve, back at work, who quietly suffered. His cough lingered, and he complained of severe headaches. Joshua had just been released, and Chloe was struggling with math. I had to go to work, and there was that horrible white stuff that fell insistently. I was starting to wonder if the light would ever return.

As February came to an end, I received a phone call while on my mail route, less than twenty minutes from our house. Steve was crying. "I can't move my right arm. I think something's wrong."

"You're having a stroke, Steve!" I tried to sound calm, though I was screaming on the inside. "Call an ambulance! I'm coming home."

I arrived just before the ambulance and found him sitting in his favorite chair. "I'm scared," he said.

I held his face. "Don't be afraid. Everything will be fine."

He tried to smile. "Spring will come. You'll have your light."

It was his persistent coughing, a flu by-product, that had triggered his stroke, a doctor told us. If it weren't for the blood thinners he'd been taking for the heart failure, he'd probably be dead. A couple of weeks after his stroke, with Steve securely under the care of an amazing staff of doctors and therapists in a facility seventy miles north of our home, I finally broke down.

But it wasn't Steve's stroke, or his heart failure, or the flu, or Joshua's bipolar illness, or working six days a week to make ends meet, that brought me to my knees. It was the snow that was the last straw. Last year I was taking pictures of daffodils and tying raspberries in March, for crying out loud. That night in 2017 we experienced an unprecedented March snowstorm. I screamed to the Goddess in the direction I knew the Moon would be rising: "I can't take anymore! Please give me strength. I don't want to lose my light."

Just then, the snow lightened and clouds shifted, revealing pinpricks of light that speckled the small opening—they were stars. And for that moment it was enough. I knew I was strong enough and that the light would come.

The Element of Fire

I like to think of the element of fire as that inner light that fuels our soul. It is the flames of courage and determination that get

us through life's pitfalls. It is that spark of creativity that inspires artists to produce great works or the mom of three to sew the perfect costume for a school play.

To work with fire's transformative power, you only have to stand in the light. Raise your hands to the Sun and absorb its healing rays, gaze into the flickering flames of a candle in a darkened room, or dance around a crackling fire on a moonlit night. Fire is masculine and its magick is energetic, transformative, and purifying. Its direction is south and its time is noon. Fire's colors are red and orange.

People born under the Sun signs of Aries, Leo, and Sagittarius are all ruled by the element of fire. These people are your visionaries and adventure seekers. They are self-motivated and natural leaders. But, like with any flame, too much fuel can cause these radiate signs to burn out of control—passion can turn to compulsion, and adventurous spontaneity can quickly become recklessness.

Harnessing Fire

Fire, unlike the other elements, does not exist in a natural state, but is born through a chemical reaction requiring air, heat, and

179

fuel. For fire to maintain its power, it must consume, and its hunger can be ravenous. I sometimes wonder what the fear and awe of witnessing fire's destructive powers in action was like for early humans and how quickly were they able to harness its power. It is thought that when humankind finally learned to control fire, true evolution began. Archeologists found what is thought to be the oldest evidence of man harnessing fire at a one-million-year-old campfire site within a cave in Northern Cape in South Africa. Charred fragments were identified to contain twigs, bone, and plant ash, and fractured stone and sediment at the site was an indication that the site was used repeatedly.

The importance of harnessing fire is apparent throughout mythology and folklore: For the Greeks, it was Prometheus who stole fire from Mount Olympus for mankind to survive. For the Cherokee, Grandmother Spider snuck into the land of light using her web to secure fire and keep it in a jar. In Maori mythology, it is the hero Maui who tricked the fire goddess Mahuika to obtain the secrets of fire.

In harnessing the magickal aspects of fire, we can utilize its transformative powers in spells to garner strength and confidence for empowerment and freedom. We can use it for purification and to ritually destroy bad habits.

Gods and Goddesses of Fire

Brigid: This Celtic triple goddess ruled over the hearth, poetry, and childbirth. Daughter of the Dagda, she was born at sunrise with rays of fire that beamed from her head. Her holy temple was at Kildare, where a perpetual flame was tended by nineteen virgins. This beloved goddess was turned saint with the coming of Christianity. Use Brigid in magick for hearth and home, clarity, creativity, transformation, and fertility.

Vesta: Vesta was the Roman goddess of the hearth, home, fire, and state. Her brother, Jupiter, granted her request of eternal virginity upon his ascension to Mount Olympus. Her temple was at the *Forum Romanum*, where priestesses known as the Vestal Virgins kept her eternal flame lit. Call upon Vesta for legal matters, strength, hearth and home, healing, and change.

Frigg: This Norse goddess of the hearth, home, childbirth, marriage, and destiny spun the clouds of fate upon a spinning wheel representing female wisdom. She was known as Bertha or Holda. Her sacred animal was the goose and later became the inspiration for Mother Goose. Use Frigg in magick for parenting, wisdom, fate, hearth and home, and childbirth.

Lugh: A Celtic solar god who was inventor of the arts, patron of commerce, and hero to the Tuatha Dé Danann for securing the secrets of ploughing and planting, Lugh is associated with Lughnasadh (meaning the "assembly of Lugh" in Irish) for inaugurating the day as an assembly in memory of his foster mother, Tailtiu, who died from exhaustion while clearing forest land for planting. Call upon Lugh for legal matters, courage, strength, art, and athleticism.

Ra: Ra was an Egyptian Sun god who brought the Sun as he traveled across the sky in his chariot. His importance to the people of Egypt is no surprise. Without the power and energy of the Sun, their crops would not grow. He was depicted sometimes as a falcon but always with a solar disk above his head. Eventually, pharaohs came to be seen as embodiments of this solar deity, gaining absolute power. Invoke Ra for strength, passion, success, and energy.

Ask the Flames

Have you ever gazed into the dying embers of a fire and seen shapes or symbols? What images come to mind when you stare at the flickering of the flame? What ghostly shapes appear in the smoke that rises with sweetly scented herbs? Pyromancy is a form of divination using fire. It is thought to go back to a time when sacrificial fires were used to interpret omens and prophecies that lay hidden within the coals or rose with the smoke.

Good or bad fortune for the coming year could be established by many factors, including the clarity of the smoke or the scent or sound it made when certain herbs or minerals were cast into the flames. Sometimes, it was the consumption of an object itself that was used to divine the future. When an object was tossed into the fire and was consumed quickly and easily, it was a good omen. On the contrary, if a flame suddenly died, this foretold of ominous consequences.

Visual projections were considered as well. What images lie hidden in the flames? A talented seer not only could see the

images that told of change or possible disappointment, but, as if the flames spoke to them, they were able to read beyond the symbols through the voice of intuition.

If you would like to give pyromancy a try, here are a few things to consider:

Safety First: If you're doing this outside, make sure to create a proper fire pit. If you are making one for the first time, remember to pick a spot away from trees and shrubbery. Dig a hole that is approximately two feet deep and four feet wide, and keep the leftover soil nearby. In case the fire gets out of control, it can be used to smother the flames. Line your pit with stone or brick. When you are done with the fire, use a bucket of water to drown out the coals.

Choose Wood Type: It really doesn't matter what kind of wood your fire is made of, but consider adding one or more of the nine sacred woods: birch, oak, hazel, rowan, hawthorn, willow, fir, apple, or vine.

Watch for Symbols: Add herbs, twigs, nuts, or leaves (laurel leaves are traditional), ask your question, and then divine using either your own interpretation of the images you see in the flames. You can also look at the color of the flames: bright red flames can indicate courage, deep red corresponds to your desire, orange flames may indicate the incentive to keep trying, and yellow flames may correspond to a lightening of spirit.

The smoke may also hold meaning: smoke that rises straight up is a positive sign. Smoke that hangs low around your fire is unfavorable. If the smoke is touching the earth, a new direction should be taken.

Interpret the Coals: Another way to practice pyromancy is to ask a question into the fire. Wait for the fire to die down and look for images in the coals that might answer your question.

Candle Revelation Spell

For this spell, we will use the flickering flame of a candle (which is lampadomancy, a form of pyromancy) to reveal an answer to a question:

You will need:
1 white tealight
Juice of 1 lemon squeezed into a small cup
Bamboo skewer or sharp stick to write with
2 or 3 slips of paper
Bowl

Set up your candle on a table that is free of clutter. You will be working with the flame and don't want to accidentally catch yesterday's mail on fire. You will invoke the salamanders, fire elementals that inhabit flame, to guide you with this spell, so as you light your candle, ask the elemental, in your own way, to join you.

Now with a question clear in your head, take the skewer or sharp stick and use it like a pen by dunking it into the lemon juice and writing possible solutions to your questions on each slip of paper. Simple answers are best (the lemon juice will be invisible). Now place the slips of paper in the bowl. Close your eyes and focus on the question. As you draw a paper, say,

Salamander of the dancing flame,
What is it that I have to gain?
Reveal the answer for me to see.
In the name of spark, ember, and flame, so mote it be.

Take the paper you have chosen and, holding it with both hands, begin to pass it closely over the candle flame (not too close—you don't want to catch it on fire). The heat will react with the lemon juice, clearly revealing your answer.

~

By utilizing the element of fire, I have learned that when life is at its darkest, we find the light—those little pinpricks of inner strength we never knew existed. Fire teaches us to forge on and reminds us to be adventurous and creative with our lives.

Another lesson, which was hard for me to learn because I pride myself for my strength, is that it's okay to fall apart at times. This is how we grow and develop that inner light and become better able to pass it on to those whose own light may have dimmed.

The Witch's Sigil: Crafting Magick Symbols for Spellcraft, Ritual, and More

by Laura Tempest Zakroff

If you are new to the path of the Witch, you've probably noticed a wide array of mysterious symbols displayed on books and tools. Some of those markings have origins dating back centuries, their meanings complex and varying depending on the culture, tradition, or lodge using them. But it doesn't require arcane knowledge of all signs mystical to create new symbols that are just for you. That's where sigil witchery comes in!

What is a sigil? A sigil is a symbol, sign, or design that is believed to have magickal properties. It can be carved, drawn, painted, inked on any surface—paper, fabric, metal, wood, wax, or even skin. Sigils are essentially a kind of metaphysical shorthand; they embody a larger, complex idea and transform it into a simplified image. You can make a sigil to cast a spell, make a mark of ownership, create a tool for meditation, invoke a deity or spirit, set up a ward of protection, and much more. It can be a symbol used by a group of people or made exclusively for personal use only.

What's wonderful about sigils is that they are relatively simple to make in terms of skill and materials. You don't need more than a pen or pencil and some scrap paper to get started, nor do you need to be an artist. If you can write your signature, you can draw a sigil.

Create a Sigil

There are multiple methods for creating a sigil. The way I'm going to describe for you here is one that I have

developed over the last two decades—combining my path as a Modern Traditional Witch with my art making. It incorporates imagery your brain responds to instinctively and emotionally with sympathetic magick. In teaching it to others, the feedback that I have received is that people find it very intuitive and easy to master.

There are four simple steps to follow:

1. Define your problem, issue, or goal.
2. Brainstorm ideas.
3. Design the sigil.
4. Apply and acknowledge.

For the first step, you are asking yourself what your goal is. What do you wish to achieve? Or what problem, situation, or issue are you looking to resolve? Your sigil needs to have a purpose. Does someone need healing of some kind? Would your home benefit from some extra protection? Are you looking to create an identifying mark for your business? Do you need to find a new job or need some additional help focusing on your studies or a project? Your purpose or issue can be physical or metaphysical.

Now, to get things started, take a blank page of paper. It can be a fresh page in your grimoire, notebook, sketchbook, or Book of Shadows. If you are working on scrap paper or loose-leaf sheets, I recommend having a folder or binder you can keep your work in so that you don't lose it. It's handy to keep records of your work for later down the line.

For a writing implement, my favorite tool is a basic ballpoint pen, the kind you can pick up at a hotel or bank—nothing fancy. It can be tempting to use a pencil, but it's best not to be tempted to erase. You're not looking to make perfect art but rather explore a process and see how it builds—in both words and lines. You can of course get fancier if you would like, but that's strictly your personal choice. The most important thing is make sure you can write with the pen!

Once you have your paper and pen collected, it's time to set things in motion. Write down the date (you think you will remember when you did this, but you probably won't) and the goal or problem.

In step 2, it's time to think about what elements are necessary to solve your problem. Take the time to consider the specific things you are looking to achieve. Magick tends to follow the path of least resistance, so it's incredibly helpful to set boundaries and identify the terms you require. For example, "I need a new job" is too vague. You're probably not looking for just any job. You most likely are looking for something more specific that you already have in mind. You want to make at least X amount of money. You may require having a certain number of hours, in a particular field of expertise. You could be looking for a better job, where you are respected and recognized for the work that you are doing.

This is how you brainstorm what you've identified in the first step. Allow yourself time to go through this process if the idea is particularly complex; it will pay off later on. You don't have to write out paragraphs (though you could if that helps). You can just make a list of words or items and edit it as necessary when you feel you're done. It's incredibly helpful to physically make this list—you can really boil it down to the exact things you need—and it doesn't have to be a long list at all. Typically, I like a minimum of three words or points, and I try to keep the maximum to ten so it doesn't get too bogged down.

Once you have finished brainstorming, it's time to get down to designing! Look at your list of words or highlight key points if you wrote out some paragraphs. With each word, consider what shape, mark, or symbol comes to mind when you think about that word.

You might be thinking right now, *Wait, I thought I didn't need to have arcane knowledge of mysterious symbols under my belt to do this!* I mean it, you don't. Before even involving esoteric symbols or alphabets, consider the simple language of lines around you. For example, a triangle can represent a yield sign, a mountain, a thorn, or a pyramid. The yield sign signifies caution, slowing down, or paying attention. A mountain can symbolize a pinnacle, a focal point, or an obstacle to be climbed. Thorns are designed for protection. The pyramid can speak to esoteric knowledge, inner focus, balance, and mystery. There are many more examples of what a triangle can represent to you. Consider what a circle, dot, square, arrow, star, heart, spiral, and so on mean to you. I will also bet you have associations with colors as well— does red mean anger, or does it mean love to you? The same is true for numbers. I often like to use the symbolism behind the various numbers found in the major and minor arcana of the tarot.

Don't overthink it, and don't be tempted to start drawing out illustrations. Just jot down what comes to mind with each word in your brainstorming list. Once you've assigned a shape or mark to each word, it's time to put it together.

To start designing the sigil, I choose the word or symbol in the brainstorming list that stands out to me most. Then I add each symbol or make a combination of them until I create a design that I am happy with. If it doesn't feel right or I mess up, I start again. This is where drawing with a pen comes in really handy, because you're able to look back at your designs and see what works best in each of them. You might like one element from your first drawing and the rest of your third drawing and find it looks finished when you put them together. Allow yourself to trust your eye and your gut. Also, it doesn't have to be a perfect drawing. Your star doesn't have to be absolutely precise. Your square can be slightly off, your circle not exact. That doesn't really matter in the larger scheme of things.

Once you have arrived at a design you are happy with, the last step is applying and acknowledging your sigil. You don't have to do anything special to "activate" your sigil—that has already happened in the finalizing of the design. Consider it like making a candle: it's ready to go once the wax is set. It's a thing ready to work. Applying your sigil is like lighting that candle to put it into use.

How you apply your sigil depends on what you need to accomplish. Is the sigil to improve your work environment? You could put it on a sticky note next to your computer or by your office door. Need invisible protection for your home? Inscribe the sigil in blessed water

on doors and windows. Have a project that you want to grow? Draw the sigil on a flower pot and plant something in it. Are you refocusing your spiritual path or dedicating yourself? Then you could make a piece of jewelry to wear with the sigil on it or perhaps choose a more permanent method: tattooing. As you can see, the possibilities are varied and endless for applying your sigil.

Acknowledging a sigil is another layer that can be incorporated into your practice, depending on the need and scope of the sigil. If it's something that you need to revisit, then you can add a ritual layer to it. If you do the flower pot suggestion, then tending to the plant daily is a regular acknowledgment process. If you get a tattoo, after it is healed, you can apply an essential oil every morning to it that aligns with your purpose. If you create a sigil for meditation, you can refer to it again and again by tracing it out with your hand. If you are using a sigil to protect your home, you could "refresh" the wards on a monthly, quarterly, or yearly basis. So acknowledging the sigil can be a very simple process that refreshes and strengthens your work—if you feel that's needed or necessary.

Sample Sigil

To help you get familiar with this process, we will create a sample sigil together.

The Scenario

Let's say you feel you are rushing through things in your life and think you're missing out on things and people you find important. Maybe you're being distracted by outside influences you don't need in your life. You want to make a sigil that helps you slow down, reduce stress, and focus on the details, while remaining goal-oriented. Being able to stop and smell the roses occasionally is better than putting it off for later—so you want to find a balance in the moment.

A Solution

In analyzing the scenario, we see the following list:

1. Slow down your pace
2. Eliminate unhelpful distractions
3. Reduce stress
4. Remain focused on your path
5. Goal-oriented
6. Balance

In assigning each point a symbol, I find the following associations:

1. Triangle (yield sign)
2. Circle (to contain/protect)
3. Wavy lines (calming energy)
4. Arrow (directional energy)
5. Star (the goal in the distance)
6. The number four (for balance)

I start the sigil design by drawing the triangle. Below the triangle I decide on a starting point (place of origin), and then draw a larger circle around it for protection. Out from the point and heading directly up through the center

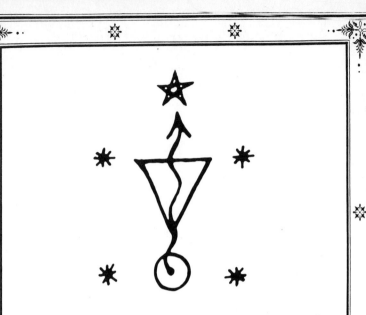

of the triangle, I draw an arrow with a gently wavy line. The wavy arrow gives direction, but slows down the pace a bit. Just above the head of the arrow, I place a five-pointed star to represent the goal. Then at four points around the design, I place asterisks. These simultaneously balance out the sigil and create an implied rectangle that also helps keep the energy focused toward the center.

After you have drawn the sigil, there are numerous ways you could apply it. It could be placed on your nightstand in a little frame by your bed or maybe embroidered on your pillow. You could put it on a sticky note on your bathroom mirror so that you see it in your periphery in the morning and evenings. It could be used as a meditation device you trace as you start your day.

I hope that you have found my method of sigil witchery helpful and put it to good use. Remember, as with all things, the more you do it, the better you will get with practice. Happy sigil crafting!

Enlighten Up:
A New Approach to Cursing

by Raven Digitalis

It's a longtime debate in magical circles: Should we use our abilities to cause suffering, even when it appears clearly justified? Even for the greater good?

Well, let's first take a look at that very term—"justified." The term implies justice and, unless we are referring to universal karma, is an objective term that requires assessment or judgment from a human being. So, who are we to judge? Is our knowledge, willingness, and ability to magically influence others reason enough to be karmic judges in any given situation? These ethical issues can be complicated and convoluted and tend to differ greatly from one situation to the next.

It's easy to be reactive in life. In 99 percent of instances, the act of cursing is entirely reactive and is ultimately unnecessary. Many people will curse—or will seek someone to curse on their behalf—if they feel even slightly wronged by another person. These divisive actions are ultimately cruel, *mundane*, petty, and usually unsuccessful.

Throughout this article I will examine a number of elements, aspects, and theories surrounding cursing, hexing, crossing, and other forms of magickal retaliation. This article will conclude with an instructional guide to "enlightening up" a violator as a more ethical—and more effective—alternative to traditional cursing.

Additionally, I propose that our magickal focus be primarily spent not on cursing the violator, but on assisting the violated, which I encourage the reader to contemplate throughout.

Injustice Be Damned

There are times when we will hear news about horrific abuses toward innocent people and animals. The sad reality is that

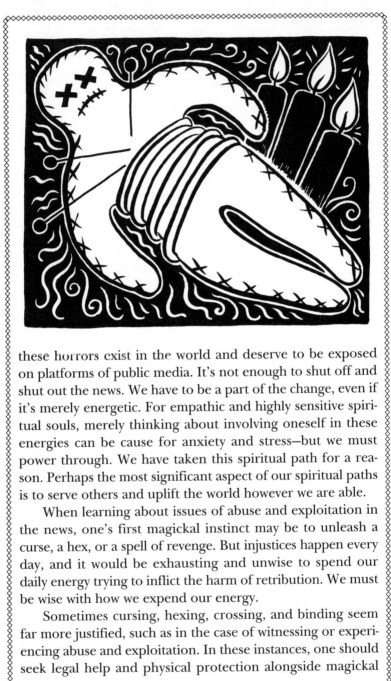

these horrors exist in the world and deserve to be exposed on platforms of public media. It's not enough to shut off and shut out the news. We have to be a part of the change, even if it's merely energetic. For empathic and highly sensitive spiritual souls, merely thinking about involving oneself in these energies can be cause for anxiety and stress—but we must power through. We have taken this spiritual path for a reason. Perhaps the most significant aspect of our spiritual paths is to serve others and uplift the world however we are able.

When learning about issues of abuse and exploitation in the news, one's first magickal instinct may be to unleash a curse, a hex, or a spell of revenge. But injustices happen every day, and it would be exhausting and unwise to spend our daily energy trying to inflict the harm of retribution. We must be wise with how we expend our energy.

Sometimes cursing, hexing, crossing, and binding seem far more justified, such as in the case of witnessing or experiencing abuse and exploitation. In these instances, one should seek legal help and physical protection alongside magickal work. In cases such as these, laying curses and "black magick" are understandable responses. Nevertheless, I feel that magick aimed at helping a violator become more enlightened "by any means necessary" is far more effective and karmically clean.

The Issue of Binding

There is a fantastic scene in the groundbreaking 1996 film *The Craft* in which protagonist Sarah binds coven-sister-gone-cuckoo Nancy "from doing harm; harm against other people and harm against yourself." You can bet dollars to donuts that thousands of teenagers performed binding spells as a result of this scene back in the nineties—myself included!

Most Witches, Pagans, and magicians agree that binding rituals can be very positive magickal acts that influence restriction on the violator and protection for the violated. Typical binding magick is different from cursing or hexing because it affirms safety for the violator and the violated, although it still directly influences a person's freewill. Like anything, binding can take numerous forms and involves a spectrum of ethics just as nuanced as cursing itself.

Cursing, hexing, and binding are all complicated subjects too vast to thoroughly explore in these pages. For readers curious about diving deeply into the ethics of these topics, I recommend reading "The Hex Appeal of Activism" on Patheos, wherein journalist Mat Auryn interviews twenty-eight public Witches and magicians, exploring the intricacies of hexing, cursing, and binding in modern practice. I wholeheartedly recommend this article for every reader, as its wisdom is indispensable for magickal practitioners of all varieties.

Contemplating Karma

Wicca is one of the most influential Western magickal paths in modern times. Since its creation in the late 1940s, the law of threefold return has been interpreted under various meanings, the most common of which assumes that a person will "get back" what they "send out," times three. However, many modern practitioners see this belief as more of a superstition than a natural law. This is because nature is balanced;

everything is an equal give-and-take. Anything beyond a "law of equal return" simply does not make sense because reality itself is a balancing act of equilibrium, not amplification.

Sanatana Dharma (Hinduism) and other Eastern mystical paths have long understood the reality of the karmic cycle. Often misunderstood in the West, the idea of karma is not an "eye for an eye," but one of universal balance and equilibrium that spans lifetimes of experience. This is not to say that every horrific occurrence in the world is "karma in action." Why? Because new karmic imprints are formed regularly.

In numerous Eastern mystical traditions, *samskaras* are understood as "karmic formations," or vibrational imprints that are created through certain actions or inactions in a person's life. Taking out the trash, for example, does not affect karma and does not create a samskara. However, intentionally throwing recyclables in the trash because it feels amusing would be something that creates a samskara or reinforces a preexisting karmic pattern. On the flipside, organizing an earth-based sustainability rally to spread education about reducing waste may also create a samskara. In other words, it's not always a bad thing. If we choose to make positive, progressive, and compassionate lifestyle choices toward ourselves and others (including our thoughts!), those energies become peacefully affixed to our spheres, encouraging more positivity day by day.

Karma is not good or bad. Like gravity or oxygen, it's a natural force that upholds existence, although its effects may not be immediately observed and can't be accurately tested in a laboratory. I should also mention here that recognizing, understanding, and resolving deep-seated karmic patterns takes lifetimes. When we humbly dedicate ourselves to a path of spiritual growth, whether Witchcraft, yoga, or something else, we become more aligned with spiritual currents that encourage the learning and settling of old karmic patterns. Seemingly "negative" karmas can be resolved through self-awareness, humility, and *seva*, selfless service to others.

Our influence on the realities of other beings crafts our own experiences. This is why karmic work and magickal work truly are inseparable and why many a wise magickal practitioner believe that cursing should not be practiced or promoted.

The Place of Mindfulness

I'm a big fan of Buddhist perspectives on mindfulness. Now a common phrase, "mindfulness" implies a certain conscientiousness and self-awareness when it comes to responding to life's ups and downs. Moreover, mindfulness can be likened more to an experience of observing life rather than reacting instinctively.

Self-awareness is greatly borne of mindfulness, and both terms imply an ability to emotionally step back before instinctively reacting to the human drama around us. Wisdom takes numerous forms and is valued in virtually all cultures and traditions. At the end of the day, I believe that wisdom and self-awareness hold little difference.

If we can more objectively look at our minds and the way we think and respond to our experiences, we can more wisely choose where and how to expend our energies and efforts. This most certainly applies to our intentional magickal practices. One of the first magickal lessons I was taught is to wait twenty-four hours after getting a magickal idea (a full Sun cycle) before actually casting the spell or performing the working. This is especially relevant to magick that has the potential to strongly affect another person's reality or one's own.

Enlighten Up!

Everyone deserves self-awareness. Many of the world's problems come from traumatic imprints latent in the spirits and psyches of individuals who, having been violated themselves, become violators. Psychological and sociological sciences of interpersonal violence, control, and cruelty are incredibly nuanced subjects. When it comes to magick of the "enlighten up" variety, the reasons, whys, and wherefores of the violator take a backseat to the desperate need for increased self-awareness.

The best part of "enlighten up" magick is the fact that it will not harm a person if they are in fact innocent in a situation.

If performed with kindness rather than malice or spite, this sort of magick will assist the other on their path of knowledge. If the person or people are guilty of causing intentional harm, however, a blast of enlightened energy may appear to them as a curse because of the intensity of the sentiment to "enlighten up—by any means necessary." It is not always easy to learn deep-seated life lessons and to get on the right track.

This form of magick is concerned with helping a person become more enlightened and self-aware so that they can stop causing harm. After all, who doesn't want more awareness? Who doesn't need more loving kindness in their life? We all need it, and we all deserve it.

I encourage attempting the following ethical alternative to cursing—one that is often far more powerful—or a variation thereof. This should only be performed alongside magickal and real-world action toward safety, protection, and criminal justice, if the case is severe. (If laws have been broken or if you or someone else is in danger, contact 911 and legal authorities immediately.)

Throughout this magickal working, make a concentrated effort not to cast any malice toward this person or people; send only peace and compassion to the best of your ability. This is often much more easily said than done. If this simply feels impossible, do not direct magick toward this person.

Keep in mind that you will, to some extent, be forcing the energy of self-awareness onto another person or people. In many ways, this can be likened to a "binding of light." If this does not sit right with you or if it feels unethical, please do not perform this sort of magick. Everything in life is situational, and every circumstance is different, so the practitioner must be entirely confident that this magick is the proper and most ethical course of action.

Binded by the Light: Performing the Steps

Get comfortable in sacred space. Perform cleansing activities such as smudging with sage and asperging with saltwater. Light candles and incense. Perform the Lesser Banishing Ritual of the Pentagram or cast a circle if it is your practice.

Call upon gods, guides, and guardians with whom you are
familiar and who you feel represent the concept of enlightenment. This type of ritual is best performed at dawn or some-
time before the Sun reaches its daily pinnacle, and it is most
potent on a Sunday. (These are merely suggestions rather
than requirements, and the practitioner should personally
tailor all magickal workings to some extent.)

Facing the east (sitting or standing) with your eyes closed,
envision the violator in your mind's eye. See their face and recall
the incidents that have led you to magically influencing their
reality in this manner. If anger, sadness, or difficult emotions
arise, allow them to exist without becoming attached to the
sensations. Try your best to become the observer of these
emotions rather than the experiencer.

Now it's time to get to work. If you are weaving a spell
alongside this visualization (such as using a photo, candle, letter, or anything else), set out your Crafting components and
perform your additional work. (Note: certain herbs, incenses,
and stones can also be utilized for this sort of metaphysical

work, including jasmine, sandalwood, frankincense, benzoin, selenite, and lapis lazuli.)

When you feel as though you have accurately tapped into the emotional energy of the situation—and the energetic signature of the violator in question—visualize yourself looking straight into their eyes.

Doing your best to cultivate acceptance in your heart (which is not the same as forgiveness), speak directly to the image of the violator. Rather than cursing them with your words, tell them the reason why you are taking a higher road in the situation. Explain to their spirit why they deserve self-awareness, healing, and enlightenment just as much as anyone else.

Invoke light. Lift up your hands and spend some time visualizing your body growing in size, extending out into cosmic space. See yourself invoking the light of consciousness, life, and the projective force of evolution. Contain these energies in a blinding white astral ball between your hands. Visualize yourself coming back down to earth with this sphere in hand.

Forcefully project this sphere toward the violator in your mind's eye or the spell in front of you. See the person physically respond to the blast of light while you declare,

Enlighten up—by any means necessary—RIGHT NOW!

Visualize this light entering every facet of their body. Come to terms with the fact that you are helping to quicken their soul's evolution.

Visualize the powerful light simultaneously opening their heart chakra (*anahata*) and their third-eye chakra (*ajna*) as well as both of their hands. See these two chakra points and the hands all connected by this astral light, symbolizing a connection between awareness, compassion, and action. To seal these energies, envision the person's face growing in astonishment. Visualize them being able to accurately perceive and realize the violations they have committed.

Finally, see the individual in your mind's eye accept this light into themselves. Place your hands in the *anjali mudra* (namaste or prayer position) and bow to them. Communicate any final wishes aimed at their enlightenment, and genuinely wish them well on their journey. If Wicca is your practice, you may now wish to repeat a mantra such as the line "An it harm none" from the Wiccan Rede.

Thank the gods and spirits at hand, and be sure to ground down your energy however you see fit. Rest assured that you have performed work that is beneficial for everyone in the situation, and be sure to follow up any castings with real-world action concerned with safety and social justice.

Resources

Auryn, Mat. "The Hex Appeal of Activism," *For Puck's Sake* (blog), July 9, 2017. http://www.patheos.com/blogs/matauryn/2017/07/09/the-hex-appeal-of-activism.

Bennett-Goleman, Tara. *Emotional Alchemy: How the Mind Can Heal the Heart.* New York, NY: Harmony Books, 2001.

Cole, W. Owen, and Hemant Kanitkar. *Teach Yourself Hinduism.* Chicago: McGraw-Hill, 1995.

D'Este, Sorita, and David Rankine. *Wicca Magickal Beginnings: A Study of the Possible Origins of the Rituals and Practices Found in this Modern Tradition of Pagan Witchcraft and Magick.* London: Avalonia Press, 2008.

Digitalis, Raven. *Esoteric Empathy: A Magickal & Metaphysical Guide to Emotional Sensitivity.* Woodbury, MN: Llewellyn, 2016.

Farrar, Stewart, and Janet Farrar. *A Witches' Bible: The Complete Witches' Handbook.* Custer, WA: Phoenix Publishing, 1981.

Hagen, Steve. *Buddhism Plain & Simple.* New York, NY: Broadway Books, 1998.

Judith, Anodea. *Wheels of Life: A User's Guide to the Chakra System.* Woodbury, MN: Llewellyn, 2006.

McNevin, Estha. Tradition materials and lesson notes of Opus Aima Obscuræ. Missoula, MT: 2017.

Paramananda. *A Practical Guide to Buddhist Meditation.* Birmingham, UK: Barnes & Noble, 2000.

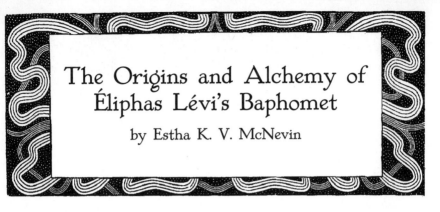

The Origins and Alchemy of Éliphas Lévi's Baphomet

by Estha K. V. McNevin

Have you ever wondered why occultists always dress in black? Why you'll never see bright colors on their back and why their appearance seems to have a somber tone? Do you know the reason for the clothes they wear? Woven into those deeply held cultural habits, Hermetic philosophy unites alchemy and the occult through symbolism. For many who seek the truth of magick, the black shroud of Baphomet is emblematic of initiation. It unveils the mystical power of rational self-education as a prerequisite intelligence; reason is mandatory in maintaining the self-preserving secrecy of the Craft. To will, to know, to dare, to keep silent—these are the powers of the magician, with which one weaves reality in accordance to the mastery of will using magick.

Occultists in the know often wear the color black in honorific recognition of the protection and self-respect that initiation affords. It is from others that we learn the one singular alchemical formula that will dominate our own journey to enlightenment: *solve et coagula*, dissolve and reconstitute. Like it or not, by way of oblivion and reformation, we humans are essentially always adapting, grappling in the darkness as we decay and are reborn according to our karmic cycles.

Shadow Boxing

Many of the profound occult philosophies are rooted in the Hindu Vedas as well as the Hebrew Qabalah. These are ye olde texts of antiquity from which astrology and the tarot have been reconstructed for the New Age of the West. Classical Hermetic arts can be hard to wrap our modern minds around because they shroud the original paradoxical principals of pagan culture from

that lost garden of chaos. Our spiritual culture upholds the psychological truth that symbols are things, images are symbols, and all things have a deeper level of meaning than what we assume from the surface. There is empathy to be found when we explore the substance of a proper noun. Personally, this sort of deep thinking saved my life from uncertain rhetoric as a student by destroying my concept of "taboo." All the while, magick has challenged my assumption that reality is authentic.

Meditating on Baphomet in my early phases of initiation and training was fundamental to my development as clergy because it helped me define my ceremonial practice as a lucid Gnostic process. Oh, the devil is there, all right, in each of us, riding our primeval impulses like a topless Babylonian banshee in the best of times. In the worst of times, however, he looms like a Satanic bank manager, more aware of our desires and limitations than we are and therefore quick to satiate instinctive self-indulgence. In an effort to out-exploit us, the devilish details are ever ready to tether us to yet another exhaustive learning curve. Elucidating our own pursuit of enlightenment, Baphomet is a symbolic essay; the image reminds us to be careful what we wish for in very deed!

These Hermetic ideas from antiquity challenge and guide seekers in the school of hard knocks, with good reason. They test the enslavement of our ego to assumption. Esoteric liberation only happens when matter-of-fact experiences yield understanding. If separation is a delusion, as swamis of Hinduism would have us believe, then *unity* is the real goal of enlightenment. Oneness excludes nothing. Baphomet looks scary, doesn't he? But he proves his truth in spades. We need every religious perspective there is to understand our shared reality; each and every path to enlightenment is necessary for someone in the collective.

Our own choices are the only ones imperative to us. At times, however, our stubborn pride, riddled with our willful ambitions, will long to know. Even our pious vows made in service can set us up for a sort of Gnostic selfish suffering, that burden of the martyr. As we grapple for enlightenment beyond self-identity, we have to work on ourselves most of all. In alchemy, the orphic aura is a glass egg filled with the black bile of our choices; our reaction to it is what affects our karmic learning curve the most. Yet in life, amid the throbbing heat of circumstance, instantaneously dissolving and reconstructing the ego is so much easier said than done—wouldn't you agree? Perhaps this little devil is trying to give you fifteen trump reasons to sort yourself out.

From French Bohemian to Hippie Occultist

Behind every obscure idol there is a human story of Gnosis, longing, and attainment. For Paris-native Alphonse Louis Constant, life in the 1830s proved itself beholden to the Roman Catholic *Ancien Régime* doctrines of the colonial crusades. They who "had," had in abundance, and everyone else was among the unwashed masses. Disillusioned during his studies at Saint Sulpice Seminary, this occult pioneer left to join a radical new movement of socialist bohemians. He went on to become a prominent Romantic writer on the Neo-Catholic socialist movement as well as Qabalah and the occult.

Many of these magickal and foreign ideas proved transformative to early occultists because they exposed them to a lost world of fantasy, planetary allegory, and astrological code, revealing the very lacework of Western mythology. It was while studying the Qabalah that Alphonse Louis Constant took the Hebrew name Éliphas Lévi around 1835. This was also when he began writing extensively on magick and the occult. Moreover, as a result of Lévi's work with planetary and zodiacal classifications of the Qabalah, the occult sciences took on a more alchemical tone, in many ways adapting a scientific model to ceremonial magick.

Lévi was rooting out these layers to the onion when he so famously divided this science into two parts in his seminal work *Transcendental Magic: Its Doctrine and Ritual.* There he introduces Baphomet in relation to the Devil, Trump XV, and provides a self-drawn sketch. To Lévi, Baphomet was a hieroglyph of occult science and magick, disguised for a Neo-Platonist Christian world hell-bent on censorship and disavowed of idolatry in the human form. Nevertheless, it still permitted all manner of scary monsters and demons of antiquity. Lévi clarifies, "adores of this sign do not consider it as do we, a devil; on the contrary, for them it is that of the god Pan."

The Anatomy of a Hieroglyphic Text

To say that Baphomet is rooted in ancient magick would be an understatement. For occultist Aleister Crowley he was the *lingam*, the regenerative male potential—primordial Shiva, the Hindu creator and destroyer. I love what modern academic Michael Osiris Snuffin says on the subject: "Baphomet is a god of the old religions and schools of thought that were active before the full advent of Christianity, and not a representation of the devil." Snuffin, like so many magicians, looks at the image created by Lévi and sees a totality of philosophy and a sort of pictorial essay on the fabric of existence. Where literalists might see a god or a fantasist would perhaps contrive a devil, the multilingual and initiated occultist relies on the symbolic reason of antiquity, which has never really fallen out of practice thanks in part to art and religion quite simply because it decodes the hieroglyphs of living and dying.

For Lévi, the figure was not a god but a glyph that held all of the admonitions of a devil as an eternal rebellious idea more related to willfully independent thinking than to a living deity or being. Over time, longing to reclaim our pagan idols, occultists have personified the Devil, Trump XV, with the Christian underworld demigod Satan, himself bound to antiquity by the Jewish corresponding force Moloch (King), the accuser and prince of primeval demons.

So many of the Golden Dawn documents, namely McGregor Mathers's chief translations of texts on the Tree of Life, were taken from the French translations of Éliphas Lévi. These documents would go on to influence Wicca and Thelema. The Qabalah provided a unique understanding of reality as multidimensional light, the medium of all magick. The planetary and astrological symbolism of antiquity was paired with Hebrew letters and myths from classical European paganism to enhance the tarot into a pictorial collection of the pagan cosmology.

By the time that A. E. Waite began to study Baphomet in anticipation of its symbolic use in his reimagining of the Devil card, ideas of Satanic occultism were flourishing amongst the early Evangelical revival communities of Europe. Subsequent generations have continued to equate Trump XV with Satan, at least on the surface, but, increasingly, the deeper alchemical philosophies have been fermenting in popular culture. From album covers to dorm room posters, Baphomet has achieved a godlike status, the likes of which Lévi himself could have hardly predicted.

Of Angels and Spirits

The original image appears, hand sketched, as black charcoal on a white background. A gargoyle or hieracosphinx, Baphomet is perched squatting on a cubic throne atop a sphere, mocking the vulgarity of the world. The image is unusual and contains a wealth of elemental and alchemical symbolism coded into the obscure body, gestures, and stance. The figure is cross-legged, right over left, and two cloven hooves are visible beneath a Saturnine shroud that is draped over the lap of the image to indicate the veil of secret initiation into the occult. The hooves identify the figure as a satyr and relate it to "IAO Pan," the occult mantra of creation of which Aleister Crowley was so fond.

From the groin, a caduceus emerges. It rises from an oval sphere of the *akasha* or aura *tattwa* of Tantric Hinduism. Behind it, watery fish scales cover the abdomen of a voluptuously breasted Roman satyr, making for a titillating goat-man. The image certainly has a way of lingering in the psyche. Two snakes entwine a rod of light, so iconic of the Upper and Lower lands of Egypt, a metaphor of contrast and union. The white curative snake Nebthet and the black toxic Aset merge in Hadit, an Egyptian symbol for Gnosis. These Greek Hellenistic themes, which evolved out of the cult of Harpocrates, are still essential in the

study of the occult, teaching magicians the ability to exercise free and rational nonbiased will secretly, in an effort to achieve a *magnum opus*, or Great Work of karmic destiny.

Resting on the twenty-sixth path of the Tree of Life, the Trump XV image relates to the nature of reality. This icon of life force is the All-father and All-mother Nuit as well, binding us to the rings of Binah, the cellular boundaries of our own karmic existence. We are slaves to our own primeval and instinctive choices. When a living rebirth is necessary, we seek out esoteric initiation and we transfigure the ego to adapt to new conditions or circumstances to elevate our own consciousness through direct effort. This force of nature is ruled by Capricorn the goat-fish, itself an anthropomorphic architect of our reality, who bestows the benefits of experimentation and applied self-education.

The Great Mother Nuit is associated with Binah on the Tree of Life, the female Saturn. Binah is the Qabalistic Sephira of understanding, and Nuit rules the Saturnine foundations of reality from her throne of creation, upon which Baphomet squats. Our fermentation within the alembic glass egg is within her realm of alchemy. This is because fusion, division, and fission exhibit the ascending and descending energy of fertility and rebirth. In occult doctrine this demonstrates the link between outer physical alchemy and our internal emotional alchemy and gives us a transcendental pictograph of adaptation designed to help us philosophically navigate our more willful choices in life.

Furthermore, Lévi gives us some real clues to the contrasting forces at work within each magician. Baphomet is fitted with eagle or angel wings that suggest the illusion of freedom, for like all winged spirits, he is bound in service and leaded to the formational earth beneath his wild cloven hooves. His arms are poised in an alchemical gesture indicative of esoteric fermentation. The right is muscular and masculine, inscribed with *Solve* (dissolve) and reaches above with the hand held in the benediction mudra used to draw angels and good spirits from the glowing first quarter Moon of pure light. The left arm is inscribed with *Coagula* (reconstitute) and reaches below with the hand in a mudra for casting manifestive or dark magick from the last quarter Moon of shadow.

The figure's chest reveals the androgyny of the image, of the breasts so evocative of fertility and having one's wishes fulfilled. The figure's goat head is a direct reference to Pan and the wild satyr gods of antiquity. The pentagram on his brow evokes the five elements that bless and protect the ajna chakra. A glowing flame of enlightenment, the Hebrew *Yod* (a Light of God) burns atop his torchlike crown. Verifying the godhead through esoteric study and experiment will reveal the truths inherent in this hieroglyph and manifest the fruits of our desires.

It is the reality of our shared human experience that we dissolve and recreate into our own image and then call it God. This esoteric philosophy is vital to the evolution of magick as well as to our own growth and adaptation, and perhaps that is why Lévi and so many other occultists turn time and again to the alchemist's idea of evolution. From images like Baphomet, we learn to read in symbolism and to daily orient our thought, speech, and actions to our highest purpose with our own brand of primitive and willful magick.

Baphomet's Tawdry List of Devilish Correspondences	
Tarot	The Devil, XV
Hebrew Letter	Ayin, O, the all-seeing eye and Nazar
Numerical Value	70
Tree of Life	Path 26, the Eye uniting Tiphareth (Beauty) and Hod (Splendor)
Global Mythic Deities	Yoruba Olodumare, Egyptian Typhon, Zoroastrian Ahriman, Babylonian Ea, Greek Python and Pan, English Herne, Celtic Cernunnos, Abrahamic Satan, Hindu Shivling (Lingam of Shiva), Hermetic Baphomet, the obscene deity of Mendes, goat of the Sabbath
Planets	Saturn, the baron Earth authoritarian devouring of life; the smothering mother inundating

Baphomet's Tawdry List of Devilish Correspondences	
Zodiac	Capricorn—goat-fish, architect, intellect; practical, prudent, ambitious, disciplined; a primal urge for order and an emotional need for chaos
Astrological House	Tenth (skill, recognition, triumph, and mastery)
Garden	Rhizomes, bulbs, roots, tubers, and stalks
Flowers	Ivy, heartsease, amaranth, pansy
Trees	Pine, elm, yew, willow, aspen, poplar, red sandalwood (chandan)
Herbs	Hemp, grape, hops, comfrey, knapweed, hemlock, henbane
Incense	Dung, dragon's blood, sandalwood, cyprus leaf, balm of Gilead
Intoxicants	Wine, marijuana, psilocybin
Metal	Silver, iron, lead
Color	Dark gray, black, dark brown, tan
Hindu Tattwa	Akasha—spirit, rising hope, aura, orbis aetherial
Gemstones	Turquoise, amethyst
Occult Hermetic Axim	*Solve et coagula*, "dissolve and reconstitute"
Alchemical Process	Fermentation within the alembic glass egg using the perpetuation of fusion, division, and reformation to achieve a refined result; Gnostic intoxication

A Journey to Call One's Own

There is more to magick than meets the eye. The levels of our culture and very depths of our history are enlightening. In studying ancient symbolism, we come to find joy and curiosity; learning is a fun adventure and is our birthright. We begin where we are, but our potential is only limited by our own fixated assumptions. There is a real liberation in feeling the power of being alive. Real magick is the lotto win, a twenty-first birthday, and Christmas all rolled into one because the universe is euphoric. Our ability to perceive and comprehend it is a miracle.

When we first feel the joy and thrilling power of magick, it feels like being wrapped up in a rainbow every day. I would love to hold life in that feeling and tell the world that everything's okay. But, like so many other occultists, I fight apathy and my own lazy ignorance, so I proudly wear black, and to conqueror my own karma I carry Levi's magick on my back.

Selected Resources

Crowley, Aleister. *The Book of Thoth (Egyptian Tarot): A Short Essay on the Tarot of the Egyptians Being the Equinox Vol. III No. 5.* Stamford, CT: US Games Systems, 1988.

Hall, Manly P. *The Secret Teachings of All Ages: An Encyclopedic Outline of Masonic, Hermetic, Qabbalistic and Rosicrucian Symbolical Philosophy.* New York: Penguin, 2003.

Hulse, David Allen. *The Western Mysteries.* St. Paul, MN: Llewellyn Publications, 2000.

Lévi, Éliphas. *Éliphas Lévi: Transcendental Magic: Its Doctrine and Ritual.* Paris: Presses Universitaires de France, 1969.

———. *Éliphas Lévi: visionnaire romantique.* Paris: Presses Universitaires de France, 1969.

Mann, William F. *The Knights Templar in the New World: How Henry Sinclair Brought the Grail to Acadia.* Rochester, VT: Destiny Books, 2004.

Moore, Thomas. *The Planets Within: The Astrological Psychology of Marsilio Ficino.* Hudson, NY: Lindisfarne Press, 1990.

Mullen, Diki Jo. "Astrological Keys." In *The Witches' Almanac.* Newport, RI: The Witches' Almanac LTD, 2016.

Parker, Julia, Derek Parker. *Parkers' Astrology: The Definitive Guide to Using Astrology in Every Aspect of Your Life.* New ed. New York: DK Publishing, 2001.

Snuffin, Michael Osiris. "Devil of Astral Light: Éliphas Lévi's Baphomet." Hermetic Library. 2009. https://hermetic.com/osiris/levibaphomet.

———. *The Thoth Companion: The Key to the True Symbolic Meaning of the Thoth Tarot.* Woodbury, MN: Llewellyn Publications, 2007.

Stavish, Mark. *The Path of Alchemy: Energetic Healing & the World of Natural Magic.* Woodbury, MN: Llewellyn Publications, 2006.

Scissors as a Magical Tool

by Mickie Mueller

The humble pair of scissors is something that we use for many everyday tasks, such as opening packages, crafting, and cutting hair, but have you ever considered those scissors to be a magical tool? Scissors can be a tool of transformation. They are used to transform cloth into clothing, poppets, or magical sachets. They transform paper into petitions for magic. They are also used as a tool to sever, cutting ties both physical and spiritual, breaking curses, bringing endings—scissors can free us. In another respect this simple tool is often seen as a symbol of opening the way. We see giant scissors used to symbolically cut a ribbon for a store opening; scissors can also be a magical tool for opening access to what you want in life. The simple pair of scissors is also a tool of harvest used to gather sacred herbs and food from the garden, which makes them a tool for abundance, hearth, and home.

You may think of scissors as a modern invention. How can they be considered a traditional magical tool? Most of us experience scissors from an early age as a plastic-handled implement that comes packed in cardboard and plastic that seems more mundane than magical, and certainly not steeped in history and tradition. If we delve a little deeper, we'll discover that scissors have their roots in ancient times. I first learned this interesting fact as a teen while browsing through a book of ornaments that belonged to my dad's art book collection. There they were among the ink drawings of shields, ancient jewelry, and mosaic details—scissors from ancient Egypt. It's believed that scissors were first invented in Egypt around 1500 BCE. Civilization has had scissors longer than we've been eating with forks!

The first scissors didn't have handles with pivots like modern scissors, but the blades were held together with a thin flat band of flexible curved bronze that allowed them to be squeezed to cut and would flex back open when released, much like simple buffet tongs. The forerunner of modern pivoted scissors with two blades connected by a screw was first made of bronze and iron in Rome around 100 CE, and the design was eventually used all over the world.

Deities Who Run with Scissors

Did you know there are actually deities associated with scissors? Atropos is a Greek deity, the oldest of the three Fates. The Fates are three sisters charged with watching over destiny and the threads of human life. Her sister Clotho is the spinner of the thread; another sister, Lachesis, measures the threa; and Atropos cuts the thread with her scissors, thus determining the length of each life. Many people made offerings to the Fates petitioning their favor for a bountiful harvest, safe childbirth, or other pivotal events.

Culsu is the Etruscan goddess who stands at the gateway of the underworld with her consort Culsans. She is described as a bare-chested winged woman who carries a torch and scissors. She is also a snake goddess, representing transformation. Culsu lights the way through the dark with her torch and accompanies the dead to the other side. Some suggest that her scissors may be a symbol of the cutting of earthly ties to the soul, thus allowing the soul to journey untethered by earthly bonds into the afterlife.

Blue Tara is revered by both the Hindu and Buddhist faiths. She is a primal goddess who transmutes anger and destroys obstacles. She is one of twenty-one Taras, who all have different aspects. Blue Tara is actually blue, has a third eye, and often appears as a fearsome presence surrounded by clouds and flames and wearing nothing but a tiger skin. Among her attributes are a sword, an axe, and scissors, all used to cut away obstacles, unwanted habits, and negative karma. She also has the power to remove the fear your enemies have over you. When a fierce blue goddess has your back, what's to fear?

Scissors of Folklore and Magic

It's considered unlucky to drop a pair of scissors. If you happen to drop yours, though, you can have someone else pick them up for you. If that's not convenient, just stomp on them once, and then you can pick them up yourself without bringing bad luck. Other beliefs suggest that dropping scissors can also predict events. If scissors fall with one blade stuck in the ground, this suggests you will attend a funeral; if both blades stick, this points to a wedding instead.

If you receive scissors as a gift, be sure to pay the gift giver for them, even if you just pay a penny. If you don't pay something for the scissors, they will sever your friendship.

If your scissors accidentally break in two while using them, it's also an omen of bad luck, so if you have any old rickety scissors that seem to be in danger of breaking, better toss them just to be safe. Some traditions attribute scissors left open in the home as a cause of strife among the people in the household, but open scissors under your doormat protect against malevolent magic. Additionally, there is another tradition that suggests open scissors under your pillow will cure insomnia, although I would probably stab myself while turning the pillow over to the cold side!

One of the most popular ways that Witches use scissors for magic is to symbolically sever something that no longer serves you, cut ties, break curses, and bring about endings. Methods include ritually cutting cords, photographs, or sigils that are charged to represent whatever you wish to cut out of your life. Two items or candles representing people who need to break a bond from each other can be tied together and then ritually cut apart with scissors. Scissors have long been used to break hexes and curses, so they can be used to cut away negative astral connections by cutting through the air around the affected person.

Another use for scissors in spells is opening access to what you want in life; scissors can magically open the way. Some ideas on how to use scissors in this way include cutting up a representation of your obstacle or wrapping up a poppet in twine or ribbon and then cutting it free with scissors. Do some image magic by printing two photos of the same size, one representing the future you want and the other of closed double doors. Place the door image on top of your goal image and use a glue stick to glue the left and right edges of the paper together. Charge the paper with your intentions and, using your magical scissors, cut the double doors open to open the way to what you want!

Scissors can be quite a handy tool for Witches when it comes to the harvesting of magical herbs. Most kitchen witches would get great use from a pair of kitchen shears both for preparing magical formulas and for magical cookery. Some kitchen shears are meant to come apart in

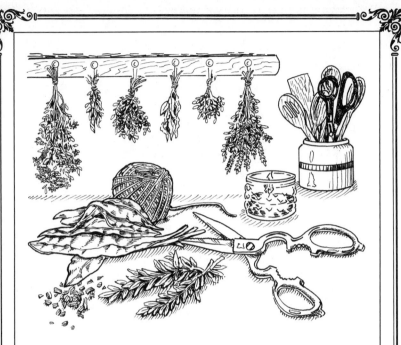

order to properly wash them when used for food. I have a pair of these, and they're my go-to scissors for kitchen witchery. These uses show that scissors are not only a tool for cutting away what you don't want, but they are also a tool for bringing things into your life that you do want, a tool of harvest, abundance, and even healing. When used to gather sacred herbs or food from the garden or even cutting food free from packaging twine, rubber bands, or bags, scissors become a tool that brings good things to us and helps nourish our lives with abundance and magic.

Most of the Witches I know not only create their own destinies through magic, but they also craft many of the things in their lives. Generally speaking, Witches are often creative people. Scissors in the hands of a crafty Witch become a tool of transformation. Fabric is cut out to create magical sachets, poppets, or even ritual robes if you are handy with a sewing machine. Paper is cut to create an ornate scrapbook style book of shadows, strips of paper for petitions, or even a sigil to decorate a jar candle with. Scissors have the power to turn an item into something else.

Slice Away That Hex Spell

If you suspect that you're under a crossed condition, hexed, or otherwise put upon by malevolent energy, here's a curse breaker that's as close as your pair of witchy scissors.

You will need:
About 2 feet of black embroidery thread
Photo of yourself
Scissors

Hold the thread in your hands, one end in each hand and state aloud powerfully like you mean it,

I summon all energies that align against me, affecting my life and working against my greater good. You are drawn into this thread. It is you, and you are it.

You should feel it filling up the black thread. Tie thirteen knots all along the length of the thread and then state,

Now you're stuck.

Begin to wrap it around your photo and say aloud,

You tried to hide. I see you now; I know you're there. I know what you've tried to do. You bound me, but no more, because I see you.

Once the thread is completely wrapped around your photo, tie it. Then take your scissors and cut yourself loose, cutting through all the thread and shearing it to pieces. As you cut, you should declare,

I'm free from you. You have no power here—you are nothing!

Once you cut the threads off, you should dispose of them by burning them, tossing them into running water like a river, or leaving them at a crossroads.

New Endeavor Grand Opening Spell

Do you have a new project, business venture, or creative undertaking that needs a kick start in order to happen? Try this spell and create your own grand opening.

You will need:

Piece of paper
Pen
Red ribbon
3 small orange candles
Scissors

Write a detailed description of your new endeavor as you envision it. Write down only positive statements. As an example, instead of "My project won't fail," try instead "My project will be a success." Carefully craft your words to describe all the positive aspects of your new endeavor. Roll the paper up and tie it with the red ribbon using three knots. Now place it on your altar or someplace where it can remain undisturbed for three days. Light one of the candles next to the scroll each day for three consecutive days. As it burns, it adds power to your vision, filling the scroll with life.

After the third candle burns down, you are ready for your grand opening. The scroll is fully charged and ready to release your intention to manifest your new project into reality. Taking your scissors in your right hand and the scroll in your left, repeat this intention:

Now the power is full. All my dreams shall unfold
At this grand opening of my future so bold!

As you cut the ribbon with the scissors, state,

I now declare this new endeavor open!

Feel free to state the name of the endeavor in your ribbon-cutting statement if you wish. You have now released the opening energy into the world. You may keep the paper as a talisman or return it to the realm of spirit by burning it.

Desperately Seeking Scissors

By now I bet you're interested in finding a special pair of scissors to add to your magical cabinet. When choosing scissors for your magic, you can choose any pair you like—whatever feels right to you. If you love a small pair of kid's scissors with glitter handles, by all means, set them aside for magic. If you prefer something more elegant, consider browsing the sewing scissors at the fabric or craft store. There are many metal scissors available and some are decorative and ornate, making them seem more like Old World tools from a bygone era. Small decorative sewing or embroidery scissors are usually great for most magical uses like cutting cords or petitions. Very popular are the vintage-style scissors shaped like a stork or crane; the bird's feet hold the handles and the blades are its beak. These designs were inspired by the scissors and clamps found in the kits of midwives and folk healers. One of the uses of such scissors would have been to cut the umbilical cords of babies after delivery. My magical scissors are a pair of dark-bronze-colored embroidery scissors in a vintage style with filigree handles; I've used them in my magic for years. Once you've found your perfect Witches' scissors, you might want to bless and consecrate them for your magical tasks.

You will need:

Scissors

Incense of your choice or a smudge bundle

Oil for blessing, such as olive oil, angelica oil, frankincense oil, or any other oil that you like to use for blessing

First, hold your scissors over incense or smudge smoke, as you do visualize any energy from other people who handled them before you and see those energies dissolving and releasing from the scissors in the smoke. Once the energy feels neutral, you may anoint your magical scissors lightly with oil and really feel the scissors in your hand. Hold the scissors in both hands and gaze at this tool of magic, making a statement of blessing and consecration. Here is an example, but you can also speak from the heart using your own words:

> *I hereby bless and consecrate these scissors as a magical tool of severing, harvest, opening, and transformation. I proclaim that I dedicate this tool of the Witch for my use in the name of the God and Goddess and in the presence of the spirits that guide my magical path. As I will it, so mote it be!*

You may now wipe most of the oil off with a tissue or soft cloth. Since scissors are metal, a small amount of oil left on the surface will protect them, but don't leave them greasy. You may wish to store them in a pouch if they came with one, or wrap them in cloth and reserve them for magical use.

Whether using scissors for magic to sever that which doesn't serve you, harvest abundance, open the way before you, or magically transform things in your life into what you need, scissors can be a treasured tool in your own magical practice.

The Inverse Cone of Power

by Jason Mankey

Building the cone of power is a traditional way of raising energy for magickal purposes in many Witch covens. Cones of Power are built by casting a strong magickal circle designed to keep energy within the circle's boundaries, and then filling up that space with magickal energy. There are a variety of techniques that can be used to create the energy necessary for building a cone of power, the most common being dancing and chanting (with those two techniques often used in tandem).

Eventually, when enough magickal energy is released, it begins to circulate around the circle, spiraling upward. If we could see magickal energy circle around us with our mundane eyes, it would resemble a cone or an upside-down funnel. When the energy inside the cone of power reaches a crescendo, it's generally released by whoever is leading ritual and then sent out into the world to accomplish whatever goal it was raised for. I often imagine this release of energy as resembling a volcano erupting.

The first mention of the cone of power occurs in Gerald Gardner's 1954 book *Witchcraft Today*. (Gardner was the first modern, public, self-identifying Witch, which makes him a rather important historical magickal figure.) In that book Gardner talks about a group of Witches in World War II Britain that "raised the great cone of power and directed the thought at Hitler's brain: 'You can't cross the sea.'"[1] Gardner's Witches seem to have succeeded with their spellcraft too—Hitler never did invade the United Kingdom. Since Gardner first wrote about the cone of power, it has become a popular tool in the magick arsenal of most Witches and is

---

1. Gardner writes this tiny little snippet about the Cone of Power in chapter 10 of *Witchcraft Today*. Since *Today* has been reprinted several dozen times, the page number will vary from edition to edition.

generally present anytime a group of Witches gets together to raise energy.

When I'm leading the rituals of my coven, I generally raise a cone of power for our magickal workings, but not everyone in our coven operates that way. Out on a walk one evening with my wife while discussing an upcoming ritual, I brought up the cone of power and suggested we use it for an impending piece of spellcasting. My wife gave me a rather blank stare and told me that's not how she would be leading our work and that she rarely ever raises the cone of power anymore. Instead she told me that she does just the opposite. She described this to me as her "death ray," but after we discussed her technique, we decided that it should probably be known as the "inverse cone of power."

So What Is the Inverse Cone of Power?

A couple of years ago my wife and I had a friend with a very aggressive form of cancer, and we performed a lot of magick for him. For several months most of our coven rituals ended with all of us attempting to send him energy, which we would then direct toward him. After thinking about the techniques we were using, my wife decided that simply blasting energy up and out of our circle like an erupting volcano seemed too imprecise. She wanted to make sure that the energy we were raising went directly to our friend and reached him as quickly as possible. This is how she came up with the inverse cone of power technique.

Instead of letting the energy of our coven spiral upward and out, my wife directed our energy downward toward our coven's altar. Upon the altar she'd set up some specific focus items designed to channel our energy out and away specifically toward our sick friend. She envisioned our magickal force as being as sharp and focused as a laser beam, which is the reason she initially called her technique a death ray. The inverse cone of power is a lot like a traditional cone of power: energy is raised and that energy is focused and

spirals around the circle, but in this instance it takes a different path out of the circle and out into the universe.

The Pentacle and the Crystal Ball

For the inverse cone of power to be effective it requires a gateway and a point of focus. Luckily, most of us already have the perfect gateway on our altars—the pentacle (sometimes called a paten). A ritual pentacle is generally a metal, wooden, paper, or clay disc with an upright pentagram drawn or inscribed upon it. Sometimes other symbols are placed around the pentagram by individual Witches, but such "extras" aren't a requirement. (The terms pentacle and pentagram are often used as synonyms; in my own personal practice I use the term "pentacle" for the working tool and "pentagram" for the symbol of the five-pointed star.[2])

The pentacle is generally used to consecrate ritual materials such as salt and water, but it has a much deeper meaning. In ceremonial magick the pentacle was used to summon

---

2. The Oxford Living Dictionary provides the word "pentagram" as a secondary definition for "pentacle," which means that in general English usage the two words are often used as synonyms.

spirits (and demons), and its use in early Witchcraft was similar. In *Witchcraft Today* Gerald Gardner writes that it was used to "command spirits," which allowed Witches to ask "departed spirits to return or communicate" with the living.[3] What this implies is that the pentacle is a gateway tool, one that can open up access to other realms and physical locations in this world. If spirits and other entities can arrive in our rituals through the pentacle, it makes sense that we should be able to send energy out and through it too!

If you don't currently own a pentacle, they are easy enough to put together. If you have access to a blank dinner plate, you can simply paint a pentagram onto it—instant pentacle! Even easier is taking a paper plate and simply drawing a pentagram onto it. It doesn't really matter how special or pretty our magickal tools are. As long as we create them with good intent, they'll work just fine.

It almost sounds silly to say that my coven uses a crystal ball during ritual, but we do! For the inverse cone of power our crystal ball serves two purposes. Crystals are excellent conductors of magickal energy, so they make a powerful focal point in ritual. When using the inverse cone technique, we focus our energy into the crystal ball, which we sit on top of the pentacle. The crystal ball absorbs all the energy directed toward it, stopping any stray energies from escaping their intended purpose.

In fortune telling and popular movies crystal balls are often used as scrying devices. Energy is directed into the crystal ball, usually so the scryer can find out something about a particular person or perhaps a future outcome. In our practice we use the ball for a similar purpose: we use it to call up the person (or persons) we are doing a spell for. We use the crystal ball to lock in on their location, which helps ensure that the energy we are raising goes to the people we want it to.

---

3. The information about the pentacle in Gardner's work can be found at the beginning of chapter 11, "Some Other Matters."

Our crystal ball is not particularly big either, about the size of a vending machine "bouncy ball." (Instead of rubbing two hands across it like fortune tellers do in the movies, I can fit it between my thumb and forefinger.) While we have a rather specialized crystal ball, any piece of crystal will do, and it doesn't necessarily have to be sphere shaped. Buying the most expensive crystal at a gem shop is no guarantee of greater success, either. Some of the most powerful crystals in our house are rather rough looking and only cost a couple of bucks!

Using the Inverted Cone of Power: The Ritual

My wife and I generally use the inverted cone of power during coven ritual, but I think it can also be used effectively by solitaries. Start by setting up your ritual space in the usual way—calling the quarters, invoking the Goddess and God, and so on, making sure to cast a circle designed to hold in magickal energy. Set your pentacle on the middle of your altar and place a crystal in the center of it.

To make sure the energy you're raising reaches its intended target, you can place a picture of the person (or goal) you are working on under your crystal. If you don't have a picture, simply writing down a name or intention upon a piece of paper will suffice. Additionally, if you have stones or herbs that you like to use that contribute to your intended purpose, you can place them on top of the pentacle, where their energy will combine with the power about to be raised.

Dancing and movement are often associated with the traditional cone of power, but won't work here (the energy you are raising will spiral around and upward). We usually chant or tone to raise energy when using the inverted cone. The best chants are generally short and rhymed ("Better you'll feel; we say heal!"), and if they end up being a bit goofy, that's nothing to worry about; it's the intent that matters.

Instead of coming up with a chant, we'll often tone instead, which is just as effective. Toning doesn't release power through words, instead it utilizes a vowel sound. In my coven we generally use a deep "O" sound, repeated over and over. While toning, you want your mind to focus on the task at hand. When doing healing work for a friend, you'd want to focus in your mind's eye on that friend and visualize their condition improving and the magick you are sending them being absorbed into their body.

While much of the energy from toning and chanting leaves the body through the mouth, in our coven we also

push it out of our hands. While we tone, we can literally feel the energy leaving our hands and being directed where we want it to go. As we tone, we all slowly inch closer toward the altar in the center of our ritual space, our hands gradually moving out toward the altar's pentacle. The closer we get to one another and the altar, the more intense our toning becomes. "Intense" doesn't necessarily imply that our toning is increasing in volume. It's the intensity of the energy being released from our bodies that grows stronger.

Eventually we all end up shoulder to should around the altar, our hands all lifted directly above the pentacle. By this point we can feel the energy in front of us, and we literally start pushing it toward the pentacle. The energy is no hypothetical here either—we can all feel it as we push. At these moments it's just as real and as tangible as pushing a door open.

With our fingertips now directly above the crystal sitting atop the pentacle, we can feel some of the energy beginning to flower through the pentacle toward its intended destination. Before we end the rite, our high priestess usually shouts "one," letting us know that we are almost done and for everyone to give her (and our spell) one final push! Here our toning reaches a crescendo, and the space around us crackles with energy. Our toning then ends in unison with no prompting, and we feel the energy we've raised being whisked away to its intended destination.

The crystal upon the pentacle has given our magick laser-like focus, pinpointing our energy for maximum effectiveness, while our pentacle has taken that energy from our ritual space directly to where it needs to go. After my coven performed this technique for our friend with cancer, he informed me a few days later that he could literally see the energy we had sent him descending down upon him like an army of golden parachutes. The inverse cone of power may not be traditional, but it most certainly works.

Hamsa

by Dallas Jennifer Cobb

There is a magical image that appears in many, many places these days: blazoned on T-shirts, stylized as tattoos, and even artistically represented in jewelry. Gaining popularity in the media, this image of a hand is being worn by movie and music personalities and popular culture figures. But what is this open-hand symbol, where does it come from, what does it mean, and how can it be used magically?

What Is the Hamsa Symbol?

The symbol of the open hand with five distinct fingers is an ancient and enduring symbol of the divine feminine called the *hamsa*. Its history is long and multilayered.

Hamsa has its origins in the Arabic word *khamsa*, meaning "five," and has also enjoyed a variety of other spellings, including *hamesh, khamesh,* and *chamsa,* which all loosely translate to "the hand" or "five." *Hamesh,* meaning "five" in Hebrew, is a sacred reminder of the five books of the Torah and the necessity to use all five senses to praise God. In Arabic, *khamesh* means five and symbolizes the Five Pillars of Islam: faith, prayer, charity, fasting, and pilgrimage.

This enduring symbol, which appears in many cultures and is woven through the iconology of most major religions, is finding new meaning and widespread use in these modern times.

Where Did It Come From?

With its origins in early Paleolithic society, the hamsa was originally known as "the hand of the Goddess." Artifacts adorned with the hamsa symbol include vessels and statues honoring Inanna, the Sumerian goddess of love, sex, fertility, warfare, and political power. Associated with the planet Venus, Inanna was honored as far back as the Ubaid period in 5300 BCE. As time progressed, the hamsa was used in Mesopotamia in approximately 3500 BCE to honor Ishtar, a goddess possessing similar qualities and powers to Inanna.

At different times, and in different cultures, the hamsa has been known as the Hand of Inanna (Sumerian), the Hand of Ishtar (Mesopotamian), the Hand of Aphrodite (Greek), the Hand of Venus (Roman), the Hand of Mary (Christian), the Hand of Fatima (Islamic), the Hand of Tara (Buddhist), the Hand of Miriam (Jewish), and the Hand of Hamesh. The Christian hand of blessing, an open hand with the pinky and ring fingers folded over the palm, also has its origins with hamsa, initially called *Mano Pantea,* meaning the "Hand of the All-Goddess." The hamsa has ancient roots in the United States too. In Moundville Archaeological Park on the Black Warrior River in Hale County, Alabama, an engraved stone pallet decorated with a hand symbol much like the hamsa was found. This site was used by Mississippian Native Americans between the tenth and sixteenth centuries.

While it is uncertain how the amulet symbol made its way into so many cultures, faiths, and religions, the transmission of the amulet's use from Mesopotamian goddess culture to Israel's

Christian culture is documented. It is said that Ishtar's priestesses used the hamsa symbol when they "performed some version of the rite each year in the temple of Jerusalem, where the virgin form of the Goddess was called Mari, Mari-Ana, or Miriam," writes Barbara Walker.

Recently, the hamsa has become a symbol of peace in the Middle East, with the image being drawn on prayer flags that flap in war-torn zones of conflict. Because it is a symbol that exists across the borders of culture, country, and faith, the hamsa is thought to be something that can bring unification through identification with a symbol that predates modern religion and is held in common by both Jews and Muslims. Hamsas for peace have become a symbol of the hope for peace in Israel and the Middle East.

Different Uses

Generally speaking, the hamsa is an amulet used to banish evil and negativity and provide protection. Simultaneously, it is used to receive blessings, good fortune, happiness, and luck. While it can be used in these very different ways, it is also used in different hand positions.

In Buddhism, circa fifth century BCE, statues of the Buddha were built showcasing many different mudras, or hand positions. It is said that the five fingers symbolize the five perfections: generosity, morality, patience, effort, and meditative concentration.

Two of these mudras could be related to hamsa: the abhaya mudra and the varada mudra. The *abhaya mudra* is the right hand held at shoulder height, with the elbow bent and palm facing out. It is much like the "stop" gesture used by traffic cops. It symbolizes strength and inner security and aims to instill fearlessness of others. The *varada mudra* is made with the left hand, with the arm hanging long by the side and the palm facing forward with the fingers extended. It is the mudra that symbolizes charity, compassion, and wish granting.

In some statues only one mudra is represented, but in many statues the varada mudra is commonly used with the abhaya mudra, with the right hand held up and the left hand held down, dispelling evil and negativity and receiving blessings at the same time.

In the Pagan tradition and for many body and energy workers the dominant hand is known as the projecting hand, and the nondominant hand is known as the receiving hand. Because so many more people seem to be right-handed, it makes sense to me that the Buddha is represented as projecting protection (and deflecting negativity) with the right hand and receiving blessings and luck with the left hand. Often, in sacred circles, Pagans will stand with one hand up and one hand down, palms facing the center, as they "hold" sacred space.

When using only one of the images, remember that when the fingers of the hamsa point up, the hand looks like what it means: stop. The fingers-up hamsa is used to ward off evil and deflect the evil eye. It can be used to protect homes, rooms, spaces, and people, sending someone's negativity back to them and deflecting anything undesirable so that it isn't absorbed. When the fingers of the hamsa point down, it symbolizes welcoming and receiving blessings, luck, fertility, and good energy. Much of popular culture's current use of the hamsa depicts the receiving hand position. Depending on what you want to use the hamsa for, you should carefully choose which position of the fingers suits your desired outcome.

Easy Hamsa Spells

Hamsa Home Protection

You can easily make your own hamsa protection symbol. Traditionally, the color red was used for protection. While in Inanna's time it was often the blood of a sacrificed animal that was used, I suggest using watercolors or tempera paint. Coat the palm of your right hand evenly and fully. Press your hand onto a sheet of paper, channeling your protective and deflective energy into the image. Carefully peel your hand away and let your hamsa dry. Hang this hamsa with fingers turned up on the front door of your home or in the window of the entry door, facing out.

As you put it up, say,

Hand of Inanna, hand of mine,
I invoke your protection divine.
Deflect evil, sadness, and pain.
Peace and safety in this house sustained.

Each time you enter or exit through that door, pause and renew the energy of the hamsa by repeating the invocation.

Personal Protection

Wear the hamsa as jewelry for personal protection The symbol is available in a variety of jewelry options—rings, bracelets, necklaces, and brooches. You can even go to your local craft store and buy hamsa beads to make your own jewelry. Again, remember to select the fingers facing up if you want to deflect negativity or send someone's evil eye back to them, and position the fingers facing down to welcome luck, fertility, and blessings.

I wear a hamsa with fingers facing up at my throat chakra to remind me to always use the gentle art of verbal self-defense. The symbol helps me remember that I don't need to accept everything said to me or about me and that I have a powerful voice that I can use to speak truth softly.

Using a regular utterance associated with the symbol can help you get in the habit of affirming yourself using this powerful symbol. Try this common hamsa prayer:

> *Let no sadness come to this heart.*
> *Let no trouble come to these arms.*
> *Let no conflict come to these eyes.*
> *Let my soul be filled with the blessing of joy and peace.*

Banishment

In sudden, difficult situations you can simply use your own hand as a hamsa. Hold it at shoulder height with your elbow bent and your palm facing forward to make a banishing hamsa. Use this mudra or gesture to stop people who are speaking negatively or in a manner that drains your energy. When you hold up your hand, let it be a symbol to you that you are deflecting their negativity back to them and not absorbing it. This will help you resist engaging with negative people and their negative messages or energy.

While the Buddha used the right hand to stop negative energy, I believe that we can use either hand, especially in a pinch. As a symbol, the hamsa helps make us conscious of our ability to deflect negativity back to its source, banishing it from our own realm.

For Fertility, Babies, and Children

With historic connections to fertility, creativity, procreation, and children, the hamsa can be used by parents wanting to protect their children (fingers up to ward off negativity), parents who want to bestow blessings on their children (fingers down welcoming luck and good fortune), and women seeking to conceive (fingers down welcoming fertility). For those who seek to birth creative babies, the hamsa can be used to welcome artistic creativity, inspiration, and ideas.

Conclusion

However you choose to use it, the hamsa is an icon of magical versatility and power. The symbol can be made with your own hand, worn on the body, mounted in the home, hung over or on a door, or even tattooed on the body. With such strong and long-enduring magical powers, the hamsa is a great go-to amulet and icon. It's no wonder it has begun to appear—or reappear—in so many publicly visible places.

Selected Resources

"Ancient Site." Moundville Archaeological Park. Accessed November 23, 2017. https://moundville.ua.edu/ancient-site/.

"Buddha Mudras: Hand Positions of the Buddha." Lotus Sculpture. Accessed November 13, 2017. https://www.lotussculpture.com/mudras.html.

Burmese Art. "Mudras: Buddhist hand positions." Accessed August 29, 2017. https://www.burmese-art.com/about-buddha-statues/hand-positions.

Department of Near Eastern Art. "The Ubaid Period (5500 to 4000 B.C.)." Metropolitan Museum of Art. October, 2003. https://www.metmuseum.org/toah/hd/ubai/hd_ubai.htm.

Heaphy, Linda. "The Hamsa (Khamsa)." Kashgar. April 28, 2017. https://kashgar.com.au/blogs/ritual-objects/the-hamsa-khamsa.

Silvestra. "Inanna—Sumerian Mother Goddess, Queen of Heaven and Earth," *Goddess Inspired* (blog), June 10, 2012. https://goddessinspired.wordpress.com/2012/06/10/inanna-sumerian-mother-goddess-queen-of-heaven-and-earth/.

Walker, Barbara G. *The Woman's Dictionary of Symbols and Sacred Objects.* San Francisco: Harper and Row, 1988.

Water Magic

Ethical Considerations for Healing Circles

by Blake Octavian Blair

As magickal practitioners, most of us have an interest and an involvement in one or more healing arts. Healing spells and candle magick, Reiki, meditation, and the recitation of mantra and prayers are just a few of the many methods magickal persons employ with the noble goal of imparting healing and blessings to others. In times of need we also like to band together as a community to send healing in circles and groups to community members and those dear to community members. Further, we often like to contribute healing energies to masses of people and places affected by world events. However, there are ethics to consider when doing any healing work. The healing circle should discuss and explore the scope of the work so as to properly assess what exactly is an ethical scope in which to send healing.

First, it should be mentioned that while there are certainly magickally minded people who are also in medical professions, that is not the type of healing we will address here. The healing methods, modalities, and ethics surrounding them that will be discussed in this piece are in the domain of spiritual healing modalities and not medical. The medical professions have their own ethical realms, protocols, practices, and governances. In fact, there is considerably more discussion and material available elsewhere to read on medical ethics than there is on the ethics for those engaged in spiritual healing. So, let's begin our discussion regarding just a slice of the ethical questions for spiritual healing, the question of the scope of healing circles.

Most gatherings of healing practitioners have a distance-healing ceremony of some kind in which healing is sent on behalf of the collected group to those who are not present.

Even gatherings that aren't focused explicitly on healing will often perform one at some point toward the end of the proceedings, even if it's a small component amid the proceedings. After all, historically if you have a group of Witches, Druids, and the like, you have a group with a natural inclination toward the healing arts at hand. It's a powerful and fulfilling experience to be part of a community that sends healing into the ethers for others, including your loved ones. This is an admirable practice, but ethics must be followed and ground rules laid, or the effort can quickly slide into the darker shades of the magickal gray area.

Obtaining Permission

Permission is a paramount issue to discuss and make sure everyone understands. Much of the rest of the scope and ethics are decided from that juncture. Do you have express permission from the person to send them healing? This is a paramount ethical tenant in the ethos of many healing

modalities. In spiritual healing it is well accepted that you cannot help those who do not want to be helped. Permission makes the intent of all involved parties clear.

The most ideal route for obtaining this permission is asking the person in need directly if they would be open to you and others performing healing for them with whatever method it is you plan to use. Often times people in need will be more than open to various healing modalities, but some people, due to their personal background, beliefs, or other reasons, may not wish to partake of certain methods. I find it is rare, but it does occur, and their wishes should be respected.

There is an oft-mentioned gray area that arises with this point, however. Many feel it is okay to ask, "May I pray for you?" and then proceed to do whatever form of healing it is they practice for the person. Those practitioners view their healing practice as their form of prayer. This is a semantics game and a definite gray area. What would I do? This depends on context and the specific case. I generally will not perform the healing and will not use a semantics guise if the person's personal morals, ethics, or beliefs are against it. I must respect them. However, if it is simply that they may not understand what Reiki is if I used the term, for example, then I'll go ahead and use the rephrasing of prayer, obtain permission, and proceed to do the Reiki. This is of course only in cases in which I know the person well enough to understand that they'd be open to it if I were in a position to fully explain it. Sometimes the moment of need is not the moment ripe for education of what a certain term means.

This leads to a common issue in group healing circles: permission is often overlooked. Facilitators fail to mention in the preface to performing the healing that any persons worked on or names placed in the healing circle need to be people that permission has been granted from. This is often an innocent omission by an experienced facilitator who knows it's common sense to ask, and it slipped their mind to be explicit. Many people, especially "newbies," might either not have been taught this important ethic, or some may be so caught up in the desire of wanting to help a loved one that they aren't thinking clearly about if it's proper to put their loved one forth in the ceremony. I've attended countless Reiki Shares with distance healing circles, and I coordinate a shamanic healing circle. I have had several participants who were asked if the person they are requesting work for has granted permission, and we arrived at an answer of . . . no. If you are a facilitator for an event with a distance healing component, please take the utmost care to remember to be explicit with the importance of permission. If you are an attendee and the facilitator does not preface with a word about permission, feel free to speak up and inquire. The reaction to this from an educated and ethical healing arts practitioner will be one of gratitude for reminding them to speak a few words on the matter.

The Gray Areas of Permission

What do we do regarding permission when we have a large tragedy? When there is a natural disaster, terrorist attack, or other situation when entire groups or populations are in potential need of healing, how exactly do we tackle the obtaining of permission? This is an important question. The answer takes a certain amount of experience to determine. This is in large part due to gray areas and various variables. Surely, we cannot in this case obtain permission for every individual in a city affected by a tragedy, for example. Also, we certainly don't want to dismiss the fact there are many people in need who are likely agreeable to receiving needed healing in such a dire time and also are not in a position to be able to grant us permission directly. So, the question is, how do we step into the gray area while doing our best not to compromise our ethics? There is a caveat that is employed by many healing arts practitioners to assist in these tricky cases. It has no universal name, but let's dub it the "highest good clause." This involves

setting your intention in your opening prayer prior to doing
the healing and inserting verbiage in your statement or prayer
that the healing only be for the person's "highest good" or
state that the person's "higher self may accept or reject as
they see fit." This is of course imperfect. However, so would
be doing nothing when we can do something, in the eyes of
many. In fact, many in the healing arts and helping professions find it unethical to not help in some way, even if small.
In situations of mass suffering, these clauses and caveats may
perhaps satisfy the gray area for you in many instances. Apply
your own judgment. I find this an easier method to stomach
in cases of groups so large or far away that we cannot obtain

permission rather than with nearby individuals, which I will address shortly.

The highest good clause, while useful when applied with a bit of judgement, can lead to a slippery slope if not judiciously used. For example, I find that when it is applied, perhaps rightfully so, in a healing circle where names are being spoken aloud into the circle, the situation can quickly devolve to people passionately and mindlessly including the name of every large group they can think of, for which permission might be grayer even under the clause. This is especially true when it comes to statements that roll out of mouths: we aim to address "all those running in the election," which moves to "our entire government," which moves to "everyone in our country," and then "everyone in the entire world!" It can be a runaway train with absolutely no discernment. Surely, the ethics of asking for healing for every person in a governmental body or country is not the best application of such a clause.

Perhaps we can use some judgment and better apply it to a group affected by a tragedy, under duress, for which no possible way to grant permission is possible. I understand there are some pretty dire situations around the world, but I hardly think we can blanket permission-slip the entire human population. We need to use discernment and apply a bit more of a thought process when it comes to permission and when to default to a highest good clause and when to hold off. I'm not opposed to its use, but people use it with merry abandon as an excuse rather than as a pragmatic tool in applicable situations. Many of the large groups of people that it gets hastily applied to have members who would not accept such efforts. Healing should have focus and benefits from it. There is power in focus, and the less focus we have by blanketing too large a group, in which many may not be in need of the work or wouldn't wish to grant permission, dilutes the collective effort. Finding an appropriate scope for such a situation can feel tricky. We'd ideally like to find the intersection of helping the most people we can ethically send healing to while keeping the group a manageable scope for focusing power.

While we are discussing the concept of the highest good clause, it is important to also examine it in the context of a single individual. Sometimes a person is unable to consciously and expressly grant permission themselves. Perhaps the person in question is a young child and cannot really make these decisions for themselves yet. Perhaps the person is incapacitated due to level of injury, or they may be in a coma. There are numerous other scenarios that could be posited. In any situation in which you cannot obtain direct permission from the person, you might have it granted by a close loved one, caretaker, spouse, adult child, or similar. Keep in mind this works best if the person responds to your permission request according to what the wishes and the views of the person in question would be.

Sometimes, we don't have an easily accessible route to permission. At that point, the highest good clause may be something to consider. It is suggested in these situations that you try to connect with the spirit of the person, their higher self, and ask permission. If you are genuinely doing this, you'll soon find that the answer is not always a clear yes. Sometimes it will be an affirmative; other times they'll decline, or there'll be a bit of discussion of sorts. Then of course once permission is obtained, a line should be included in your intention or prayer at the outset, such as "for their higher self to accept or reject as they see fit."

When Permission Isn't Granted

After all we've discussed, what if we've not obtained permission and cannot ethically engage in the healing work? This may leave you feeling helpless, unable to assist, and as though your hands are tied. It shouldn't leave you feeling this way, though having pangs of such emotions is understandable. Remember, it is honorable to act from an ethical

place. It may feel as though we are unable to help, but even when somebody outright declines healing work, you may have provided the person something very valuable. People who end up in situations in which they are institutionalized, whether that be in a hospital, a nursing home, a mental health facility, or far more simply, temporarily bedridden with an illness, have often had the ability to make simple choices and decisions stripped from them. By approaching the person for permission, giving them a choice, and then honoring their decision, you serve to restore a bit of that power and autonomy back to them.

However, you aren't completely left in a place of inaction. In situations when permission is unclear, not provided, or simply too broad to obtain, an acceptable alternative course of action is to do a simple prayer for peace. To pray for a person or even a large group of people to be at peace simply means to experience compassion and express the desire that, whatever their situation, they may reach a state of calm, balance, and understanding. This isn't forcing healing upon a person who wishes not to have such intervention. Perhaps not having the intervention will allow them to be at peace. This action isn't trying to metaphysically sway an entire political body to make policy in a very specific direction to our individual desires but rather encourages that their decisions bring peace to all. It is not inaction toward a terminally ill person; it is wishing them peace and compassion with their situation and decisions and giving them respect. To be at peace is to be free of strife. To be at peace is to have mutual harmony. Everyone's best interests are met when peace is achieved.

An Ethical Conclusion

The discussion of what constitutes an ethical scope for healing circles and what the nuances are of having permission granted could well fill an entire lengthy volume of its own. However, hopefully this short piece has given you the contemplation points in order to navigate these waters yourself. I have offered a few of my personal opinions on what I may do; however, they are not applicable to every situation and may change depending on individual circumstances of specific situations. In the end you will have to arrive upon your own responses and develop your own moral compass in healing work.

An exploration of even moderate depth into the ethics of almost any topic will quickly lead into gray areas that will need navigation. Many have come before you with varying opinions to give you reference along the path, but when it comes to a real-life situation . . . it is you who will have to apply your moral compass, knowledge, and experience to the questions in front of you. Hopefully, what you've read here will assist you in that. I wish you and those you come in contact with peace, compassion, and good health!

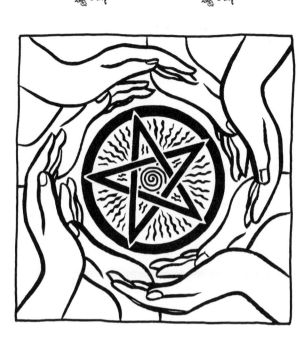

So You Want to Start a Coven?

by Alexandra Chauran

So you've decided that you'd like to start your very own coven of Witches. Perhaps you've been practicing the solitary lifestyle, meaning that you've been a Witch practicing magic or worship alone for a while, and now you'd like to try working with other Witches on your own terms. Perhaps you're new to this whole Witchcraft thing, but you have an enthusiastic gaggle of friends eager to learn alongside you. Maybe you've enjoyed a coven before, but circumstances such as a move, a new baby, too many people, or ideological differences have caused you to part ways. Whatever the reason, you're embarking on an incredible adventure that will teach you more than you can learn from any book. Make no mistake—there will be problems along the way. You're probably in for a lot more work than you anticipated. Starting a coven is an act of service, so if you take on the attitude of service as your mantle, you'll be just fine.

I remember when I first decided to start a coven. I had always been drawn to worshipping in a group of Witches. My parents drove me to witchy workshops and rituals when I was a teen. As a young undergraduate in university, I founded a Pagan student group. By the time I was in my early twenties, I was ready to settle down and let somebody else take the lead and teach me what I was supposed to be doing, in a traditional sense. Thank goodness I was wise enough to reach out to those who had gone before. After reading exemplary articles and books such as "Trollspotting" by Eran and *A Teaching Handbook for Wiccans and Pagans* by Thea Sabin, I stepped things up by watching other coven-leaders in action. I believe that the third step had to be from my gods, thrusting me into the leadership role once again.

After experiencing personality clashes and personal mistakes, I became a newly minted elder in my tradition in what was considered a foster coven, a place for me to learn and grow while I decided whether to return to my old coven or do something else. Suddenly, a highly regarded priest in my Wiccan community was diagnosed with cancer and made it known that starting a coven was on his bucket list. Since in my tradition a priest needs a high priestess to run a coven, I eagerly stepped forward to help a friend and to try to seek my heart's true home. What I found in starting a coven was so much more than I could ever have dreamed. I forged a bond with my coven-mates that was closer than family, and I unwrapped my faith like a present of many layers.

Important Steps to Starting a Coven

Since my steps toward starting a coven worked for me, I'm going to present them here for you and share a few of the lessons that I learned the hard way.

Step 1. Research and Fix Your Mind on Your Goal

Figure out what you really want from practicing Witchcraft in a coven. Are you looking forward to becoming a teacher yourself? If so, you'll want to form a "teaching coven." A teaching coven is one that focuses on paying forward the gifts and knowledge that are received from the coven. As a member of a teaching coven, you can look forward to regular and increasing public outreach as you search for students, as well as frequent changes to your coven membership as your coven hives, or splits into two smaller covens, when it gets too large.

Conversely, you may be interested in a "working coven." We're Witches, right? That means we can focus our force of will on what we want in life and make it happen.

In the beginning of your coven formation, you'll need to fully visualize what sort of coven bonds and practice you want to form. What will you actually do in your coven, and how will you treat each other when you gather?

Step 2: Find a Mentor

In many areas of the world, books are the only windows to the wisdom of those who have walked a path before you and chose to tell the tale. Reach out if you are lucky enough to have access to an experienced coven leader, called a queen; coleaders, which might include a magus, the high priest of the coven; a maiden, who is the understudy to the queen; or a summoner, who is the communications face of the coven. Learning from another coven can take the form of a Wicca 101 class, a book club, glorified ice cream social, or even just hanging out with the coven leaders in their homes.

In any case, the key to your learning is to ask the right questions. If two people were learning from the same coven mentors at the same time, the person who asked the most questions would learn the very most. So, lay aside your pride and bring up whatever questions spring to mind as you learn. As you see what works and what doesn't, you'll revise the initial image of what you're going to be doing with your coven.

Step 3: Find Your People

If you don't already have wannabe Witches beating down your door, you'll have to reach out to find some members for your coven. Keep in mind that your coven won't be right for absolutely everyone. There might be people out there willing to cause harm, or at least trouble, to your coven and household.

If you're meeting strangers, it is essential that you make your first meeting outside of your home. Post flyers anywhere you want, such as metaphysical bookstores, coffee shops, festivals, or online. Interview newcomers in a coffee shop, pub, library, or bookstore to determine whether they have the same goals and to make sure they're respectful and responsible. Set a date and a time on the calendar and get started.

Step 4: Reflect, Be Flexible, Learn, and Grow

You'll need to be flexible to the needs of your coven and to your own boundaries as a coven leader. You may find yourself in the position of asking a coven member to take a break, often called a sabbatical, or even to leave the coven to find their own way or to be placed in another coven that you recommend. Be brave, and make the decision that best benefits your coven, your practice, and your gods.

∼

In conclusion, I'd like to encourage folks to avoid some common mistakes that I have learned the hard way. Treat all your mentors with respect at all times, and consult them first even with your disagreements in their teachings, so that misunderstandings can be corrected before feelings are hurt. Don't set ultimatums, spread gossip, or cause drama. If you find yourself needing to shop around for a new coven, make sure you do so with the full knowledge of your existing coven.

Starting a coven can be a rewarding way to learn and to serve one's gods. I pray that you serve others well as a teacher and always temper your power with humility.

Conjuring the Silver Thread: Cultivating a Spiritual Bond with the Ancestors of Our Craft

by Storm Faerywolf

Working with spirits is a hallmark of the Witches' Craft. Whether we see those spirits as being the spiritual consciousness within a plant, a stone, an animal, a place, or even that of a faery, an angel, an ancestor, or a deity, Witches place themselves in a position to engage these nonhuman intelligences to learn the deeper magical secrets of nature. But of all the spirits with whom a Witch may choose to work, none are as deeply personal—or as eerily fascinating—as those of the dead.

Honoring the dead in Witchcraft is twofold. On a personal level, we honor our ancestors, whom we poetically refer to as the "beloved dead." These are family members (both biological and those made by marriage and adoption) and are usually considered to be those spirits who are "closest" to us, meaning that they are more immediately accessible. On a transpersonal level, we honor the spirits of those Witches and Warlocks who have gained enough power in this life to be able to retain an astral pattern of consciousness postdeath and now exist in a state in which they offer assistance to living Witches. These are the "mighty dead," and they might be specific to a particular lineage or tradition or could be those luminaries who affected the course of the Craft and continue to work toward bettering the Craft from the other side.

Honoring and working with the dead has long been a core practice of the Witches' Craft. While it is a popular observance for Witches to honor the dead at Samhain (when the veil between the living and the dead is said to be at its

thinnest), we work year-round to cultivate and deepen our bond with them.

The following ritual is really just the beginning of a practice aimed at forming an intimate relationship with the mighty dead. While the first part of the rite is to be done at your altar, the second part (and the subsequent practice that it begins) will require an outdoor place where you will plant one or more seeds and maintain a living plant. If you have no outdoor space or your environment will not support the growing of a sunflower, you may use an indoor pot instead.

This rite relies heavily on your ability to enter and maintain an open trance state as well as to practice automatic writing. If you need additional tools or practices to accomplish this, please feel free to add them to this working.

The rite can be used at any time of the year, especially special markers of the year such as your birthday or New Year's, or whenever else you feel you wish to embark on this journey. Since this rite involves planting and nurturing a seed, make sure your local environment will be harmonious to cultivating a small plant at that time or else adapt the ritual to grow it indoors.

You will need:

Photo of, or personal belonging from, one of your beloved dead

White or red candle

Photo of the mighty dead with whom you wish to work (or you can create a sigil for them)

Silver candle

Offerings for your dead (such as food, whiskey, etc.)

1 or more sunflower seeds

Incense burner and charcoal

Copal resin

"Spirits of the Dead" oil blend (perhaps one that includes anise)

Black candle

Ritual blade (optional)

Pen or pencil (You can also use special inks, if desired, such as dragon's blood.)

Paper for drawing

Short length of silver thread

Pitcher of water

Spoon or spade

Setting Up

An ancestral altar should be placed in the west and have these items arranged in the following manner: the photo or item belonging to your beloved dead on one side along with the red (or white) candle, and the photo or sigil of your mighty dead on the other with the silver candle. Place their offerings near their photos and the sunflower seed(s) in the center of the altar. Encircle the seeds with the silver thread. The incense burner may be placed anywhere you would like. Have the other items nearby.

The Ritual

Ground and center. Perform whatever preliminary prayers you feel are appropriate. Light the incense.

We will open the western gate, which is the poetic term for a magically created portal between the worlds of the living and the dead, giving us more immediate access to the ancestors and the dead. Face west and contemplate the dead. Think of any friends or family members who have passed on and allow yourself to feel the loss of them. Anoint the center of your forehead with the oil and imagine it assisting you in opening up your inner sight to the dead.

With your breath slow and deep, light the black candle and make a statement of intention, such as,

> *I stand between the worlds of fate*
> *And summon forth the western gate.*
> *By my blade (or hands), I part the veil.*
> *Across the sea we set our sail.*

With your blade, make a vertical gesture from above to below, imagining that you are slicing through the fabric of space and time, revealing the hidden realm beyond. See this like a watery, ghostly light just beyond this imagined opening you have created. Still focusing on your breath and the presence of the dead, physically and psychically reach into that opening. With an outward sweeping motion of your arms, cast open this gate, imagining it becoming wide open before you. Say,

> *By moon that hangs low in the sky,*
> *By ancient sea, the earth's own womb,*
> *I call the gate to open wide,*
> *That leads to life beyond the tomb.*

Take a moment to feel this power shine upon you from the gate and know that *you* are the gate; the opening is but an extension of your own spiritual power.

Light the white (or red) candle and call out the name(s) of your beloved dead, along with any titles or descriptions of accomplishments that are relevant to their personal mythology. Take some time to honor their presence. Silently send them love and awareness of the offering you present to them.

In their presence, we are brought closer to the mysteries of death. And so here we now call to our mighty dead; those spirits of Witches and Warlocks passed from this life. They offer to us the silver thread—the connection and magic of the spirits—so that we may better learn the magic of our deep ancestors and the magic yet to be known in this world. Their passing from this world offers up the seeds of renewal . . .

and with their guidance, we plant those seeds that they may grow into power for the coming year. Light the silver candle and say,

> I call to you, O mighty dead,
> To enter through the western gate
> And weave here now the silver thread
> That guides me toward the Witch's fate!

Be open to their presence now. As assuredly as the wind does blow, they are with us. Call to them with an open heart! Send them love and awareness of the offering you give to them. Ask them to extend to you the silver thread of their spiritual knowledge. Imagine taking that thread and following it toward that which you need to know . . . what the Mighty Dead wish to tell you . . .

> Mighty dead, I call upon your guidance.
> Empower me to receive your message.

Maintaining your trance and that sense of connection, take your pen and paper and begin automatic writing. Just write whatever comes through. Try not to judge it in the moment. You may begin just doodling, drawing circles, shapes—just allow the energy to come through while you are moving pen against paper. Spend as much time as you need writing and drawing, imagining the mighty dead guiding your hand through the connection of the silver thread. You may wish to chant something to keep the energy moving.

> Ancient Witches, mighty dead,
> From you I take the silver thread.

When you feel you are done, look at your paper. This is your message from the Mighty Dead. It could be a word, phrase, or perhaps a symbol. Or it may appear to be nothing more than gibberish. But if even so, it is a start. You need not understand it. Whatever you see, know that the ancient and mighty ones of the Craft have given you this message that you may use to strengthen your own connection to the ancestors of our Craft and to deepen your own power in the coming year.

Now, take the silver thread and hold it in your hands. Be open to the presence of the mighty dead and ask for their guidance. Close your eyes and feel them here with you. Feel their presence in the silver thread that you hold as you claim that connection to them. Holding their presence in your heart, take three breaths of power and then blow life force out onto the thread with each exhale, while tying a knot to bind that presence there (three breaths, three knots).

Now, go to your outdoor space with your message paper, your seeds, and the small pitcher of water. (Or go get a pot filled with potting soil.) Take the message paper and breathe out three times upon it. Fold it in half toward yourself, rotate it 90 degrees clockwise, breathe on it three more times, and fold it toward yourself again. Repeat this process one more time and then roll the paper toward yourself, wrapping and tying it with the silver thread while you chant,

Ancient Witches, mighty dead,
From you I take the silver thread.

Using a spoon or spade, dig out a small amount of dirt and then place the thread-wrapped message paper inside the hole. Place some of the soil on top of this, and then scoop up the sunflower seeds and breathe three breaths of power over them. Plant them in the soil about one inch deep and about six inches apart if you are planting more than one, all the while repeating,

Flower of the golden Sun,
The seed of life that comes from death,
Awakened by the Witch's breath,
Arise! The magic has begun!

Continue to chant until the last seed is planted. Now, place your hands over the pitcher of water and charge the water with energy. Focus on this water being a catalyst for the spiritual power to "take root" in this plant that you will now grow. Water the seeds with this water, and repeat the process of watering the seeds with charged water every day for a week.

End the ritual by closing the western gate: imagine the gate closing as you sweep your arms closed, and then trace a pentacle over the area with your hands or your blade. Proceed as you would normally, making sure to thank all the spirits you have invited and extinguish the candles safely. Allow the offerings to remain in place for twenty-four hours and then dispose of them in a reverential manner.

As the flower grows, so will your spiritual connection to the mighty dead. The plant's petals, leaves, and seeds will be potent tools in your continued work with them when used as part of your spells, such as in a charm bag, a poppet, or an incense or bath blend. You can also use the plant as a meditative portal, allowing your consciousness to travel down its roots into the underworld for trance journeys with the dead as it provides a symbolic anchor for you to more easily return. As you work with the plant, both its spirit and that of the mighty dead will guide you.

Io Evohe! Blessed be.

Processing Grief
by Charlynn Walls

Though death is a part of the natural cycle of life, it is still a difficult process to navigate through. It can be especially painful for those individuals who have lost a spouse, child, sibling, or parent. While I have written on the topic of death and dying previously in the almanac, those essays were geared toward getting over the initial shock of the loss.

We will discuss what happens beyond that devastating event. What do we do after the initial shock has passed and we try to move forward again? As we all know, grief is a process that must be worked through. Grief does not always abate quickly or easily. It is sometimes necessary to take it one day at a time.

One Day at a Time

Each day brings new opportunities for change along with the challenges. Some days are much easier than others. I lived with my grandmother while I attended college directly after high school. She and I were very close. While I was not present for the episode that required her transportation to the hospital, I was the one who held the hospital staff accountable for following her living will. There were days that I felt comfortable with that decision. On those days breathing seemed easier. There were also days when I questioned if I should have gone a different route, and one of those days was a burden I carried like a lead weight on my chest.

There were times when I lacked motivation to proceed with my daily life. I had to do small daily meditations that gave me a moment to focus and recharge so that I could face the mundane tasks of the day. One daily devotion that I started after the passing of my grandmother was to greet the day. I literally faced the day as it broke over the horizon and absorbed the light and energy from the Sun. Now, I realize not everyone wakes at dawn. On those days when I could sleep in I did, and when I woke I would do the same thing. That daily devotion allowed me the ability to get out of bed, and, believe me, it was sometimes a challenge.

Personal Care

This leads into the importance of self-care. We are kind to those around us and take their feelings into consideration. However, we rarely afford ourselves the same consideration. It will take you a while to feel like yourself again. That is okay. You may also feel like you are not quite ready to face the world. That is okay. You will know when the time is right for you to reemerge.

In the meantime, you can do small things for yourself:

Rest: Take the time to rest. There are many times when we throw ourselves into work or other activities to take our minds off the loss, but this can have negative health effects. Go to bed at the same time each night. Even though you may not be able to sleep at first, you will find that your body will relax a little more each night you do this. Finally, sleep will come.

Eat: I know the thought of food can be repulsive when you are in the throes of grief. However, if you do not at least take small bites of food here and there, you will run yourself down. If you are run down, your immune system becomes compromised and you are more prone to illness. You are not good to yourself or others if you are sick.

Exercise: If your mind will not quit racing, give it something to think about. This might be lifting weights, running, or just taking a walk around the block. I often go for a walk on the walking path near my home when my mind is mulling over a problem. The physical activity makes me tired, and then it is often easier to rest. It provides the added benefit of physical strength and health.

Take Some Downtime: This suggestion can be the hardest for us to do. Downtime looks different to everyone. This can be a day off from work to do an enjoyable activity. I personally like to read, as it allows me to enter another realm, where my problems no longer exist. This could also be seeing a movie or hanging out with friends. It could also be an hour of quiet solitude. Whatever lets you unwind, take the time to do it, and it will help you to recharge and prepare for another day.

Grief Jar Ritual

In addition to the mundane things we can do to help us cope in our time of need, we can also take a magickal approach. Rituals help us traverse intense feelings and can bring an element of clarity.

You will need:

Altar

Empty dish

30 dark-colored stones (These should fit in your pocket and hand easily.)

Large jar (Size is dependent on the size of the stones you choose, though a large quart-size mason jar works well for this purpose.)

Dark-colored cloth or dark-colored cloth pouch (to store the stones in before carrying them with you)

Container of black salt

Dish of water

Gather all the items that you need prior to beginning the ritual and place them on the altar. I recommend that you place the empty vessel in the center of the altar with the pouch or cloth with the stones directly behind it. You can then place the black salt to the left and the water to the right side of the empty vessel. This allows for easy access to all the components for mixing and blessing items.

The first step will be for you to cast a simple circle. I suggest that you cast the circle in the manner you feel the most comfortable with. When I do this, I tend to close my eyes and envision myself surrounded by a sphere of white light. I can make my circle as small or wide as I need. Make sure that you have enough room for the altar and for you to work comfortably. Once you have established your circle, take a deep breath and exhale.

Call the quarters. Feel free to create your own quarter calls or expand on what is provided here. I typically begin in the north based on my experience in the tradition I follow. You may have a reason for calling the quarters in a different order, and that is fine.

North: *Hail to the guardians of the north, the guardians of stability and strength. Grant me the ability to find firm footing along this unstable path. Welcome!*

East: *Hail to the guardians of the east, the guardians of knowledge and transitions. Grant me the understanding to accept the changes that are in motion. Welcome!*

South: *Hail to the guardians of the south, the guardians of will and action. Grant me the ability to continue moving forward. Welcome!*

West: *Hail to the guardians of the west, the guardians of emotion and healing. Grant me serenity in the eye of the storm. Welcome!*

Invite in the God and Goddess. You can use any pantheon that you are comfortable working with. I suggest using deities associated with transitions and the underworld as they are appropriate to deal with death and dying.

Lord and Lady, gather near and offer your insight and council. Welcome!

Face your altar and the items that you have gathered. You will now want to bless and charge the stones so that they are ready for their purpose of absorbing negativity and grief. Take the black salt and water from their separate vessels and combine them in the empty dish. Once they have been mixed together and the salt has dissolved, sprinkle the mixture onto the stones while chanting the following. The stones are now cleansed and ready to be blessed and charged.

Chant,

Lord and Lady, feel my anguish and despair; lessen my load and make it easier to bear.

Once you feel that enough energy has been raised, you can release it and direct it into the stones. They are now blessed and charged for their purpose.

Now it is time to release the quarters.

Lord and Lady, thank you for lifting my burden and making the journey easier. Stay if you will; go if you must.

West: *Guardians of the west, thank you for helping me find my emotional balance. Hail and farewell.*

South: *Guardians of the south, thank you for enabling me to push past the paralyzing fear of the unknown. Hail and farewell.*

East: *Guardians of the east, thank you for the ability to approach the situation with a rational mind. Hail and farewell.*

North: *Guardians of the north, thank you for providing me strength to go on. Hail and farewell.*

Finally, it is time to close the circle. Close your eyes and hold in your mind the white sphere of your sacred space. Watch the sphere shrink and dissolve into a thin line of a glowing circle around you. See it weaken in intensity until the sphere is completely gone. Take a cleansing breath and release it as the last of the circle dissipates.

Though the stones are now prepared, the real work is set to begin. Each day that you get up and go about your day you will take a stone from the pouch that they were in and place it in your pocket or purse. Carry it with you. This is a daily reminder of the grief you also carry. You can feel the weight of it in your hand or as you carry it in your pocket. As you feel those momentary spikes in your anxiety or despair, funnel it into the stone.

At the end of the day take five minutes to reflect on those times during the day that you felt overwhelmed. Understand that it was a momentary feeling but that you will never forget your loved one. When you feel ready to let go of the day and the grief associated with it, place the stone in the jar. Notice that your chest feels lighter, it is easier to breathe, and your mood lightens as you do so.

Each day you will repeat the processes. At the end of the month you will need to take the jar and let moving water run over the stones to cleanse them of the despair and remaining grief. You will remove the metal lid from the mason jar and replace that with the cloth or pouch you used to store the stones in and fit the metal ring around that. This creates a semipermeable membrane that will allow water to flow in and out.

You can utilize water running from your faucet in your bathroom or you can visit a nearby creek, stream, or river and allow natural water to run across the stones. Either way, you will want to hold the jar in the running water and visualize the emotions that you stored in the stone being released and flowing out of the stones and away from you.

You can continue the daily and monthly process until you feel you are relieved of your burden. At this time, you could open the jar and deposit the stones permanently into a stream to truly let go of the grief.

Conclusions

Mentally, I feel that we understand that life follows the cycles of life, death, and rebirth. Emotionally, it can be much more difficult to let go of the person we loved. We miss their spirit, laughter, and companionship. We have to go on doing the work of living even after those individuals have left us.

The work of living after loss is a process. Each day has its own unique set of experiences and choices. We must be willing to feel the emotions and work through them. Only by doing so will we be free to move forward.

Back to the Basics: Self-Care with the Elements and Your Tarot Deck

by Melissa Cynova

I have an anxiety disorder. I never learned how to properly deal with stress, so my brain instead built up this elaborate catchall of "what to do when stuff goes sideways." My brain instructed my person that if I clean the entire house at 2 a.m., I definitely won't get laid off. If I eat a salad instead of that fantastic taco, I will suddenly feel better about my body and myself. It seems that if my family or friends are under stress or experiencing a loss, I feel the need to pile more things on myself to create some sort of hyperaware force field around them. If I stress out, everyone will be just fine, right?

Well, no. That's actually really stupid, but it's the way that my brain works. Whether that's a fixed neurological pathway or really ingrained behavior, I'm not sure. What I do know is that if I need it to stop—that constant braying of *fix it, fix it, fix it*—then the best thing I can do is sit down.

After I sit down, I try to get back to the basics. What can I control? What is clearly and wholly outside of my control? Usually, the problem is like 99.9 percent out of my control. What I can handle, though, is me. And since I'm me, and I'm a card-slinger, I can control my tarot cards too. I decide which part of my life this particular problem belongs to. Since I am a Witch, I use the elements to do this.

Earth: Home

If, for example, your mother-in-law gifted you all of your Great Aunt Rita's (may she rest in peace) furniture and antiques and tchotchkes and whatnot, and they're currently taking up residence in your already crowded house, this can cause stress. You don't want to upset your mother-in-law, but you know that breathing in your own house is important. So what do you do?

You get your tarot deck out and decide what you're going to keep or share with a family member. Or are you going to sell or donate the item? For each item or set of items, you pull a card:

Major Arcana: This is meaningful and needs a decision. Do you keep it? Find a home for it in the family?

Minor Arcana: See ya! It goes on its way.

Now, I'm sure you're ahead of the game already and see the cards as an extraneous decision-maker, but that's what you need in this situation. How often have you looked at a chair and wanted to get rid of it, but the guilt made you hold on? If you pull a card on it and find that you're arguing with the decision you've made, you know exactly what to do with that chair, right?

After you've gone through one room at a time (just one at a time, mind you—this is not a reality show, so no hurry needed), give that room a good once-over with a sage stick or some sweetgrass and reset the energy. It will make everything feel better.

Air: Mind

Are you bored? Are you frustrated or disengaged at work? Some folks are the most destructive when they are bored. That "do something" energy spins around, knocking over lamps and messing with relationships. The best thing to do when you're anxious or bored about work or even when you just need to refresh your mental acuity is to visit your brain objectively.

Hello, brain. How's it going? Ooh, not so great, huh? You've been doing this work for four years, and it's become completely tedious? And you work with a bunch of jerks? How frustrating. Tell me, then, the following things:

1. What do you really like to do?
2. Do you need more education to do that?
3. If you're doing what you want, can you do it somewhere else?

I encourage you to pull out your cards for this exercise. Let them confirm and tease out what the problem is. And then— and this is really the important part—do something about it. Change your job. Go back to school. Find a new position.

Whatever you do, remember that the whole point of it—over everything, really—is to be happy. It's difficult to achieve happiness when you spend more than forty hours a week at a place you don't like or can't thrive in.

Fire: Body

I could write a whole book about body issues that people have (and I am, actually, in the middle of writing one in which the body takes up one-fifth of the space).

A simple exercise to get to the base of your physical self is one of gratitude. Draw a map of your body, and on it draw all the scars, bumps, wrinkles, fissures, scuffs, and stretch marks that you can.

For each event (for that's what all of these were—events), I want you to pull a card telling you how that event changed your life, for good or for bad. That childbirth, that broken leg, those fifty pounds gained, lost, and gained again. I want you to ask the tarot one question: "How did this shape me?"

You'll find that even the rough patches were for a cause and that those events led you to who you are today. Say,

Thank you, body, for getting me here. For protecting me. For coming out on the other side.

Say thank you and burn the picture, letting the ashes fly away with your gratitude.

Water: Emotions

A lot of times emotional overwhelm is either from an overabundance of emotional drama or from not knowing what your baseline feels like. As I mentioned earlier, I have an anxiety disorder, so my baseline runs high. I can tell (or my partner can tell) if things are going wackadoo on me because I exhibit certain behavioral tells. I have circular thinking, I get upset over small things that normally wouldn't matter, I am short tempered, and so on. When these things start up, I have a seat with them and pull out the suit of cups from a deck of tarot.

The cups are aligned with emotion, and I use them to tell me what is a big deal . . . and what is not. What I can control, and what I cannot.

Make a list of up to five stressors, write them down, and pull a card for each. You can put the cards back in the deck after you've written which card goes to each stressor. When I do this, I ignore the standard meanings of the cards and go for the numbers. If I pull a 1 through 5, things are manageable or I can put them down. Cards 6 through king are ones I need to tend to. After I put them in order (crisis/king first), I get to work.

These rituals are simple but powerful. It's important to remember, however, that the power comes after you start the work. It isn't enough to recognize that there is a problem. You also have to do something about it.

Spirit: Soul

A lot of my clients are surprised when I ask them what their relationship with spirit is. I suppose it is an unusual question. I see matters of religion and spirituality as hugely private, and so don't often go there with my clients.

I have found, however, that I can tell if there is a lack of spiritual alignment. You can have the best job, have the best partner, and take care of your physical self in an amazing

home, but if you don't have a spiritual element to your life, there is something lacking.

This doesn't mean go to church, temple, or synagogue every week. This means find a practice outside of your day-to-day, outside of *you*. You can volunteer, go for a walk in the woods, spend some time with friends once a week. Whatever it is. If you do decide to go for a more traditional spiritual exercise, though, try asking your cards these questions:

1. What is missing in my life spiritually?
2. What spiritual baggage can be removed from me?
3. What can I add to my life to enhance my spiritual connection?

Remembering that a connection to other, to outside, is a spiritual connection. You can find answers in books, in a sacred space, or in a walk in the woods. You can even find it across the table from a dear friend, talking smack and cracking jokes. Spirit can be structured or loose, intense or relaxed. As long as it exists, you will see a difference in your life.

A Glamour Dinner Party Rite

by Deborah Castellano

If you are unfamiliar with glamour as a magical con-cept, your mind may immediately go to Sephora or current Hollywood faves. While they are a part of what makes up the whole of glamour, the additional part to consider is what makes you interesting and exciting to yourself and others. Magically speaking, you would use your glamour to give your intention a push (. . . some-times a shove). Glamour is used to help you see doors that are about to open to you, recognize potential allies, and see potential outcomes more clearly, and it gives you the ability to figure out how to be perfectly charm-ing as needed, as one of my mentors would say.

Why do you do magic? If you are doing magic minus the spiritual worship aspect (which also a completely valid practice, of course), you Want something.

No, no. I just–

No. You Want something. You Want something so badly that you're willing to get into a chicken fight with the universe to get it. You Want something so badly that you're willing to admit to desire. You Want something so badly that you're willing to use means and methods that are laughed at by 75 percent of the first world's population. You Want something so much that you can't sleep, you can't eat, you're sick with it.

Let's break down why people do magic:

- Protection
- Revenge
- Love
- Sex

- Power
- Money
- Fame

You can couch it however you like, but this is what it boils down to. In what scenario would glamour be a hindrance? Here's a hint: *um, none of them.*

Protection: Who gets more protection—someone who people feel inclined to help and protect or someone who people don't feel inclined to help and protect? Why do they feel inclined to protect you? You have the attractive or exciting quality that makes certain people or things seem appealing or special.

Revenge: When you want an eye for an eye and you're looking for the universe to salt the earth on your behalf, what would make goddesses and spirits more inclined to help you over someone else? The attractive or exciting quality that makes certain people or things seem appealing or special.

Love: What makes you interested in someone else? What makes someone else interested in you? The attractive or exciting quality that makes certain people or things seem appealing or special.

Sex: What makes you want to get down with someone? What makes someone else want to hook up with you? The attractive or exciting quality that makes certain people or things seem appealing or special.

Power: When describing powerful people, what words are often used regardless of appearance? Magnetic, forceful, commanding, influential. What makes someone all of those things? The attractive or exciting quality that makes certain people or things seem appealing or special.

Money: How do you get hired for a job over someone else? How do you get more of an inheritance than

your cousins? How do you get insider investing tips? Through the attractive or exciting quality that makes certain people or things seem appealing or special.

Fame: How does someone get famous even though it's a scientific fact that there are many people in this world who work harder, have more talent, and have more influence and better connections? Through the attractive or exciting quality that makes certain people or things seem appealing or special.

Host a Dinner Party

Who do you think is going to win in the chicken fight with the universe? The person who is using glamour as part of their magical practice or a person who is doing the same practice but without glamour? Coffee's only for closers, and you, my friend, need to be a closer.

So let's have a dinner party and take your glamour out for a trot so you get comfortable using it. Bonus: now your guests will have a foot in the door with glamour too!

Step 1: Select the Guest List for Your Party

Everyone should be able to fit comfortably around your table. While each guest doesn't have to be a Witch, it will work better if you pick people who are either Witchcraft-adjacent or tend to be game for anything. You want a mix of people who get along well and perhaps one unexpected guest—someone from out of town, someone new to you, someone's new significant other. Children would probably be difficult to manage for your first magical dinner party, though you may be able to figure out how to include them for a magical brunch in the future with some practice.

Step 2: Choose Your Intention

Let's start small. You can have as many dinner parties as you like, *n'est-ce pas*? You can always go bigger later. Maybe you want to get a piece published in a small magazine, maybe you want to sing at an open mike, maybe you want a meeting to go well, maybe you want to attract a partner, maybe you want a flirty vibe with your current partner. It's up to you. Make it tangible and set a time frame to accomplish it. Prep your guests to do the same.

Step 3: Set the Scene

Make sure your house is in good order and you have the table arranged as simply or as extravagantly as you would like. Mason jars full of fresh flowers, tiny succulents, fresh herbs in heaps, seasonal fruit in a vase, seashells, natural stones, tealights—whatever strikes you. Consider if you want to burn some incense beforehand. Ponder music choices. If you want to create a cohesive wardrobe for everyone, suggest that everyone wear black or white. Most people have either or both in their closets, so there shouldn't be too much whining.

Step 4: Set the Menu

What food is both glamorous and affordable to you? In my circles, it's usually an epic-size antipasto plate that takes up most of the table with bread, different cheeses, olives, artichoke hearts, dried meats, fresh figs, bruschetta, and cold beans. I always enjoy that because it's affordable and even my pickiest and most diet-restricted guests can usually find something they'll eat.

If you're not into antipasto, think about setting a grazing table with vegan treats, carnivorous delights, fresh light nibbles, heavily decadent tiny dishes—whatever would please both you and your guests the most. Eating with your hands and dipping with bread adds glamour to the event. Pinterest and Instagram are going crazy with how photogenic grazing tables are even if you have a small budget and a small table.

Consider a signature cocktail for the evening or bottles of champagne. I often serve Verdi or a champagne from my local grocery store, both of which are less than five dollars a bottle. If your guests aren't drinkers, consider a variety of fruit- or herb-infused waters.

Have your guests each bring a dessert that will add decadence to your glamour, which is always a good mix. On a magical level, when everyone contributes something that everyone will consider eating, it makes for a stronger *egregore*.

Step 5: First Ritual

Before you eat, have small bowls or teacups at each guest's place. One should be filled with salt, one should be filled with fresh spring water with a little rose water in it, and one should have some fresh sage leaves in it.

Put an extra napkin by each person's plate. Have your guests take a moment to remind themselves of their individual intention. Have your guests consider what's keeping them from their intention. Then have your guests touch the salt to their lips. Have your guests pick up the sage leaves and smell them. Have your guests then dip their fingertips in the rosewater and touch their fingertips to their foreheads.

Step 6: Second Ritual

After dinner, have everyone consider their intention again and focus on obtaining it. Teach your guests the

mantra ॐ नमः शिवाय, *Om Namaḥ Śivāya*. I bow to the divine within me.

Say it three times together, each focusing on opening your glamour to the universe so that you can manifest your intention.

Step 7: Third Ritual

After dessert is finished, have everyone draw an omen for their intention. It could be using tarot, bibliomancy drawn from each guest's selection from your bookshelves, drawing runes, a screw eye on a thread that you make for each guest as a pendulum for yes or no questions. My personal favorite to use with a group is the Golden Moth Illumination Deck because there's not a set interpretation for each card, which makes it much more novice friendly.

Step 8: Farewell!

When it's time for your guests to leave, when you say goodbye, take a moment with each other to wish each other well in your respective intentions. Be sure to catch up in the weeks to come to see who has manifested what for themselves!

Bad Magickal Breakups
by Najah Lightfoot

Betrayal. Revenge. Promises broken, vows tainted. I would bury thee, I would spit at thee, I would rail at thee. I would take thine image, carve it into a candle, and bury it in a graveyard. I howl at the Moon. I weep, I cry. I tear at my hair, burn my clothes. The Sun sheds no light upon me and I am trapped in an eyeless fog. All is suspect. I trust no one. Jealousy, envy, rage, and anger are my constant companions.

What has happened to me?

I've had a bad magickal breakup. It happens. It happens in covens, groves, groups, and communities. It happens between friends, teachers, and your best magickal buddies. And when it happens to you, as oft times it will when you set upon the magickal path, it can break your heart and burn your soul.

It's a hush-hush subject. No one wants to talk about it or admit it has happened to them. A bad magickal breakup leaves you feeling vulnerable and scared. It can haunt your dreams and cloud your waking moments.

Loss and Separation in the Magickal Community

Separation for any reason is hard. Lovers leave us, spouses get divorced, and friendships fall apart. Breakups are some of the most difficult things we experience as social creatures. As human beings, we long for family, community, society. The desire to come together is encoded in our DNA. Since the dawn of our species, we have come together as tribes, clans, families, and partners. We thrive when we come together.

When those ties are broken, it can take us a lifetime to recover, if we ever do. It can take days, weeks, or months of soul-searching therapy. It can take ten thousand nights of crying on a best friend's shoulder or even picking up and moving away to a new place to recover. It some cases it may even take more than one lifetime to recover. However long it takes, one thing is for sure: it takes courage, strength, and long, hard, and sometimes painful work to pull yourself up and move forward. And once you do move forward, it can be extremely difficult to trust someone again.

Now take the power of those romantic, familial, or friendship breakups and add magickal vows or covenants to them. Add the vulnerability of trusting a teacher, a leader, a high priest or priestess, a guru, a mambo, or a hougan with your magickal training, your scarlet cord or soul in a clay pot. If the relationship works, you've got a recipe for success, trust, and guidance on the highest level, but if it doesn't, you can be left with a burnt casserole that will reek forever and never taste sweet again.

The path of a seeker, novice, or apprentice can be a hard, lonely, rocky road. It twists and turns, leads you down dark paths, and constantly makes you second-guess yourself. It tests your strength, your will, and your passion. As seekers, we long for guidance, but it can be extremely difficult to find teachers or people you can trust and believe in to guide you and help you grow in your chosen path. There are many people out there who say they can and will lead, but sometimes you end up with charlatans or someone in the position for their own selfish and egotistical gains, who harms countless people and damages many a soul, while they pump up their own false images of pomp and grandeur.

As we travel our magickal paths, we need to be careful. We need to use discernment. But even the most cynical and jaded of us will get our fingers burnt and our hearts torn from time to time. Perhaps it doesn't happen to us as often because we've got callouses on our hearts to protect us, earned from surviving setbacks, betrayals, and disappointments.

More often than not the ones who get really hurt are the new ones, the novices, the seekers early on their path, who mistakenly get trapped by hooded robes, "secret" knowledge, and vague promises—promises given but rarely kept.

Yet all the great ones have been down this road and survived it. Those who walk their path with integrity and substance have fallen into the snares, been caught in the brambles, and clawed their way out of the stink and emerged as true leaders and trusted members of the community. They've earned respect. They've dealt with the pain of betrayal and broken promises and turned it into something good. They've maintained good relationships and kept bridges intact, none of it easy, none of it worthless.

Sadness and Betrayal: How to Cope When You Lose a Magickal Teacher

So if bad juju gets dumped on you, what can you do? How can you survive it?

First and foremost, swaddle yourself in the most loving environment you can find. Lean on a trusted friend. Don't tell everyone; maybe only one or two people you believe you can trust, and definitely don't blast it on social media. Social media rants can harm you, your family, or innocent people in ways you may not have considered.

Shut down, shut in. If there aren't people in your circle of friends and family you can trust with your emotions and situation, find a therapist. There's nothing better than spilling out your heart to a trained and licensed professional who has no skin in the game other than to help you heal.

Work empowering magick. You may need to burn magickal items, which connect you to the person. You may need to deeply cleanse your home with salt and vinegar and burn smudge bundles to smoke out negative entities. You may need to sit in a graveyard and cry, and then bury a candle that contains all your hurt feelings. You might even need to carve your words of hurt onto a figural candle, light its head on fire, and then flush the remains down the toilet!

Remember, you are a magickal person. Even though you have been harmed, had your soul burnt and singed, the magick belongs to the universe, and you can still use it for your own healing. Even if you took vows or covenants with persons, groves, organizations, temples, or houses, the knowledge you gained ultimately belongs to the universe and is there for all who choose to seek it. Your deities, gods and goddesses, guides, and angels still

love you. They will be there when you call upon them. If you no longer choose to work with the powers you used when you were in the relationship with those who hurt you, that's okay too. The magickal universe is a vast place, and you may find a better fit with new deities and guides as you heal yourself from the pain of bad juju.

As your heart burns and smolders, you may feel called to work spells of revenge. Caution! Even the best and justified intentions can boomerang. Take much time and thought before you venture down that path. Be very sure of your intentions before you act upon them, for even if the work is justified, it will still come at a cost to you. Be ready to do much cleanup and face fear within yourself if you choose this route. Take a breath, write your feelings down, and throw tarot cards. Pour your feelings out in a forest or a sacred grove of trees. You may also find this simple spell helpful:

During a waning Moon cycle, write down all your negative feelings and emotions. Try not to censor your feelings as you write them down. Allow your pen to be your magickal wand of power. Take a moment and read what you have written. Embrace the power of the moment and anoint the paper with eucalyptus essential oil. Light the paper on fire and burn it in a fireproof container. Carry the ashes to a crossroads and dump them. Take a different route home. Feel the power of giving your worries to Spirit.

Last, take some time and walk away. While we can expend much energy trying to change other people, in the end we can only change ourselves. It's hard to walk away. It's hard to let go. But sometimes after you've done all that is magickally possible to heal yourself, walking away can be the best answer. Nasty people deserve to be with nasty people. Let them eat each other while you dine somewhere else. You never know what bright, shiny treat may be waiting for you in a different restaurant.

And give yourself a break. Try not to beat yourself up too much. What has happened to you has probably happened to other people who came in contact with that person, group, or organization. You may find that when you move on, others who have had similar experiences will show up in your life, and you may be able to build solid new relationships with those who suffered similarly.

In the end, try not to give up on your magickal path. You were called to it for a reason. Sometimes the bad shows up to test your commitment, courage, and faith. Sometimes you're becoming a stronger Witch and for your growth you need to be tempered in the fires, even though it hurts like hell. There's a reason why the mystics and ancient ones had to face dark caves, minotaurs, nights buried in graves, and vision quests on lonely mountaintops. These tests of the soul build spiritual strength and confidence.

Should you choose to carry on after your heart has been broken and healed, know you will be a stronger, more capable Witch, priest or priestess, healer, or conjurer. Know your trials and tests will not have been in vain. After all is said and done, you never know what goodness may come. Perhaps one day you may be the one to help someone else when they fall into the snares of broken vows and covenants.

About the Contributors

ELIZABETH BARRETTE has been involved with the Pagan community for more than twenty-seven years. She has served as managing editor of *PanGaia* and dean of studies at the Grey School of Wizardry. Her book *Composing Magic: How to Create Magical Spells, Rituals, Blessings, Chants, and Prayers* explains how to combine writing and spirituality. She lives in central Illinois. Visit her blog *The Wordsmith's Forge* (ysabetwordsmith.livejournal.com) or website PenUltimate Productions (penultimateproductions.weebly.com).

BLAKE OCTAVIAN BLAIR is a shamanic practitioner, ordained minister, writer, Usui Reiki Master-Teacher, tarot reader, and musical artist. Blake incorporates mystical traditions from both the East and West with a reverence for the natural world into his own brand of spirituality. Blake holds a degree in English and religion from the University of Florida. He is an avid reader, knitter, crafter, pescatarian, and member of the Order of Bards, Ovates, and Druids (OBOD). Blake lives in the New England region of the United States with his beloved husband. Visit him at www.blakeoctavianblair.com or write him at blake@blakeoctavian blair.com.

DEBORAH BLAKE is the award-winning author of the Baba Yaga and Broken Rider paranormal romance series and the Veiled Magic urban fantasies. She has also written *The Goddess Is in the Details, Everyday Witchcraft* and numerous other books, along with a popular tarot deck. She writes the ongoing column Everyday Witchcraft in *Witches & Pagans*. Deborah can be found online at Facebook, Twitter, her popular blog (*Writing the Witchy Way*), and www.deborahblakeauthor.com. She lives in a 130-year-old farmhouse in rural upstate New York with various cats who supervise all her activities, both magickal and mundane.

DEBORAH CASTELLANO is a frequent contributor to occult/Pagan sources such as the Llewellyn annual almanacs, PaganSquare, and *Witches & Pagans.* She blogs at *Charmed, I'm Sure.* Deborah's book, *Glamour Magic: The Witchcraft Revolution to Get What You Want,* was published with Llewellyn in the summer of 2017. She resides in New Jersey with her husband, Jow, and their cat.

Dr. **ALEXANDRA CHAURAN** (Port Moody, BC) is a second-generation fortune-teller, a high priestess of British Traditional Wicca, and the queen of a coven. As a professional psychic intuitive for over a decade, she has served psychic apprentices and thousands of clients. She received a master's in teaching from Seattle University and a doctorate from Valdosta State University and is certified in tarot. She can be found online at SeePsychic.com.

CHIC AND S. TABATHA CICERO are Chief Adepts of the Hermetic Order of the Golden Dawn as reestablished by their mentor, Israel Regardie. (Visit www.hermeticgoldendawn.org.) The Ciceros have written numerous books, including *The Essential Golden Dawn, Self-Initiation into the Golden Dawn Tradition, The Golden Dawn Magical Tarot,* and *Tarot Talismans.* Both are prominent Rosicrucians: Chic is currently Chief Adept of the Florida College of the SRICF and Tabatha is Imperatrix of the SRIA in America (www.sria.org).

DALLAS JENNIFER COBB practices gratitude magic, giving thanks for personal happiness, health, and prosperity; meaningful, flexible, and rewarding work; and a deliciously joyful life. She lives in paradise with her daughter in a waterfront village in rural Ontario, where she regularly swims, runs, and snowshoes. A Reclaiming Witch from way back, Jennifer is part of an eclectic pan-Pagan circle that organizes empowered and beautiful community rituals. Contact her at jennifer.cobb@live.com.

MONICA CROSSON is the author of *The Magickal Family: Pagan Living in Harmony with Nature* and *Summer Sage*. She is a Master Gardener who lives in the beautiful Pacific Northwest, happily digging in the dirt and tending her raspberries with her husband, three kids, three goats, two dogs, two cats, many chickens, and Rosetta the donkey. She has been a practicing Witch for twenty-five years and is a member of Blue Moon Coven. Monica is a regular contributor to Llewellyn's annuals.

MELISSA CYNOVA is owner of Little Fox Tarot and has been slinging tarot cards and teaching classes since 1989. She can be found in the St. Louis area and online for personal readings, parties, and beginner and advanced tarot classes. Her first book, *Kitchen Table Tarot,* was released in 2017. Melissa lives in St. Louis with her outstanding kids, her sweet husband, Joe, two cats, two dogs, and a tortoise named Phil. When she's not slinging cards, she's enjoying her tribe and probably watching a superhero movie while reading a book. Find her on Twitter, Facebook, and Instagram.

AUTUMN DAMIANA is an author, artist, crafter, and amateur photographer. She is a Solitary Eclectic Cottage Witch who has been following her Pagan path for almost two decades and is a regular contributor to Llewellyn's annuals. Along with writing and making art, Autumn has a degree in early childhood education. She lives with her husband and doggy familiar in the beautiful San Francisco Bay Area. Visit her online at www.autumndamiana.com.

RAVEN DIGITALIS (Missoula, MT) is the author of *Esoteric Empathy* and three other books with Llewellyn. He is a Neopagan Priest and cofounder of a nonprofit multicultural temple called Opus Aima Obscuræ (OAO). Raven has been an earth-based practitioner since 1999, a Priest since 2003, a Freemason since 2012, and an empath all of his life. Visit him at www.ravendigitalis.com and www.opusaimaobscurae.org.

STORM FAERYWOLF is a professional author, teacher, Warlock, and coowner of the Mystic Dream, a spiritual supply store where he teaches and offers services to the public. An initiate of the Faery tradition with over thirty years' experience practicing Witchcraft, he has been teaching for more than twenty-five. He holds the Black Wand of a Master and is the author of *Betwixt & Between: Exploring the Faery Tradition of Witchcraft*. He is a founding teacher of the Black Rose school of witchcraft and travels internationally teaching the magical arts. Visit faerywolf.com.

KATE FREULER lives in Ontario, Canada, with her husband and daughter. She owns and operates www.whitemoonwitchcraft .com, an online witchcraft boutique. When she isn't crafting spells and amulets for clients or herself, she loves to write, paint, read, draw, and create.

JUSTINE HOLUBETS is a Solitary Wiccan practicing ancient Egyptian sacred traditions living in Lviv, Ukraine. She holds a tarot certificate from the British Astrological Psychic Society and works as a tarot and lunar rhythms/astrology consultant for Zodiaclivetarot.com in the UK. A published author focused on philosophical, social, and gender issues, she currently studies psychology at University of Roehampton online and prepares courses to help women maintain healthy, dignified intercultural relationships. Visit http://www .zodiaclivetarotreading.com/tarot-reader?id=129.

JAMES KAMBOS became interested in magic as a child after watching his grandmother perform spells she learned growing up in Greece. He has a degree in history and geography from Ohio University. He lives in the rural hill country of Southern Ohio.

TIFFANY LAZIC is a registered psychotherapist and spiritual director with a private practice in individual, couples, and group therapy, and the owner of the Hive and Grove Centre for Holistic

Wellness in Kitchener (Canada). She created and teaches two self-development programs and is a frequent guest facilitator at Transformational Arts College of Spiritual and Holistic Training in Toronto (Canada). Tiffany is the author of *The Great Work: Self-Knowledge and Healing Through the Wheel of the Year*. Visit www .hiveandgrove.ca.

NAJAH LIGHTFOOT is a writer and contributor for Llewellyn Publications. She is a sister-priestess of the divine feminine, a martial artist, and an active member of the Denver Pagan community. She keeps her magick strong through the indigenous practices of her ancestors, the folk magick of Hoodoo, Pagan rituals, and her belief in the mysteries of the universe. Find her online at www.twitter.com/NajahLightfoot, www.facebook.com/Najah Lightfoot, and www.craftandconjure.com.

JASON MANKEY is a Wiccan Witch, writer, and wannabe rock and roller. He has been a part of the greater Pagan community for over twenty years and has spent nearly half that time teaching and speaking at Pagan conventions across the United States and Canada. He has written *The Witch's Athame* and *The Witch's Book of Shadows* and is also the channel manager of Patheos Pagan online. He lives in Sunnyvale, California, where he and his wife, Ari, help lead two local covens. Because they don't want to be outnumbered, Ari and Jason only have two cats.

ESTHA K. V. McNEVIN (Missoula, MT) is a priestess and ceremonial oracle of Opus Aima Obscuræ, a nonprofit Pagan Temple Haus. She has served the Pagan community since 2003 as an Eastern Hellenistic officiate, lecturer, freelance author, artist, and poet. In addition to hosting public rituals for the sabbats, Estha organizes annual philanthropic fundraisers, Full Moon spell-crafting ceremonies, and women's divination rituals for

each Dark Moon. To learn more, please explore www.opus aimaobscurae.org.

MICKIE MUELLER explores magic and spirituality through art and the written word at her home studio and workshop in Missouri. She is the author/illustrator of *The Voice of the Trees*, the illustrator of Mystical Cats Tarot and Magical Dogs Tarot, and author of *The Witch's Mirror* and *Llewellyn's Little Book of Halloween*. Since 2007, Mickie has been a regular article and illustration contributor to Llewellyn's almanacs and annuals and many Llewellyn books. Her art has been seen as set dressing on SyFy's *The Magicians* and Bravo's *Girlfriend's Guide to Divorce*. Visit her online at MickieMuellerStudio.etsy.com

DIANA RAJCHEL has practiced magic since childhood. She lives in San Francisco, where she runs the Emperor Norton Pagan Social and handles the oft-squirrely city spirit. She is the author of the Mabon and Samhain books in the Llewellyn Sabbat Essentials Series and of the Diagram Prize–nominee *Divorcing a Real Witch*.

SUZANNE RESS runs a small farm in the alpine foothills of Italy, where she lives with her husband. She has been a practicing Pagan for as long as she can remember and was recently featured in the exhibit "Worldwide Witches" at the Hexenmuseum of Switzerland. She is the author of *The Trial of Goody Gilbert*.

CHARLYNN WALLS resides with her family in Central Missouri. She holds a BA in anthropology with an emphasis in archaeology. She is acting CEO of Correllian Education Ministry, which oversees Witch School. She is an active member of the St. Louis Pagan Community and is a part of a local area coven. She writes for *Witches & Pagans*, in Llewellyn's annuals, and on her blog, *Sage Offerings* (www.sageofferings.net).

CHARLIE RAINBOW WOLF is happiest when she is creating something, especially if it can be made from items that others have cast aside. Pottery, writing, knitting, astrology, and tarot are her deepest interests, but she happily confesses that she's easily distracted, because life offers so many wonderful things to explore. She is an advocate of organic gardening and cooking and lives in the Midwest with her husband and special-needs Great Danes. Visit her at www.charlierainbow.com.

STEPHANIE WOODFIELD (Brookfield, CT) has been a practicing Witch for over fourteen years and a priestess for ten years. Her lifelong love of Irish mythology led to a close study of Celtic Witchcraft. A natural clairvoyant and empath, she has worked as a tarot card reader and is ordained as a minister with the Universal Life Church.

LAURA TEMPEST ZAKROFF can be described as a professional artist, author, dancer, designer, muse, mythpunk, teacher, and Witch. She has been a practicing Modern Traditional Witch for over two decades and blogs for Patheos in *A Modern Traditional Witch* and *Witches & Pagans* in Fine Art Witchery. She is the author of *Sigil Witchery* and *The Witch's Cauldron* and coauthored *The Witch's Altar* with Jason Mankey. Laura resides in Seattle, WA, and can be found online at www.lauratempestzakroff.com.

NATALIE ZAMAN is the author of *Color and Conjure* and *Magical Destinations of the Northeast*. A regular contributor to various Llewellyn annual publications, she also writes the recurring feature Wandering Witch for *Witches & Pagans*. When not on the road, she's busy tending her magical back garden. Visit Natalie online at nataliezaman.blogspot.com.